How to Find That

Quality Tenant

The Five Simple Steps of Tenant Selection

Don Conrad

Blue Collar Publishers
VALPARAISO, INDIANA

Although the author and publisher have made every effort to ensure the accuracy and completeness of information contained in this book, we assume no responsibility for errors, inaccuracies, omissions, or any inconsistency herein. Any slighting of people, places, or organizations is unintentional.

Disclaimer: The author is not a lawyer and so cannot guarantee the legality of every contract and addendum in every locale. Readers are advised to double-check any contract or addendum with their real estate attorney.

First printing 2007
ISBN-13: 978-0-9786294-3-4
LCCN 2006927537

ATTENTION CORPORATIONS, UNIVERSITIES, COLLEGES, AND PROFESSIONAL ORGANIZATIONS: Quantity discounts are available on bulk purchases of this book for educational, gift purposes, or as premiums for increasing magazine subscriptions or renewals. Special books or book excerpts can also be created to fit specific needs. For information, please contact Blue Collar Publishers, 814 Concord Street, Valparaiso, IN 46385 or email DonConrad@FindThatQualityTenant.com.

DEDICATION

First and foremost, I dedicate this book to my wife, Kris—who toiled by my side to make this dream a reality and whose support I couldn't do without. I love you.

To my friends and family who believed and stood by me as I completed this task, often keeping the faith when I couldn't.

And I dedicate this book to you, the reader, because without your willingness to take the chance to prosper, I wouldn't have been able to take the chance either.

My sincere thanks to all.

TABLE OF CONTENTS

Step One: Prepare

Outlines what to do to attract quality renters.

Step Two: Prequalify

Helps landlords weed out prospects who don't fit their criteria.

Step Three: Paperwork

A highly qualified tenant prospect needs to fill out the necessary paperwork to obtain the dwelling. Step three helps the landlord understand that process.

Step Four: Process

This step explains how to follow up on and evaluate all the information filled out in the paperwork step. The previous forms are analyzed in the following order:

Step Five: Payoff

Proper use of the first four steps should yield a highly qualified tenant. This step details the forms needed to place the new tenant in the rental.

INTRODUCTION

Rental real estate is often touted as the most steady, surefire way to a secure future. The concept is simple: Locate a desirable home in a decent neighborhood, purchase that property, and put in a tenant who pays down the mortgage, covers the related costs, and provides a little cash flow. All this happens as the property appreciates in value. As an added bonus, you get to depreciate the dwelling against your other income. No drawbacks. A no-brainer. Right?

Maybe in Monopoly. But in real life, there *are* drawbacks. Toilets leak. Houses don't appreciate. Property taxes skyrocket. And tenants cause problems. Sometimes lots of them. In fact, I believe the fear of tenant problems, more than other fear, is what keeps people from investing in real estate. I also believe it is the main reason most people get out of real estate investing once they start.

If you're nodding your head "yes" as you read this, I can sympathize. I too have had tenant problems. And although I do agree that tenants can be problematic, I don't think they are the one and only cause. I think part of the problem is you, the landlord.

Don't take that the wrong way. Even though you are part of the problem, it most likely isn't your fault. Look at it this way: You can turn on the TV morning, noon, or night and probably find an infomercial telling you: "Buy with no money down!" "Become a millionaire!" "I made X number of dollars in X number of days using this system!" These infomercials sell you the glamour and the hype. They appeal to your sense of wanting a better retirement, a better lifestyle, a better future. And you know what? They're not lying to you; these things do happen. The gurus' systems can and do work, if you are willing to put forth the effort.

Likewise, go to a major bookstore and count the different real estate investing titles on the shelves. There are likely 50 or 60—maybe more. Then go to the service desk and ask them to pull up all available titles on the subject. Hundreds more.

Think of all the people you know who are financially better off than most. Many will have done it through real estate.

Whether you realize it or not, for years you've been bombarded and therefore unconsciously programmed by these messages telling you to invest in real estate. You're conditioned to the idea that wealth building is easy. The problem is that a lot of this hype promises to set you on the glorious and wealth building path of investment real estate, but doesn't always give you the tools to *control* that real estate: especially the tenants, which you must have if you own rental property. Well I'm here to tell you, the best way to keep control of your rentals is to pick the right tenants to occupy those rentals in the first place.

Sure, most real estate investment books devote a chapter here or there to the subject of selecting tenants. And most do warn you to pick quality tenants because a bad tenant will ruin your investment appetite. You might also read a paragraph or two about running credit checks, talking to a previous landlord, or filling out a lease. But this information isn't enough. When I was starting out, I wanted to know how to truly find quality tenants. I wanted to know how to *read* a credit report, not just obtain one. I wanted to learn what step to do first, then second—and when to do them. I wanted more. I wanted a tenant selection system, but I couldn't find one.

So I built one.

It took a few years of tweaking but through trial and error, I've come up with a system that works exceptionally well for me. Since I've been in this business, I've never had a tenant vandalize my property. I've never had one skip in the night. I've never been threatened, and it took more than twelve years before I had to finally start an eviction process.

I'm proud of my system. It was developed by a small-time landlord to help the small-time landlord—the beginner, the person who has a few properties to supplement their retirement: probably *you*.

How to Find That Quality Tenant: The Five Simple Steps of Tenant Selection is my system. This book contains five steps of tenant selection. They are as follows:

- Step One: Prepare
- Step Two: Prequalify
- Step Three: Paperwork
- Step Four: Process
- Step Five: Payoff

How to Find That Quality Tenant is devoted to educating you and improving your chance of finding a good, quality tenant. That is all the book is designed to do. You won't learn how to evict. You won't learn how to handle tenants who break the rules. You won't learn how to run your properties. This book concentrates only on helping you find a quality tenant, and it does that by offering a step-by-step system. Use what you need in step one, then proceed on to step two. Complete step two, then move on to three. By the time you've started step five, you should have a tenant of higher quality and more suited to your needs than before you read this book.

This doesn't mean you won't have a quality tenant whose life circumstances change, therefore becoming a problem. That can and will happen. You just don't want it to happen in the first month you rent out your dwelling. And you don't want it to happen very often. This book is designed to prevent many problems before they have an opportunity to arise.

In Closing

The main goals of this book are to educate you about tenant selection and to help you realize you need some sort of system to find quality tenants: a tangible, workable system. If you don't have one, I'm offering mine in its entirety. If mine doesn't fit your needs, use what you need and build your system around it. Whatever you choose, I hope you discover what works for you and I hope I have been of some help. Good luck.

And thanks for buying my book.

Step One: Prepare

F or many things in life—whether you are climbing Mount Everest, re-painting a classic car, building your dream home, or planning your wedding or retirement, preparation is the key difference between a successful success and an acceptable success. At one time or another, probably all of us have taken on a project that we failed to properly prepare for and were gravely disappointed in the results. Good early preparation could have yielded a better outcome.

As I explained in the Introduction, there are five steps in my tenant selection process. Step 1—prepare—is important if you are going to successfully locate a quality tenant, and it sets the groundwork for the other steps in the process. In this step, you will learn to prepare the rental unit so you attract the best possible tenants. Next, you will prepare your standards or qualifications the tenant prospect must pass if he or she is to be a candidate for your dwelling. Finally, you will prepare your advertising to draw potential tenants into your selection pool.

CHAPTER 1

Preparing the Dwelling

When landlords think of the preparation needed to find a tenant for their rental dwelling, they usually think in terms of cleaning and painting the property or writing an ad that brings tenant prospects by the truckload. Although both of these factors do require preparation (and I will cover them in this section), there are other things to do to prepare for a tenant search.

Finding and choosing a quality tenant for your rental dwelling requires work. It is going to take time and play havoc with your emotions. You will be misled, frustrated, ticked off, and discouraged, among other things. You may want to quit and you may question your sanity, or at the very least, your desire to be a landlord. All this is normal. All this comes with the territory, so it's important to prepare yourself first.

Preparing Yourself

With good preparation and understanding of what lies ahead, you will be able to adjust and cope with any negatives that creep in. Proper preparation will give you a boost of self-confidence, a better attitude, and a more professional air as you search for that quality tenant.

How do you prepare yourself? For starters, realize why you are searching for a *quality* tenant and not just any tenant. The difference between the two can be the determining factor between success and failure in this business. To help you better understand that difference, let's first define quality tenant.

Defining "Quality Tenant"

A quality tenant can best be defined as someone who pays their rent on time or very close to on time. They don't call with pesky, minute problems. They don't call to complain about a slight noise or other trivial matters. They don't call just to chat. They do call to tell you when they see a problem that could cost you money now or cause a real problem in the future (for instance, a plumbing or roof leak or the initial signs of property deterioration). They are communicative, but they are not whiners. They follow the house rules, stay on the right side of the law, and don't disturb the neighbors. They may not live the way you want them to live as far as their personal lifestyle goes, but they make you money with very minimal effort. To me, that is a quality tenant. And it is these tenants who make landlording a fulfilling and enjoyable vocation.

On the other hand, a tenant who fails to fit these ideals will cause you varying degrees of grief, headaches, and sleepless nights because their problems somehow become your problems. Inferior tenants waste your time, elevate your blood pressure, and make you dislike the business. They destroy your property and cause unnecessary turnover by skipping out in the night. They are prone to evictions and judgments and in general will cost you money every time you turn around.

Finding a quality tenant will make all the difference in the world and you need to be prepared to continue your search until you find them. Uncovering such a tenant will take extra time and extra effort. Unfortunately, all this time and effort will happen in the beginning of this journey at a time your rental property is empty and costing you money each and every day. This is a disheartening time in your landlording career and you may be tempted to rent to any breathing body. Don't. Prepare yourself to be strong during this time and stick to your goal. Commit yourself to giving extra time and effort now, in the beginning of your search, because the stress and anxiety you feel at this point will only be a small fraction of the stress and anxiety you will experience with a problem tenant living in your rental dwelling. And *that* stress will gnaw at you twenty-four hours, seven days a week. Also keep in mind that the hours used to deal with those problem tenants will equal ten or twenty times the hours you would have spent to find a quality tenant in the first place

Economical Classes of Tenants

The next area in which to prepare yourself is the understanding of the social and economic standings from where quality tenants can come. Contrary to popular belief, your renter's income level does not matter. There are quality tenants in all income brackets. I should know, I have had tenants in almost every bracket.

Tenant Mentality

Next, you should prepare yourself for understanding the average tenant mentality. Many tenants have never been homeowners and never will be. Others are just leaving the nest and have no clue as to what is required to be responsible for a home. And a few believe that the tenant way of thinking is the only true way of thinking, making landlord/tenant communication difficult. Whichever of these mentalities crosses your path, you want to be ready. If you can learn a little about how a tenant's mind works, you'll be better prepared to find quality tenants in addition to solving or avoiding tenant problems that come your way.

To better understand the tenant mentality, be willing to step into the shoes of your tenant periodically to better view their perspective. I would advise trying to do this at least once in each step of the tenant selection process. If you are finding this difficult, take yourself back in time to when you first rented a place of your own. Do you remember how you felt about that rental property? Did you take care of it like you owned it? What did you think of the manager or landlord? What did you dislike about him or her? Were you treated fairly and professionally?

If you remember the true answers to these questions, you may realize that your current view of rental properties and landlords is far different from back then. When you were a tenant, you may not have cared if things got damaged. You likely didn't realize the cost of repairs and even if you did, you figured that your security deposit would cover any and all damages. And when it came to rent payments, I bet you assumed your landlord was filthy rich and greedy with his rent demands; a thought that I'm sure entered your head with every rent increase.

Now that I have you thinking, I'll let you in on a little secret: Tenants haven't changed. Your personal scenario from tenant to homeowner to landlord may have changed, but the tenant mentality of today is in many ways identical to the tenant mentality ten or twenty years ago.

This doesn't mean most tenants are bad, it just means they think differently than you. They think they understand you. But they don't. How could they? They have probably never walked in your shoes. They don't have the experience dealing with the things a landlord deals with. Don't hold this against them. Just keep in mind how they think—how they view renting and how they may act as renters. If nothing else, commit this thought to memory: *Most landlords have been a tenant, but most tenants have never been a landlord.* Use this knowledge accordingly. Approach tenant selection as a live game of chess. You want to analyze both playing fields, even though you only represent one side of the board.

Preparing the Rental

Similar to getting yourself prepared to find a quality tenant, you will need to prepare the rental unit to attract the type of tenant you desire. Keep in mind that the general public, whether as homeowners or renters, usually wants the same qualities in their lodging. These qualities can be broken down into three categories: safety/security, cleanliness, and habitability. To help you better understand these categories, let me cover them one-by-one, briefly explaining how tenant preparation is done in each category.

Safety and Security

By and large, the days when most people felt safe leaving their doors unlocked, whether they were home or not, are pretty much over. With the rise in crime in most areas of the country, home safety has become an increasingly bigger issue; therefore, I urge you to make tenant safety and security a priority when preparing a dwelling for rent.

First, walk around the exterior of the dwelling and look for anything that could aid a criminal in targeting your dwelling. Things like overgrown weeds or shrubs, especially near basement or easy to access windows, often become a hiding place for someone with ill intent. Spending an hour or two trimming these areas will usually eliminate the problem.

Doors/locks. The next item of concern are entry doors, which need to be of solid and durable quality to deter break-ins. Either steel or solid core wood is your best choice. It also is important for each door to have a strong set of locks, preferably a keyed entry and a deadbolt.

Pay attention to the following items when handling locks on a rental dwelling:

- Locks should be changed in front of the new tenant or just before they take possession of the property. Tenants should know that they and the landlord are the only ones with keys to their residence.

- If there is any window close to an entry door or in the door itself that can be broken (allowing a perpetrator to reach in and unlock the door), make sure all locks are key operated from the inside. This way, the tenant can remove the key and decrease the chances of a criminal being able to let him or herself in. (There can be exceptions to this rule as stated below.)

- This thought somewhat goes against the previous one, but it still is worth mentioning. Unless close to a window, the deadbolt on the inside of the house is best when you can latch it without a key. Some deadbolt locks require a key on the inside of the house to lock the door; if possible, you would rather not have this. The reason is that if a fire were to break out, and that key was not in the deadbolt lock, your occupants could not escape the house. By having a deadbolt lock with a flip type of lock on the inside, an emergency escape is still possible.

- Add safety chains and peepholes to any door that you must open to see who is on the other side. You want tenants to be able to identify who is at the door before they open it up.

- For added insurance against a door being kicked in, I recommend substituting 3½ inch or longer screws in some of the door hinges and all the lock latch plates on all entry doors. These longer screws should drill through the door jamb and into the 2 x 6's of the house, making it much more difficult to break down a door.

Here is a quick story on locks. Earlier in my career, I did a lot of side work for banks on their REOs—real estate owned properties, which are

bank-held foreclosed houses. This work included breaking into their properties and securing them for the bank. I can tell you from experience that
many of those homes had locks so cheap, I could knock off the knob with
a hammer, punch out the lock's inner guts, and open the door, often in 60
seconds or less. Other times, I would notice every door in the house had
quality locks on them, and I would never even attempt to enter. I would
just call a locksmith.

The lesson here: Do not buy the cheap locks that are available at most
discount stores. The locks you choose must be of high quality. They must
be strong, heavy-duty, and tamperproof. Do yourself a favor and contact
a locksmith to find out which locks they recommend against break-ins.

Windows. Just like doors, windows also need to be secure. This is
done by having good working locks on all windows. If these windows are
side-to-side sliders or large patio-type doors, you would be wise to add a steel
bar in their tracks to prevent someone from sliding the window in the case a
lock does not work properly or the window is left unlocked. Although, keep
in mind this could be a safety hazard, especially in case of fire.

You also may wish to make sure that you have good screens on all
windows.

I'm sure you're wondering what good screens have to do with security.
As far as I am concerned, screens in no way offer any type of security. But
I am bringing this subject to your attention because there has been case
law involving landlords who had missing window screens in their rentals
and intruders broke in though those windows. The courts ruled that the
landlords did not supply adequate security because of the missing screens,
and therefore were partly responsible for the break-in from the intruder.
Even though I do not agree with this verdict, I take the lesson to heart,
and recommend keeping screens on all windows.

There are other things you may do for added security in your rental
dwelling:

- You may choose to offer a security system, and then charge the ten-
ants for that system by increasing the rent.
- Another idea is to give the illusion of a dog living on the premises.
This can be done with the dog dish and dog toy outside in plain

view. Also a "Beware of dog" sign can add some impact. Understand that this is just an illusion, and may do nothing to protect against an intruder, but might offer a tenant a bit of psychological security.

- You may want to start a neighborhood watch group. Many locales, with the help of local law enforcement, are using such groups as an added security measure for their neighborhoods.

Even though no one can guarantee someone else's security, you as a landlord can do many things that will improve the security standards of your rentals. Take the time and provide the most secure environment that you can.

Electrical. Another item concerning safety involves a house's electrical system. Unlike most other safety issues in a dwelling that can often easily and cheaply be repaired, updating an electrical system can be very expensive—sometimes running into thousands of dollars. Even so, there are still things you can do to improve safe electrical usage in your home. One is the installation of GFCIs. These outlet-type devices are installed in kitchens and baths or other areas of heavy water usage. These devices shut off an outlet's circuitry if someone tries to plug something into the outlet with wet hands, eliminating the chance of that person receiving a shock.

You should also make sure all switches and outlets have the proper covers on them. At the same time, check for wires or clumps of wires that are improperly exposed. These problems need to be contained in some type of electrical box where they are unable to start a fire or be accessible to human touch.

Depending on the age and quality of the electrical system in your rentals, there could be many safety issues worth addressing. Besides those mentioned previously, you'll want to watch for the following:

- The main electrical panel has fuses instead of breakers.
- Wrong or faulty breakers on circuits.
- Aluminum wiring in the house.
- Overloaded circuits for microwave, air conditioning, and other appliances.

If any of these conditions exist, I advise you to have a certified electrician evaluate the situation for your sake as well as your tenant's.

Smoke detectors. Another issue worth mentioning when covering the topic of dwelling preparation and safety is smoke detectors. Good quality smoke detectors provide more bang for the buck in the safety department than probably anything else you can do to your dwelling. Simply place a minimum of one on each level of the house, preferably by the bedrooms. Make sure each smoke detector works properly and has a light and fresh batteries. For added peace of mind, you may wish to have your electrician wire smoke detectors into your house's electrical system. This task is pretty simple to do, especially if you have an accessible attic area. I've done this to my last few houses and the cost is worth the peace of mind it provides. I no longer have to wonder if my tenants are disabling a smoke detector, which jeopardizes their safety and my property.

Other hazards. Generally, with the exception of electrical, most other items you deem unsafe in a dwelling can be remedied

I was assembling some gas pipe in a crawl space on a house I was working on for Christmas in April, a charity in our area. Unbeknownst to me, there was a piece of exposed wiring where I was working. It was hiding in the shadows near a corner of the house. As I tightened the pipes, my hand or pipe wrench connected with this wire, providing me with quite a shock. I later found out the homeowner knew this wire was activated by a light switch by the backdoor. She failed to tell any of the volunteers this, and naturally, someone hit the switch. I was lucky the crawl space was dry and my shock was minimal. I'm telling you this story because more dwellings than you realize have these hidden hazards, so repair as needed.

fairly easily. Take a stroll through the house, both inside and out, and look for these potential safety issues. Fix them immediately.

- Loose handrails, railings, or steps.
- Address numbers on dwelling and mailbox are easy to read and illuminated at night so emergency personnel can locate the property.
- Loose floorings, carpet, decking, or other tripping hazards.
- Flammable or poisonous liquids that need to be properly disposed of.
- Adequate lighting at all doorways, hallways, and stairwells. I like all light fixtures inside a dwelling to have a minimum of two light bulbs. In case one burns out, there is still adequate illumination for safety purposes. I also like outdoor motion lights because they have two bulbs and provide more light than normal. You can never have enough light in a rental.

Even though everybody is in charge of his or her own personal safety, it is your duty as a landlord to ensure that your rental dwelling is as safe as you can make it. Check for safety each and every time you prepare your property for rent. Your tenants will appreciate it and you will sleep better at night.

Cleanliness

If there was only one thing that you as a landlord could do to guarantee you have your fair share of tenant choices, it is to make your dwelling as clean and eye appealing as possible. This begins with what is referred to in the industry as curb appeal. Simply stated, curb appeal is how the property looks from the street.

Outside. To achieve good curb appeal, I highly recommend spending a little extra preparation time on the front of the house. Start with the yard. Cut back low-lying branches. Trim the bushes. Put in a few hostas or similar easy-to-grow plants or easy-to-manage seasonal bushes. Edge them out and spread a little mulch around. Pick up loose trash and pull the weeds, especially in the cracks of the driveway and sidewalks. Take time to grow grass in the bare spots in the yard. Mow the lawn.

With the house itself, start by washing down the exterior. If the house looks drab, splash on some color by adding shutters to the facade. The easy-to-install shutters sold at most discount/hardware stores are inexpensive and will change the look of your rental with a minimal amount of effort. If, after you add shutters, you still wish to add more pizzazz to the dwelling, paint the front door the same color as the shutters. To finish off the look of the house, add a decorative flag or classy lawn ornament to give a little character.

When you are done, step to the curb and look at your property as a whole. What you see is what the tenants will see. The very first thing they will see. Will they be impressed, or will they walk away?

Inside. Cleanliness inside the home is also extremely important. Nobody wants to begin living in their new home surrounded by someone else's filth. For this reason, everything needs to look, smell, and feel clean. Begin by making sure all walls, ceilings, and trim work are freshly painted, void of holes, and free of cobwebs. Noncarpeted floors should be swept, mopped, and polished.

Carpeted areas should be professionally cleaned between each and every tenant, no matter how short their tenancy was. Carpets hold dust mites, odors, and about every other germ imaginable. Parents hate the thought of their kids rolling around on someone else's germ-infested carpet.

I know many landlords have their own carpet cleaning machines and prefer to take on this task themselves and pocket the savings. I tried this too but was very unhappy with the results. It was a lot of work, and I never seemed to get out the stains and dirt that the pros can. They have better equipment and superior knowledge to attack stains and other problems. For these reasons, I recommend you use professional carpet cleaners.

As you can probably guess, in addition to cleaning the carpet, walls, and trim, extra effort should be used in preparing the kitchen and bathrooms. These rooms can make or break how your house rates on someone's clean-o-meter. Dirty kitchens and baths give tenant prospects illusions of germ infested environments and unhealthy living. Substandard cleanliness in these two areas is the surest way to lose potential quality tenants. Spend extra time cleaning kitchens and baths. If the thought of cleaning other people's messes repulses you, hire someone else to do it.

Miscellaneous. While you are cleaning the house for display, don't forget those often overlooked, neglected areas: ceiling fan blades and lights, fingerprints around doorknobs and light switches, all vents and grills, behind and underneath appliances, mirrors, windows, windowsills, and any other place you would normally forget to clean.

As landlords prepare their dwellings for rent, they generally concentrate on the visual aspect of the task. Most people fail to remember that the sense of smell is a very powerful sense, especially in women. I recommend you remove all possible sources of unpleasant odors days in advance of the first showing. Pet odors, musty and mildew smells, and smells left behind by cleaning products, to name a few. It is worth the effort to place a couple of air fresheners around the inside of the rental. Try using the kind you plug into an outlet, which slowly release an attractive smell for a month at a time. The key to success is to have the place smell nice before a single tenant prospect walks though the door.

Habitability

Keeping rental property up to par can get expensive and require hard work, but when you accept rent from a tenant, you are agreeing to provide decent and adequate housing in exchange for the monies received. Different landlords have opposing views on what constitutes decent housing, so let's establish some guidelines for you to follow.

Besides the aforementioned safety and cleanliness issues, make sure that roofs don't leak; windows open, close, and latch properly; fire extinguishers are present and working; and the plumbing coming in and going out of the house is functioning without leaks or defects. Make sure there is adequate heat in the winter and, if possible, cool air in the summer. The rental should not be in disrepair in any other major areas such as fading or peeling paint, torn-up carpet and flooring, rotten boards on decks, or anything of that nature. Make it a dwelling that you yourself would live in. It may not be the size you desire or in the area you want, but its condition would not chase you away. Your tenants deserve the same thing. In fact, remember this: Every tenant has the absolute right to a habitable place to live. This right is protected by law.

You don't have to provide the Taj Mahal or the amenities that go with it, but keeping your rental in above average condition is fair to your tenant and a good idea for you. Your tenant wins because they receive decent housing for their buck and you win because your property should steadily increase in value and you should be able to raise rents on a consistent basis to keep up with the market. Keep in mind that the best time to do repair and maintenance work on the rental is between tenants.

To consistently find quality tenants, you need to perform more dwelling preparation than simply slopping on some paint and wiping everything with bleach.

While you are at the vacant property and it is convenient and on your mind, fix all those little nuances that make day-to-day living in that rental a drag. Tighten screws. Hang a new ceiling fan or light fixture. Change out a leaky kitchen faucet. Fix a broken cabinet. Rehang that loose closet door.

My Personal Goal

It has always been my philosophy that when I prepare a unit for rent, I want it in such good working condition I shouldn't have to go back to do repairs for months—maybe years. It makes more sense to solve those pesky problems when there are no tenants in the dwelling. You don't have to worry about making small talk with them. You don't have to work around their personal belongings. You don't have to worry about accidentally breaking, staining, or damaging something. And you don't have to do extra fixes a tenant might ask you to do while you're there—things like hanging a picture or moving something heavy.

Finally, in preparing your rental, remember that attention to detail can often make a difference when you are showing your property to prospective renters. Little things count. For instance, add a new shower curtain and set of bath towels to the bathroom. Maybe a couple area rugs on the hardwood floor would look nice. Natural drapes and/or blinds in all bedrooms add a homey touch. Put welcome mats by the entry doors. Anything to help potential tenants envision the rental as a home—their home—can be useful.

Now that you and your rental are prepared for a new tenant, proceed to the next chapter where the search begins.

CHAPTER 2

Major Tenant Qualifications

After you fix up your rental unit, you need someone to occupy that property, pay the rent on time, and hopefully keep it in the condition it's currently in. This someone has to be a special someone, so you need criteria to help you recognize when you've found that person. I can tell you from experience that when the phone starts to ring, you will get all kinds of prospective tenants with varying lifestyle habits and problems. Many of these callers you will not want or need to have as your tenant. Those callers need to be eliminated at the beginning of the rental process.

This leads us to the all-important question: How do you eliminate those callers who could potentially cause you problems? The answer can be both simple and complex. The simple part is you interview the caller to see if he or she meets the standards you want for a tenant. The complex part is *developing* those standards.

Define Standards

Simply stated, standards are the minimum criteria or qualifications that a landlord will expect from a tenant to qualify for the rental. These qualifications cover the major topics of concern for landlords. Topics such as income, credit, pets, rent and job stability, evictions, and convicted felonies are generally the main ones to consider.

The Tenant Qualifications Form

This chapter and the next detail a form designed to assess tenant qualifications. The main purpose of the form is to help you, as the landlord, develop the qualifications you're looking for in a tenant. This will prepare you for when you begin speaking to tenant prospects. These qualifications cover many important areas and become the standards by which all tenant prospect calls will be judged. This form acts as your compass in your interviewing process to keep you on course to find a quality tenant. You will use these qualifications as your guide and source of reference as you speak to and interview all prospective tenants. Failure to meet a qualification will eliminate the tenant prospect, allowing you to move on to the next. The Tenant Qualifications form and its correct use can vastly improve your chances of finding good tenants. I've been using this form for years and I can say with confidence it has made my tenant selection task a lot easier and a lot more professional.

Besides preparing the rental unit, filling out this form is the first thing you will do when it comes time to search for a tenant. You will fill it out before you advertise, show the dwelling, or place a sign on the property. This rule is extremely important since filling out the form during or after the search for a tenant has begun can lead to problems. You will better understand this rule as we proceed through this book.

Developing qualifications

When the time is right for you to begin to fill out the Tenant Qualifications form for your rental unit, you will need to make decisions on what you will or will not accept in terms of requirements for your tenants. These requirement decisions are tough ones since there are *so* many things to consider when setting up these guidelines. For this reason you are probably asking yourself, "How do I choose and develop the best guidelines possible?" Well, here's my answer, and I'm sure it's going to surprise you: You are going to have to practice discrimination.

Before you get upset about that last statement, label me as a bigot, and throw my book away, let me explain. The Fair Housing Act of 1968, and the amendment to the Fair Housing Act of 1989, state that you are not allowed to discriminate based on things such as age, race, religion, sex, physical handicap, and children. The act and its amendment are very worthwhile laws. In fact, it is one of the better laws ever passed. Its enactment has brought an opportunity for homeownership to millions of people who previously had problems owning a home because of acts of discrimination and redlining.

Title VIII of the Civil Rights Act of 1968 (Fair Housing Act), as amended, prohibits discrimination in the sale, rental, and financing of dwellings, and in other housing-related transactions, based on race, color, national origin, religion, sex, familial status (including children under the age of 18 living with parents or legal custodians, pregnant women, and people securing custody of children under the age of 18), and handicap (disability).

The following is an excerpt from the government booklet entitled *Fair Housing—Equal Opportunity for All*. It is quoted from the section "What Is Prohibited?" on pages 1–2.

What is prohibited?

In the Sale and Rental of Fair Housing: No one may take any of the following actions based on race, color, national origin, religion, sex, familial status, or handicap (disability):

- Refuse to rent or sell housing
- Refuse to negotiate for housing
- Make housing unavailable
- Deny a dwelling
- Set different terms, conditions or privileges for sale or rental of a dwelling
- Provide different housing services or facilities
- Falsely deny that housing is available for inspection, sale or rental
- For profit, persuade owners to sell or rent (blockbusting) or
- Deny anyone access to or membership in a facility or service (such as multiple listing service) related to the sale or rental of housing

In Addition: it is illegal for anyone to:

- Threaten, coerce, intimidate or interfere with anyone exercising a fair housing right or assisting others who exercise that right
- Advertise or make any statement that indicates a limitation or preference based on race, color, national origin, religion, sex, familiar status or handicap (disability). This prohibition against discriminatory advertising applies to single family housing that is otherwise exempt from the Fair Housing Act.

This list is an exact duplicate of the list from the Fair Housing booklet in regards to renting property. There is also a section on mortgage lending in this booklet, but I did not feel the need to reprint it here.

Legal Discrimination Versus Illegal Discrimination

Even though the Fair Housing Act prohibits discrimination from areas covered in the law, the FHA of 1968 *does not* stop you from discriminating based on other areas of activity. This is the difference between illegal discrimination and legal discrimination. Articles not covered by the Fair Housing Act can legally be discriminated against, although I must warn you, this can be a very fine line and a very confusing issue. Often people discriminate against those protected by the Fair Housing Act totally by accident with no ill intent. Unfortunately, those are not excusable reasons for violation of the Fair Housing Act laws, and if you are caught doing so, you could face some stiff penalties.

To help you better understand the concept of legal discriminatory practices and hopefully provide you with the knowledge to abide within the law, let me give you a couple pieces of information to remember. Please memorize them and take them to heart. The Fair Housing Act protects people from being discriminated against on personal levels. It protects their right for equality among all humans. Never discriminate against this right. As a landlord, you want to *discriminate against things or habits (not individuals) that can, do, or could affect the profit and safety of your landlording business and if taken to court, would be recognized as such.*

When I speak of practicing legal discriminating, I am talking about areas that are covered by the latter statement. For instance, can you refuse to rent to someone who is being evicted because they have not paid rent? Can you refuse to rent to someone who has a pit bull? Can you refuse to rent to someone who moves every two months? The answers to the above questions are yes, yes, and yes. These areas and many others are not protected under the Fair Housing Act, and under these circumstances, you are allowed to discriminate against these issues, as long as you do it equally to each and every tenant prospect and don't break the laws of the Fair Housing Act in the process. In other words, don't refuse to rent to a single mother because she owns a pit bull then proceed to the next prospect and rent to him and his pit bull. If you refuse to rent to someone because of a qualification, that qualification has to extend to everybody.

Other Fair Housing Guidelines

Keep in mind that the laws of the Fair Housing Act are nationwide, with the only exception to that law being if a certain locale decides to give *more* protection than is covered by the federal law, that locale coverage is recognized. Simply stated, the Fair Housing Act is the minimum guideline to follow.

Also keep in mind that case law, which is a judge's ruling on a particular case, can alter the Fair Housing Act—or at least the interpretation of it. On rare occasions, the case law verdicts can cause unknown problems for you. I mention this not to scare you, but to let you know things constantly change in our laws.

To better understand the Fair Housing Act and all it entails, go to a seminar, class, or lecture offered on fair housing and learn as much as you can. You also may want to find a competent lawyer who is knowledgeable about fair housing and its case law.

Rest assured, where applicable, I will make several references to discriminating laws as we learn and discuss the five steps of tenant selection. If you ever have any questions about the FHA, call the Housing Discrimination Hotline at 1-800-669-9777 or visit their website at http://www.hud.gov/offices/fheo/.

What the Tenant Qualifications Form Does

With all that said, the line between discriminating legally and breaking the law is a fine one. To give you a better chance of not crossing that line, you need a written guide. This is where the Tenant Qualifications form comes into play. Next to your lease, it is probably the most important paperwork you will fill out. By filling out this form with your decisions on what you will or will not require from people who wish to rent your dwelling, you will have established a written guideline to direct you through your tenant search. With a written guideline, you are less apt to intentionally or accidentally break any Fair Housing Laws as you eliminate callers who fail to meet your legal discriminating qualifications.

The Tenant Qualifications form will be the most difficult of all those discussed in this book. At first, you may feel confused or overwhelmed. Please don't run. This form is the most important form of any in this book. It compels you to think about the many possible problem scenarios that can come your way in your career as a landlord. Filling out this form before you rent forces you to make decisions and choices that will help avoid tenant problem scenarios in the future. In a nutshell, this form helps to control the urge to rent to the first "warm body with a dollar" who comes along and enables you to find a good, quality tenant. Now let's look at and discuss this form.

The Tenant Qualifications Form

The Tenant Qualifications form begins with two important disclaimers printed directly under the form's title. I purposely placed these disclaimers before the actual qualifications because of the important jobs they do. I wanted you to see them first, each time you fill out the form so you'd never forget what they mean.

The first sentence of the disclaimer is as follows: *If applicant intentionally lies, falsifies, omits, or hides pertinent information during any stage of the tenant selection process, applicant can be denied rental of said property.*

I added this disclaimer to the form after I went through a period where it seemed all my applicants were constantly fibbing. I'm not talking a little lie such as having a pet fish when they told me they had none—but major stuff.

For example, one of my qualifications is acceptable credit, which I always ask about. During one interview, I had a couple tell me their credit was pretty good—no major problems. Upon running the usual credit report, it was revealed that the husband's wages were being garnished to the tune of $200 per month for a judgment he lost. In addition to that, his wages were being garnished another $400 per month to help pay back years of child support. If $600 in monthly garnishments wasn't enough (this $600 represented about two weeks of his monthly take-home pay), he had also established credit with five creditors and on his credit report,

STEP ONE

Tenant Qualifications

Page 1 of 2

(If applicant intentionally lies, falsifies, omits or hides pertinent information during any stage of the tenant selection process, applicant can be denied rental of said property. If applicant is not of legal age, or if applicant does not have a Social Security number or other form of government issued ID, applicant can be denied rental of said property.).

Address _____ Date _____

Rent	+	Sec. Dep.	+	Last Mo. Rent	=	Total	Date	Initial
	+		+		=			
	+		+		=			
	+		+		=			

Major Qualifications

1) INCOME Minimum per month Gross pay $_____ Take Home pay $_____

Notes   or government assistance Y/N Must pass **"Cash Flow"** form Y/N

Notes _____

2) CREDIT Credit check Y/N Cost single $_____ married $_____

A) Good established credit Y/N

Rating _____ or higher Bankruptcy _____ years or longer

B) Other/Problem credit Y/N

No/new credit Y/N

Other bankruptcies Y/N _____ months or longer

Other credit problems Y/N

Landlord credit problems Y/N

*Problem credit w/extra security Y/N How much $_____

Notes_____

3) ACCEPTABLE CRIMINAL BACKGROUND CHECK Y/N

Notes_____

4) PETS (Exception: Animals covered by Americans with Disabilities Act)

Dogs allowed _____ Y/N Cats allowed _____ Y/N

Extra sec dep $_____ per pet Extra rent. $_____ per pet per month

Notes_____

5) EVICTION (Exception: owner needing house back) Y/N

Notes_____

all five were rated as unpaid as of that date. On top of all that, he made only two payments on a car he wrecked because as he later said to me, "I can't drive it. Why should I pay for it?"

Since I was certain that anyone who lied to me before they rented my dwelling would definitely lie to me after they moved in, I needed an out— a way to at least have the option of automatically removing anyone with dishonest scruples since on occasion they seem to somehow pass my qualifications. (Of course they did. They lied to do it.) Anyway, I wanted this "out" to be in writing and visible at all times, which is how it came to be on this form.

The second sentence of the disclaimer states: *If applicant is not of legal age, or if applicant does not have a Social Security number or other form of government-issued ID, applicant can be denied rental of said property.*

Many states and locales address the issue of age when it comes to renting a place to live, with the age of eighteen as the general legal age recognized to do so. It is illegal to rent to someone under this established age with a few exceptions: if he or she is in the military, an emancipated minor, or legally married.

Although it's not illegal to rent to someone who does not have a valid form of government-appointed identification, such as a Social Security number or green card, it is unwise. Should you rent to such a person and he or she somehow causes you a problem and hits the road, leaving you holding the bag, you want some kind of ID number to pass along to the proper authorities. Having such a number is not guaranteed to provide justice for you, but it can offer a small glimmer of hope where there would otherwise be none.

Reviewing the Tenant Qualifications Form

Now that we have these reminders out of the way, let's begin to review the meat of the Tenant Qualifications form. Please feel free to make reference to the form in this book as needed.

Filling in Dates

Following the disclaimers, you will begin to fill out the form. The first line is the address of the property being rented followed by the date you made out the tenant qualifications. Please don't skip this line as this information can prove to be important, especially the date. The dating of your forms will give an accurate timeline of things as they happen, which can be of utmost importance if you ever end up in litigation during your landlording career. If you don't think a timeline is important, watch some of the court shows that are on TV during the day, such as *Judge Judy, People's Court,* or *Judge Mathis.* One of the most important things these judges do is try to establish a timeline of the events to determine if they corroborate with the stories of the defendant and plaintiff. If you watch these shows regularly, you will notice that whoever has the dated paper timeline almost always wins. Get in the habit of always filling in the date anywhere it is required.

Of course, should you use it in a court of law, it is possible someone could accuse you of falsifying the date when you filled out the Tenant Qualifications form. If you wish to add a layer of protection, besides dating this form you could clip the top of the front page of the newspaper (you want the date saved) on the day you fill out the form and attach it accordingly. This way you have some concrete proof that you filled out the form when you said you did.

If you are one of those people who really wants to know you've protected yourself, you can do one very simple, easy thing. Make a copy of your filled-out Tenant Qualifications form and mail it to yourself. Make sure on the front of the envelope, across the bottom, to write down the address of the property and date the form was filled out. When this envelope arrives, do not open it. Put it in the rental property's file for safekeeping and should you ever need absolute proof of when you filled the Tenant Qualifications form out you will have the answer on the postmarked envelope the form is in.

Monies Required

Following the address and date is the area that covers the amount of money needed by the tenant to rent the property. The amount of first and last month's rent and the security deposit are generally included here. You will decide what categories and dollar amounts you wish to collect in each. Take a look at the form, and you'll see headings for the following:

- Rent
- Security deposit
- Last month's rent
- Total (rent + security deposit + last month's rent)
- Date
- Initial (yours, for each item)

Rent. Here is where you decide how much rent to charge for the dwelling. I advise you to use care when choosing your rent amount. Asking too much will keep your rental empty and renting too low will slowly eat at your potential profit each and every month. Either way you lose money. Gage your rent amount by comparing it with other rentals in the area.

Security deposit. A security deposit is the upfront money collected in case the tenant causes any damage to the rental during their tenancy. This deposit amount is generally equal to one month's rent, but can be more or less depending on circumstances. A general feeling about security deposits is to have the rent and security deposit listed as two different dollar figures. This helps discourage tenants from thinking their security deposit can be used as the last month's rent. Be aware that some states and locales put a cap on the amount of security deposit a landlord can require.

Also, some states have tight restrictions on what that security deposit can be used for. If your state is one of those, see if the term "indemnification" would be a good substitute for the word "security." You would be wise to check with your local legal advisor to see what the security deposit amount or usage guidelines are in your area.

Last month's rent. As previously mentioned, some tenants try to use their security deposit to cover their last month in the property. Asking for the last month up front is one way of avoiding this problem. Just be aware that many renters cannot come up with large sums of money at lease signing, so use care in the amounts for which you ask.

There are three separate headings to collect for instead of one because I recommend you collect a separate payment for each category on the day of lease signing. For instance, if you're just collecting rent and nothing else, then you only need one check or money order. If you're collecting rent and a security deposit, then you need two checks or two money orders, and so on.

Personally, I collect individual monies because I keep separate accounts for these monies: one for rent and one for the other categories. The reason for this is because the security deposit and last month's rent are not yours to keep until you are legally entitled to them. Because of this fact, I recommend keeping those monies in a separate, no interest-bearing account until they are either returned to the tenant or yours to keep.

Total/date/initial. Once you have established what categories you will collect money for and how much in each, you'll want to know the total dollar figure an applicant will need to rent your dwelling. Fill in the total and date on the line provided.

Looking at the form, you will also notice that there are three identical lines. When you first begin to fill out the form, start on the top line and if you realize at some point during the rental process that you need to alter your dollar figures, do so on the next line. Then date and initial that line. You will find it is only natural as you are learning your area's clientele and your rental's earning potential, you'll need to make some adjustments. Adjustments are allowed and encouraged, just back them up with good documentation by recording and dating the change. See the following example:

Rent	+ Security +	Last Mo. Rent	= Total	Date	Initial
$800	+ $800	+ $800	= $2,400	8/3/07	DC
$750	+ $800	+ $0	= $1,550	8/17/07	DC

Once completed, filling in the above section covers your decision regarding rent, security deposit, and last month's rent. Unfortunately, these items are all most average landlords ever think of as qualifications. But you want to be an above-average landlord with above-average tenants residing in your rentals. To accomplish that goal, you need more, and this is where the Tenant Qualifications form begins to shine.

Major Qualifications

To simplify the form, I've split it into two sections: a major section and minor section. This chapter covers the major section and its qualifications. I would *never* rent a unit out to anyone without knowing how they qualify in the major qualifications section. It is these five qualifications wherein 90 percent of your problems will emerge. Keep in mind that you may choose to use all, some, or none of the major qualifications. The choice is yours. I will say, however, that *the more major qualifications you use, the better your chances of finding a good quality tenant.*

If you choose to use nothing on the Tenant Qualifications form, that's fine, too. At least read this chapter in its entirety so you'll have an idea of the areas and issues covered in this step. I hope you will acquire some information that will be useful to you in your rental selection.

Another thought to keep in mind: It's important to use qualifications to find the very best possible tenant, but if you make those qualifications too stringent, no one will ever meet your standards to rent the unit because you will find some fault in everyone. You need to pick your qualifications and your battles wisely.

Let's take a look at each of the major qualifications listed on the Tenant Qualifications form.

1) *Income*

The first and probably most important qualification is income. As a landlord, what you *have* to know is if the tenant has the income to pay the rent *consistently* every single month. You'll want to know the minimum income needed by a prospective tenant to accomplish that rent task on a regular basis. This income can be earned income, steady pensions, regular alimony, and so forth—basically, any money that is a consistent income stream for the tenant. You need to know this qualification probably more than any other. Without money coming *in* to them, it is not going *out* to you. Remember, the key here is *steady* income: week after week, month after month.

Minimum gross pay. You may be asking, once you've decided on the desired rent, how do you decide on minimum income required? The simplest way is with percentages, just like the lending industry. These percentages are a balance between a person's income and what the lending institute believes the average borrower can safely handle in payments. Some mortgage brokers will allow a house payment to be one-third of a person's monthly gross (33 percent), while others, such as banks, use a more conservative number like 28 percent. At this time in the tenant selection process, you are just trying to get in the ballpark regarding a prospect's income, so you want to keep things simple. After you have actually found a prospective tenant, you will do a much deeper investigation of the tenant's income and spending habits to determine if he or she can pay the monthly rent.

To keep it as simple as possible, I take my determined rent price and multiply it by 3. A multiple of 3 times the asked rent figure means that 33 percent of a tenant's income can be assigned toward that rent payment. Again, this 33 percent ratio is along the same lines as what a broker might use to determine loans for houses. Naturally, this multiple is not set in stone so you could use a higher multiple, such as 3.5 or 4, if you so choose. If your multiple is too high, however, it will mean there will be fewer people who will qualify since the higher multiple means the tenant will need a higher income, resulting in a smaller tenant pool. Likewise, you could use a lower multiple such as 2.5, but here you need to understand that while a lower multiple will allow more people to qualify based on their income, this lower ratio could result in qualifying people who are more likely to have trouble paying bills (and rent) if money gets tight.

I believe a multiple of 3 is a safe starting point, and I would recommend you begin here. I also recommend you never go below a 2.5 multiple. The range of 2.5 to 3.5 is a good range within which to work.

The dollar amount of the rent ($800, in our example) times your multiple (3) will determine the gross income needed. Once you've established this figure, you can place that dollar amount next to the heading "gross pay."

Take-home pay. Next, you need to determine the figure needed for "take-home pay," which is the income a wage earner actually gets to keep once taxes have been removed from that paycheck. You will want to establish this figure because many tenant prospects will tell you their after-tax, or take-home pay, when you inquire about their income. To arrive at the take-home figure, simply subtract 25 percent of the gross income to give you a monthly take-home figure. This 25 percent will represent

Uncle Sam's tax take. If the monthly rent for your unit is $800, the first line under "income" would look like this:

Minimum per month   Gross pay $2,400   Take-home pay $1,800
                            ($800 x 3)   ($2,400 x .25)

Keep in mind that there are different tax brackets starting at 10 percent and working up to 35 percent or more. I use 25 percent because I feel this percentage is a safe portrayal of what most middle-income families pay in taxes. If you live in an area where the average income of the average renter is in a higher or lower tax bracket, then feel free to adjust the tax percentage multiple accordingly.

Or government assistance—Y/N. As you may know, there are many government assistance programs to help lower income people with their housing needs. Often these programs can be great for a landlord because the government is paying most, if not all of the rent. Payment to you is virtually guaranteed because you essentially have a partner for your tenant's rent—the federal government.

The line "or government assistance Y/N" is where you decide if you will use one of these government programs. You will also notice the word "or" in front of "government assistance." The reason for this is that with a guaranteed payment, a prospective tenant's income is less important since someone else is paying all or part of the rent. The result is the total income may be exempted or altered. Unfortunately, the subject of government housing assistance programs is too large to cover in this particular chapter, or even this book. However, there is an appendix in the back of the book detailing how government assistance programs can affect the tenant selection process. If you are interested in using government programs for your rentals, please read that appendix, as these programs can have their own pitfalls and disadvantages in addition to their advantages.

Must pass Cash Flow form—Y/N. The next decision to make is "Must pass Cash Flow form Y/N." The Cash Flow form is its own separate entity, and it is covered extensively in chapter 11. It is an important form and has a lot of detail. But the short version of the form's function is this: Once you have a prospective tenant, you need to find out in greater detail where their money goes each month. By getting details on their spending habits, you'll have a much better idea if they have enough cash each month to regularly pay rent after they pay their other obligations. To state it simply, if they have enough to pay rent, they have passed the form. I highly recommend using this form because it acts as a check-and-balance system, or a review of how a tenant handles money. Some people make an above-average income but still spend more than they make, resulting in late rent payments to you, the landlord. This form will help detect those people.

Notes. The next section is for "Notes." This line is for any exceptions you are willing to consider in the income area of the tenant sheet. This line is here because there may be some differences in what you feel you might need for an income qualification. Since it is impossible for me to know and therefore list all those differences, you would make any adjustments or additions you feel you personally need or desire for your own qualifications on this line.

For future reference, every qualification on the Tenant Qualifications form has the "notes" line to be used when needed. You can personalize, customize, or rewrite any of these qualifications as you see fit. In fact, I encourage you to do so. Just please remember not to discriminate illegally in the process.

At this point you have developed your first tenant qualification on the form. The procedure for developing the rest of the qualifications follows the same path. Take a moment and refer to the completed sample form on page 46 to better understand the process. Do this with each qualification.

2) *Credit*

The second major qualification to develop is credit. This subject has changed drastically in the 10 years I've been renting units—and not for the better. As I write this book, northwest Indiana (where I'm from) is number two in real estate foreclosures in the state and number one in bankruptcies all stemming from a downward shift in our economy. This also means we have a higher than normal amount of people with credit problems. Whether the economy is good or bad in your area, it stands to reason that you need to decide how to approach the issue of credit because a person's credit will best reveal if he or she is responsible in paying bills. Checking a person's credit by means of a credit report is by far the best way to detect a tenant prospect's credit history. By looking at credit history you will uncover many useful tidbits of information regarding the tenants' finances that will help you choose the best tenant possible. Too often a landlord skips this vital qualification and the resulting aftermath is often disastrous. Please do yourself a favor and always run a credit report.

Credit check—Y/N. The credit section begins with the decision to run a credit check on any prospective tenant. As I've already stated, I highly recommend circling Y and then running a credit check.

Credit checks cost money, and I advise you to have each prospective tenant pay for their report upfront. So you need to write in how much it will cost each single adult and a married couple to run their credit in the space provided. Call one or two of the credit bureaus in your area to figure this cost. Generally, two single people living together are treated as two single fees because credit checks are usually searched by last names. Two last names—even among married couples—means two individual credit checks.

Also, remember, when you charge for a credit check, you are allowed to tack on something for your time—$5 or $10 is acceptable. Just add it to your price as you fill out the Tenant Qualification sheet and remember this extra charge is income to you and should be reported as such.

I run a credit check on everyone, including people who have no credit or are just establishing credit. I include this no credit group when checking credit for two reasons: I don't really know if the tenant prospect is telling me the truth, and some people really don't know what constitutes good or bad credit, so they may misrepresent their credit standing. These people might have a lease, student loan, or car payment, but because they do not own a credit card, they believe they have no credit. Again, I run a credit check on everyone. Period.

Once you have established the credit check requirements, you need to decide on where you will personally draw the line on what you will or won't accept in the credit qualification. This will be accomplished by establishing two categories for credit: Good established credit, or Other/ Problem credit.

Good established credit—Y/N. You can ask 10 different people what constitutes good credit and you will probably receive 10 different answers. A banker's good credit standards are different from a mortgage broker's standards, which are different from a credit card company. How you view credit as a landlord will most likely be different from another landlord. This leaves us with the question, what is "good established credit"?

As far as I'm concerned, good established credit means just that: The person the credit report is about has no or very few current discrepancies and has at least three solid credit listings in their credit history. These criteria should be easy enough to figure out by obtaining a credit report, but many people have some inaccuracies or even unknown problems on their reports. You must understand that the credit reporting industry is so complex that many items reported on a report are incomplete, inaccurate, or just very confusing for the average untrained eye to read. How can you, as a part-time landlord, figure out if your tenant prospect has good credit or not?

You can do this by rating your applicant's credit. Actually, your credit reporting agency may do this for you. Generally, the rating will be a number such as 550 or 600 or 730. In the world of credit, this number is referred to as the "credit score." The higher the score, the better that individual's credit. For example, a score of 680 and up is very good and considered low risk, whereas a credit score of 515 would probably be regarded as high risk.

Rating ___ or higher. If you wish to use credit scoring in your qualification, you must pick a score, or number, and use that number as your separation between "good" and "bad" credit. Let's say your established number is 600, which represents someone just below a medium risk but is a high enough score to give an adequate separation between the two credit categories. You would write your selected number in the space provided.

At this point in time, don't worry about what number to choose for your separation point. For now, stick with a 600 score and understand why this separation exists. There are other chapters in this book on credit reporting that explain in detail the aspects of reading and understanding these reports and they will answer many of your questions.

Bankruptcy _____ years or older. When looking for a good quality tenant, it is hard to find people with exceptional credit who wish to rent. Generally, people with topnotch credit own a home and may never become renters.

What you will find when looking at tenant prospects is a group of people who are renters for various reasons. Some are new to the renter's world, while others are lifers for whatever reasons. Others are slowly rebuilding their credit so they cannot buy a house at this time, while others will live each day with bad credit, never striving to improve. Often, you will rent to people who are coming back from bankruptcy and rebuilding their credit. These folks have gone through bankruptcies for various reasons, but currently are on the clean path to better credit health.

When I receive a credit report that looks good and has a decent score, I often will notice there are older bankruptcies on these reports. These older bankruptcies followed by a new and improved credit history are fairly common, and depending on the age of the bankruptcy may not be a huge problem. Even though I'd rather not see any bankruptcies on the report, any bankruptcy over three years old—which I recommend as a minimum length of time—is acceptable to me. Whatever minimum length of time you accept, write your standard in the space provided in the area covering bankruptcies.

Other/Problem credit—Y/ N. Depending on your rental mar-

Many people with a decent credit score above a medium or so risk will probably not be looking to rent, as most of these folks own their own home, especially after the last few years of low interest rates. When rates start to climb, fewer people can afford a house payment, so you will then begin to see more applicants with higher scores. The ideal score for a cutoff point is the one where people just miss the boat in obtaining a home loan. Work in this area or slightly below.

ket and local economics, you may find there are some gray areas to consider as you develop your qualifications. One of these gray areas could be other/problem credit. This generally boils down to four specific issues listed below. It is up to you to decide whether or not you want to deal with each particular credit issue when selecting a tenant.

No/New credit—Y/N. A tenant prospect with no or new credit can be risky because the person with this issue probably hasn't learned to exercise good saving and spending habits yet. I say "probably" because I have seen no/new credit candidates that paid cash for everything, resulting in a wonderful tenant prospect, although, I must say, these tenants are few and far between. But if you did find such a prospect, he or she would be your best case no/new credit scenario.

Another potentially worthwhile no/new credit scenario could be this: Your tenant prospect just graduated from college or vocational school and is guaranteed a steady, good-paying job. Your rental, which is one block away from her employment, is just what she needs. Even though she is new to the concept of credit, her situation looks promising, so she could very well be a decent prospect.

My point is that even though a no/new credit prospect is probably learning how to handle money and therefore, could be more risky for you as a landlord, don't necessarily shy away from this group as a potential pool for prospects. Just realize there is a bigger risk with this group and adjust for this risk. I will show you how to do that shortly.

Other bankruptcies—Y/N. The next issue is one we talked about briefly a couple of pages back, but we will now discuss the issue as it applies to problem credit.

After the March 2000 stock market peak and decline, then the terrorist attacks on September 11, 2001, followed by the Iraq war and economy slowdown of 2003, I noticed that many more of the tenant prospect calls I received involved a recent bankruptcy. Unfortunately, there are few signs indicating this trend will slow down anytime soon.

Also around this time, I began to notice I was receiving a lot of medical-caused bankruptcy calls, and I suspect it will be a continuing trend. Today's fast-rising hospital and insurance costs make it common to see someone struggling to pay their bills after an unexpected bout with cancer or other medical tragedy. Too often this forces otherwise financially stable people into the bankruptcy courts.

Overall, the growing number of bankruptcies caused me to sit back and evaluate how they would affect my tenant selection process. I eventually reasoned that after a person has gone through a bankruptcy, their sensitivity to personal spending and bill paying may be greatly improved, and therefore, he or she may not be such a severe risk.

In short, it didn't take me long to realize that if I didn't accept these bankruptcy calls, my pool of prospects would be infinitely smaller. All this led me to decide to accept more current bankruptcies based on certain qualifications and criteria.

I've already mentioned that you should look for bankruptcies that are a minimum of three years old, but what about those that are less than three years? At this point, you must decide if you'll accept a more recent bankruptcy and if so, what standards you'll accept. Let me recommend that you only accept "established" bankruptcies—in other words, bankruptcies that have been filed and have had some time to pass since the filing. How much time must have elapsed since they filed? Personally, I will usually accept their bankruptcy if it was established 12 months ago or longer. After a year of paying bills following a bankruptcy, people should be back in control, and if not, I feel I will be able to locate current problems through their credit report and Cash Flow form.

To lessen some of the risk of these more recent bankruptcies, you can ask for more security deposit from your tenant prospect. This will be discussed in detail later.

Of course, if you are refusing bankruptcy, simply circle N and don't worry about elapsed time. If you wish to accept only specific criteria such as medical bankruptcies, simply write in "medical bankruptcy only" in the notes section.

Other credit problems—Y/N. The third credit issue deals with everyone else who has credit problems, including those whose credit score falls below your minimum or people who are currently having trouble paying bills but have yet to file bankruptcy. From a landlord perspective, I believe someone not paying his or her current bills is a much higher risk than someone with no credit or new credit, or someone who has filed for bankruptcy. The reason is that these people are still responsible for coming up with that money owed. Once people start to slip behind financially, it is extremely hard to catch up, so if they are struggling with bills now, there is a great chance they will continue to struggle with their bills—including rent—in the future. I have witnessed people getting behind on their bills, and I have seen few turn it around successfully.

In fact, here are two statements I guarantee you will hear when discussing these credit problems with potential tenants. First, people in the previously described situation will *always* tell you they pay rent on time. Maybe they do, maybe they don't. You don't know them from Adam, so you should probably bet on "maybe not." Let's face it. They're not paying anyone else on time, so why do you think you'll be their one exception?

Second, many times people in this credit group will tell you they *plan* to file for bankruptcy. I don't doubt their sincerity, but the problem with that idea is that it takes money to file and money is the one thing they are currently lacking, so filing for bankruptcy could take a while, if it happens at all. Also, once they have filed, there is still no solid proof they will be able to handle their finances and keep from falling into the same situation that led to bankruptcy in the first place. Unless your clientele dictates you accept these credit problems, I would circle "N" for this choice.

Landlord credit problems—Y/N. The one area I recommend never taking on a past credit problem is when there is a problem with a past landlord. As far as I'm concerned, anyone who owes money to a past or previous landlord in any way, shape, or form is not conducive to your goal of making money in the rental game. I'm not saying all people who have or had financial discrepancies with a landlord are bad or even in the wrong. What I am saying is that being a landlord is how you make your money and people who owe past landlords are a higher risk to you and your business. Therefore, I would think twice about accepting anyone with this credit issue.

Problem credit w/extra security—Y/N. As you may have figured out by now, anyone who falls under the category of other/problem credit has some risk associated with them. Those at the top of the list are less risky than those at the bottom of the list. Remember when I mentioned that risk was okay as long as you adjusted for that risk? Well, now is the time to let you in on how to do just that.

There are a couple of ways, but the absolute best is to collect more security deposit. When more security deposit is required, say two or three times the base security (or whatever the maximum is that is allowed in your state), you'll have a much stronger financial net should your tenant begin to have trouble with his or her obligations to you. The reason this idea is the best is because if something *does* happen, then that money has already been deposited in your escrow account, where you are in

> In October 2005, the laws applying to bankruptcy changed. One of the new side effects of the changes in the bankruptcy laws that went into effect is that the cost to file has increased because of higher attorney fees and other associated costs. This means the filer will now need even more money than before the law change to file, and again, money is the one thing they don't have.

control of it. Having these extra funds on hand can go a long way toward giving you added peace of mind on any risk you take. Just make sure your lease states that the landlord can use the security deposit for rent if the tenant defaults on those payments. Although, let me give you a warning: Only use this on tenant applicants who pass the rest of your qualifications. Do not use it as a reason to put a truly bad tenant in your rental.

If you wish to collect extra security deposit, be sure to indicate on the form how much extra you are going to collect from those with problem credit.

Also keep in mind that the potential rental clientele in many areas of the country simply can't afford extremely large security deposits. Be careful with how much you ask for. Also, if you are dealing with a renter's market, too high of a deposit could force people to look elsewhere to rent. Use common sense on this issue for each situation.

There is one other solution to "problem credit" I'd like to mention, and that is cosigners. Many landlords depend on having a cosigner when they rent to people with credit problems, and I say bravo if it works for you. But for those of you who've never dealt with a cosigner, let me bring up a couple of issues: Cosigners can be hard to find. Many people refuse to cosign for anyone. Have you ever heard the saying, "You can't get blood out of a turnip"? Well, try to get blood out of *two* turnips. It can be twice as frustrating. Sometimes with cosigners, you just end up with two people to chase for money instead of one.

But good cosigner situations *do* exist, and if you ask for one and are successful in securing one, I recommend filling out a Cash Flow form and running a credit check on the cosigner. The reason you ask for this information from a cosigner is because he or she could end up paying the rent, and you want to guarantee that this person pays his or her bills and can cover your prospective tenant's rent if it becomes necessary.

One last possibility is to have the cosigner front the extra security deposit. This gives the cosigner a reason to help make sure you get your rent paid. This idea also gives you the best of both worlds: an extra security deposit and a cosigner. If you decide to ask any of this from your cosigner, write in the notes area what you require. It might look like this:

Notes: Cosigner okay by passing cash flow and credit qualifications.

One other item you may wish to add to the notes section is the absolute *lowest* credit score you will accept. For instance, in the good credit section, you might have decided that anything above 600 is okay by your standards. But what about those people who make your overall qualifications but miss the score by a few points? It would probably be worth your time to write an exception allowing for a lower credit score with extra security deposit. It might read something like this:

Notes: Credit scores 530 to 599 acceptable with extra security deposit.

To best pick a number, stay away from the high-risk scoring as established by your credit reporting agency (to be better explained in future chapters) and use the medium-risk scores to help you avoid hard case credit problems.

If you have problems understanding any part of the credit sections we've discussed, view the sample on page 46.

3) *Acceptable Criminal Background Check*

I previously spoke of the legal right to discriminate against areas or things that could affect the profitability or safety of your landlording business. So far, the first two qualifications—income and credit—could drastically affect the financial stability of your rental business. The third qualification has to do more with safety.

America has the highest lawsuit rate of any country in the world. Every day, thousands of lawsuits are filed in our court system with most plaintiffs suing for some kind of damage recovery, generally equating to money. Naturally, to have a chance of being awarded money, the plaintiff needs to sue somebody with money (or lots of insurance). Whether it is true or not, as a landlord, you are believed to have money, especially by tenants and their attorneys. This automatically makes you vulnerable to a lawsuit.

Another thing to think about is that our prison system is bulging at the seams with too many inmates and not nearly enough money or room to continue to house and rehabilitate them all. Consequently, as the years go by, many of the less harsh offenders will be back on the streets looking to re-enter society.

With this discussion, it is not my intention to change anyone's view of landlords, or to criticize our judicial system, or even to judge anybody who has served their time for any kind of misconduct. I bring up these points

You will notice a lot of the times the "notes" space is the area you do your creative problem solving in advance. By filling in solutions to the main gray areas you may see and be willing to work around, you will have them in front of you when you speak to tenant prospects. This way you are not trying to find solutions under pressure since the decisions have already been made.

because as a landlord, if you unknowingly rent your house to a convicted child molester, rapist, murderer, or drug dealer, and this person decides to strike again, someone could easily point the finger at you and say you helped to place this offender in that particular neighborhood, apartment complex, and so on, so you are partly responsible for the crime. Needless to say, you could very easily find yourself on the defender side of a lawsuit. Therefore, I recommend running a criminal background check on all applicants to give you a layer of protection against such allegations.

At this point in time, not all states, jurisdictions, and locales are linked on one easy-to-use system for criminal background checks, as this takes time and money to accomplish, so it is quite possible to run a check and not uncover a previous offense. Given a little more time, I think you will see a super system for this task that will include all major cities and extend to the smallest rural communities. Even so, until that time arrives, you'd be wise to run a criminal background check and keep it in the tenant file as it will prove, if nothing else, that you are a professional landlord who tried to take the necessary precautions. I believe every landlord owes it to their neighbors and neighborhood to check the background of each adult resident who will live in their rental.

4) *Pets*

The subject of pets is another area with potential for safety issues. How would you like to rent to the person who raises exotic snakes and reptiles and sells them to the local pet store? Or possibly the guy who raises dogs for the underground dog fights that continue to grow in popularity? Not sure if any of these scenarios makes you comfortable? That's why this qualification covers the topic of pets.

Before I get too deep in this subject, let me state that I love animals. Always have. Probably always will. Growing up, I was always surrounded by a minimum of three pets at any given time. In fact, at the peak of pet ownership, my family had two dogs, one cat, two ducks, two parakeets, and several fish. Because of my family's love of pets, I understand pet owners. And as a pet owner, I understand that pets become members of the family; consequently, that is why I believe the issue of pets must be handled with care.

But touchy or not, this book is about finding the best tenant possible—one who makes you money and causes few problems. From the viewpoint of landlord profit, pets take on a new meaning. They become potential liabilities for a couple of reasons: Pets possess the ability to destroy property, and pets can sometimes pose a threat to public safety. Pets can and do cause these problems and more. Animals have natural instincts and a mind of their own, so it doesn't matter if the tenant tells you his or her pet won't bite somebody, never does his duty in the house, and has never, ever chewed anything. There is *always* a chance something will happen to prove the tenant wrong. But if you want the largest number of people to pick a tenant from, you might want to include pet owners. I do, and I've been pretty happy with the results.

Let's take a look at the pet section on the Tenant Qualifications form and cover each pet area along the way.

Dogs allowed/cats allowed—Y/N. Here you simply circle "yes" or "no" for your choice on allowing dogs and/or cats in your rental unit. The choice is yours and you can allow dogs or cats, neither, or even both in your dwelling. And since dogs and cats are the pet of choice for probably 90 percent of people who own pets and the pets most likely to cause damage to the rental, you'll want to make your decision intelligently when deciding on accepting these pets or not. Understand, the choice is totally yours, as this is one area you can legally discriminate against.

Some things you might want to consider when making the decision for allowing these pets or not could be:

- Age and quality of carpeting in the unit
- Condition and quality of hardwood and other flooring
- Condition of woodwork
- Whether the animal will make noise and bother neighbors

Extra security deposit/extra rent. If you choose to accept cats or dogs, you must figure out if you will charge an extra security deposit and/or extra rent for the privilege of dog or cat ownership in your house, and if you do, then you will need to fill in the lines that cover collecting these monies on the Tenant Qualifications form. The collection of extra rent and extra security deposit is often an area of opposing thoughts between landlord and tenant. Therefore, let's look at the problem from both perspectives, beginning with the tenant.

Many tenants think it is unfair to charge both extra security deposit and extra rent for the privilege of pet ownership and I will tell you why: If someone wants the pleasure of a pet (especially a dog or cat) an extra security deposit is nothing to pay for that pleasure. Most tenants understand that the extra security deposit is taken in case the pet somehow damages the rental unit. If they *do* damage something, the landlord pays for repairs out of that money.

Now when a landlord charges extra rent for a pet, are they charging it because the pet will be taking up more living space, use more hot water, or flush the toilet? No. They are charging extra rent because the pet could possibly cause damage to the property.

Therefore, when a landlord charges extra security deposit for wear and tear for possible damage *and* extra rent for those same reasons, many people believe they are being double-charged for the pleasure of owning a pet. And nobody likes to be double-charged.

On the other hand, from a landlord's perspective, charging the extra rent for the privilege of pet ownership is smart business since the risk of damage is definitely higher, and the tenant should compensate for that risk. Let's say you feel $25 a month is enough for compensation, so you add that to the rent. This additional $300 per year somewhat eases your mind.

Let's say six months into the lease the tenant moves out. Upon their departure you discover Fido had a weak bladder and consequently ruined all the living room carpet. The $150 you collected in extra rent ($25 per month times 6 months) will not cover that replacement and because you didn't receive any extra security money up front, you lose.

The basic thought to keep in mind from a landlord's perspective is a pet that has a bad day can do hundreds of dollars of damage to a property during that one day and collecting $25 or even $50 per month to cover that bad day just is not enough insurance—especially if this damage happens early in the tenancy. For this reason, it makes perfect sense from a landlord's perspective to charge both extra rent and extra security deposit for a pet.

Therefore, although tenants may believe you are double-charging them, in reality, the combination extra rent and extra security deposit is really an attempt to cover all scenarios—and rightfully so. Ultimately, it is easier financially on the tenant because most tenants will not have the extra money for a much larger security deposit, such as a full month's rent. Although this combination leaves you with a little more risk in the beginning of their tenancy, this risk is reduced with each passing month.

The one advantage about collecting extra rent is if upon departure, the tenant's pet really did little damage, then you've made more money since the extra rent is yours to keep no matter what.

Dogs from dangerous dog list—Y/N. Once you've made your decisions regarding extra security deposit and/or rent, you need to decide on a much more difficult topic. This topic covers dangerous dogs.

Certain cities in the country are labeling certain dogs as dangerous, and there are different trains of thought on how to handle the potential liability these dogs could create. Some of these cities now have ordinances that say if you own one of these dogs, you need a $500,000 insurance policy, a 6-foot fence to contain the dog, and a kennel. They also say if the animal is out of the kennel, it needs to be muzzled.

Other cities have no such ordinance, but this doesn't mean these dogs are any less dangerous. It just means nothing extremely traumatic has occurred within the city regarding these dogs that would result in such an ordinance being established.

Also, let me warn you, nowadays, certain insurance companies are refusing or canceling homeowner's insurance if you have what is considered a dangerous dog living on the property. If you own the property and a tenant has a dog that bites someone, but that tenant doesn't have adequate insurance to cover the dog bite, you could be held responsible and your homeowner's insurance may not pay. This alone should be enough to make you consider banning these dogs from your property.

This issue brings up another question: What if the tenant has a dog they keep insured? As far as I'm concerned, the answer is a complicated one. Some people say if a landlord's tenant is insured for the dog and something happens, then the landlord is legally off the hook. I don't agree. In a modern society where people can win multimillion-dollar settlements for hot coffee spilled on them, anything can happen in a lawsuit. I wouldn't want to chance it. When a victim receives a dog bite or worse, someone has to compensate the victim. I guarantee you that the owner of the dog—in this case your tenant—probably has zero in assets to compensate the victim. You, the landlord, however, are probably worth millions—at least in the jury's eyes—so you could very well be listed in that lawsuit. Landlords have assets. If you want to protect them, be careful about these dogs. (For more information on the subject of dangerous dogs, please visit www.FindThatQualityTenant.com.)

Others with written consent—Y/N. I accept other pets in my rentals but only with my written consent. I recommend you do the same.

The first two pets worth talking about are birds and fish, which by the way, are the favorite of the great real estate guru Carleton Sheets, whose pet policy is best summed up as, "The pet must swim or fly." Frankly, there is some wisdom in that statement as these two pets are generally popular and usually trouble-free from a landlord perspective, although when allowing a fish tank, you might want to ask for more security deposit. The reasoning is that if a tank breaks or leaks (although this is very rare), it will spill gallons of water on the floor. It doesn't matter how hard a tenant will try to clean it up; those gallons of water can still cause damage to drywall, trim, carpet, wood floors, and underlayment, leaving in their wake mold and mildew residue that is hard to get rid of. Mold is the next big scare in real estate, so do all you can to prevent it in the first place. If you ask for extra security deposit for fish, make a note of it in the notes area under the pet qualification.

When you give consent for any pet, you need to make your decision based on safety (both pet and human), potential damage to your rental unit, the owner's ability to care for that particular pet, and the local laws governing pets. Many farm, game, and wildlife animals are allowed as pets under strict licensing and permit restrictions. Check with your local government agencies if you have questions concerning unusual animals as pets. Overall, you want to know what is going on with these pets so you don't one day end up with a snake, tarantula, or rabbit farm on your property.

As far as collecting extra money for the other pets, most people will not pay extra for a rabbit, bird, or hamster, and I have to agree. They generally are pretty easy on a rental as far as maintenance goes. I've never had to replace carpeting because of a parakeet or goldfish. Use good judgment and get extra money for the pets that most likely will cause damage. And don't lose a good prospect trying to collect security deposit for a pet that has little chance of damaging your rental.

There is one notable exception to the rules regarding pets and it stems from the Fair Housing Act. This act states that a tenant is allowed to have a "companion" or "service" pet if the tenant needs one. Most people know a blind person's seeing eye dog is allowed everywhere but what most people, landlords included, don't know is that the law extends far beyond this definition. Animals are used to help people with other disabilities, such as deafness or severely limited movement, and can even be legally requested for "companionship" or accommodation. Also note that animals covered under this act are not considered "pets" but "aids" to someone with a disability. Therefore, you cannot charge extra rent or a security deposit under these conditions.

Should you ever have someone request any kind of animal under this need, you must consider the request and grant it if it is true and reasonable. To determine the validity of such a request, you should get professional verification from the tenant's doctor, therapist, or other health care provider. Remember, if you have any questions or concerns, call your local Federal Housing Authority office for answers.

The decision about pets is a tough call when you are trying to be a successful landlord. Use good judgment, common sense, and always keep in mind that it's your house so you must be able to live with your decisions. Pick your standards carefully.

5) *Eviction*

The subject of eviction is the last area of major qualifications to consider. I don't take evictions—legal or otherwise—with one notable exception. That exception is if the tenant had to move out because their current landlord had another use for the residence they were renting, such as selling the house or moving back into it. Actually, this is not a true eviction, but when you ask a tenant if they've ever been evicted, many in the above scenario will state that they have.

Don't be afraid to ask about evictions or requested vacates. I've asked and had people tell me they were moving out because they didn't pay rent. I even had one caller tell me he got evicted because he got rough with a landlord. Do either of these sound like a good prospect for your rental unit?

At this point, you have finished with the major qualifications, which should go a long way in finding a qualified tenant for your rental unit. Please feel free to study the sample qualifications on page 46 to better understand this chapter. If you think you've got it, and wish to have a little more strength in your qualifications, proceed to the next chapter and read about the minor qualifications.

STEP ONE

Tenant Qualifications

(If applicant intentionally lies, falsifies, omits or hides pertinent information during any stage of the tenant selection process, applicant can be denied rental of said property. If applicant is not of legal age, or if applicant does not have a Social Security number or other form of government issued ID, applicant can be denied rental of said property.).

Address __712 Oak__   Date __8/3/07__

Rent	+	Sec. Dep.	+	Last Mo. Rent	=	Total	Date	Initial
$800	+	$800	+	$800	=	$2400	8/3/07	DC
$750	+	$800	+	0	=	$1550	8/14/07	DC
	+		+		=			

Major Qualifications

1) INCOME   Minimum per month Gross pay $ __2400__   Take Home pay $ __1800__

or government assistance   Y/(N)   Must pass **"Cash Flow"** form   (Y)/N

Notes _____

2) CREDIT   Credit check (Y)/N   Cost single $ __25__ married $ __35__

A) Good established credit (Y)/N

Rating __600__ or higher   Bankruptcy __3__ years or longer

B) Other/Problem credit   (Y)/N

No/new credit   (Y)/N

Other bankruptcies   (Y)/N __12__ months or longer

Other credit problems   Y/(N)

Landlord credit problems   Y/(N)

*Problem credit w/extra security (Y)/N   How much $ __500__

Notes __Co-signer must pass credit and cashflow__

3) ACCEPTABLE CRIMINAL BACKGROUND CHECK   (Y)/N

Notes _____

4) PETS (Exception: Animals covered with Americans with Disabilities Act)

Dogs allowed _____ (Y)/N   Cats allowed _____ (Y)/N

Extra sec dep $ __300__ per pet   Extra rent. $ __25__ per pet per month

Dogs from dangerous dog list Y/(N)   Others with written consent Y/N

Notes _____

5) EVICTION (Exception: owner needing house back)   (Y)/N

Notes _____

CHAPTER 3

Minor Tenant Qualifications

W hen Hollywood has a good thing going, they love to make a sequel; often they even make a sequel to the sequel. Look at *Indiana
Jones* or *The Godfather* series. How about *Rocky*? He may fight until he's
seventy! Sometimes a movie and its sequels are so popular Hollywood
starts making prequels. If you don't believe me, think about the *Star Wars*
franchise, which as of this writing is a $13-billion industry. I think it is
fair to say that when Hollywood comes up with a good thing, they like to
capitalize on it.

In the last chapter, you had a good thing going with the major qualifications. The use of these qualifications will go a long way toward improving
your tenant selections, but just like Hollywood, you could benefit by having a sequel.

This chapter is a sequel to the major qualifications in the last chapter.
The plots are pretty much the same, but there will be different characters.
Those characters are classified as minor qualifications. Just as with the
major qualifications, you use the minor qualifications to fine-tune the profile of the type of tenant you want for your rental. Again, each qualification
sets a standard for the topic it covers. Let's begin with a look at the first
minor qualification. Refer to the sample as needed.

Minor Qualifications

6) *Occupancy Guidelines*

If you are like most landlords, whether new or seasoned, when you
first entered this business, you had little if any money. This situation is

STEP ONE

Tenant Qualifications

(If applicant intentionally lies, falsifies, omits or hides pertinent information during any stage of the tenant selection process, applicant can be denied rental of said property. If applicant is not of legal age, or if applicant does not have a Social Security number or other form of government issued ID, applicant can be denied rental of said property.).

Minor Qualifications

6) **OCCUPANCY GUIDELINES** (Max 2 per bedroom +1)

No. of bedrooms _____   Maximum no. of occupants _____

Notes _____

7) **ACCEPTABLE PREVIOUS LANDLORD REFERENCES** (if applicable)   Y/N   How many? _____
Current landlord references   Y/N   Establishing landlord references   Y/N

Notes _____

8) **ACCEPTABLE PERSONAL REFERENCES** Y/N   How many_____ per adult

Notes _____

9) **JOB STABILITY** How long?_____ mos. or longer

Notes _____

10) **RENTING STABILITY** (if applicable) Last _____ residence(s)   How long?_____ months each

Notes _____

11) **SMOKING** Y/N   Extra rent $_____ per mo.   Extra sec.dep. $_____

Notes _____

12) **EXTRA QUALIFICATIONS**
_____

not unusual and, in fact, is often the reason people acquire rental property in the first place. This lack of funds generally means that when you are first buying rentals, you often are forced to purchase smaller, older homes. These homes are often 1,000 square feet or less, with bedroom sizes of approximately 10 feet by 10 feet or so. When these homes were first built, their occupants lived a lifestyle that fit those homes. Today, however, we as a society have a yearning to want bigger—bigger televisions, beds, furniture, and so on. In smaller rental homes, these larger items take up space and less space means more crowding, especially when it comes time to add occupants to the mix.

As a landlord, you want to rent the home to the correct amount of occupants that the particular home can handle. Too many people occupying too small of a space almost always results in wear and tear that is more than normal. This additional wear and tear may be caused by quite natural usage, but when you have ten people wearing and tearing instead of two, the repair bills add up quickly.

Often, when it comes to occupancy, it is a tenant's mentality that spare porches, unfinished basements, and three sofas in the living area are all good sleeping quarters—in addition to their idea of three or four occupants per bedroom. It is your right and duty as a landlord to set a precedent on the maximum number of people who should be allowed to live in the rental. Your occupancy guidelines standard is where you will do just that.

This is your first minor guideline in the minor qualification section, and even though it is extremely easy to fill out, it definitely requires some in-depth discussion.

In doing research for this book I called the Department of Housing and Urban Development (HUD), which is the governing body that presides over the Fair Housing Laws and also oversees the Section 8 program. I asked how HUD determined occupancy and was told that at one time they used different bedroom guidelines than they do now. I was also told that they used to use the ages and genders of children as well as the number of adults living in the dwelling to compute how many bedrooms that family would require. The representative also went on to state that HUD gave up that practice as it was too difficult to put to practical use. She advised checking the local jurisdiction and following their guidelines for occupancy.

As I conducted further research on this subject, I spoke with another HUD representative who told me that this original practice could be considered discriminating against families. This representative said that the only people who could decide who sleeps where, are the family members themselves.

Number of bedrooms/maximum number of occupants. Of course, all this information is interesting enough, but none of it gets us any closer to deciding what limitations to set regarding the number of people we allow to live in what size rental unit. Fortunately, also during my phone conversations, it was mentioned on more than one occasion that the accepted practice was limiting occupancy to two people per bedroom. Using this guideline, a standard two-bedroom home could comfortably handle four occupants and a three-bedroom home could handle up to six. This is probably the minimum standard I would use to set for your occupancy qualification.

Some landlords and governing bodies, however, are loosening the standard just a tad and saying occupancy is based on two per bedroom plus one. In other words, a studio apartment can sleep three, a two-bedroom dwelling can sleep five, and a three-bedroom dwelling can sleep seven, and so on. The use of this rule will better protect you from discriminating against families; consequently, that is the qualification we will use here.

Naturally, just because I've established this as the guideline for this qualification, doesn't mean that you must adhere to it. You could cross out "+ 1" on the form and simply use "max 2 per bedroom." You could place an N/A across the qualification and not use it at all or you could write your own complete qualification in the notes section provided for the occupancy guidelines. Whatever you choose to do, it might be wise to check with the HUD department and local governing agencies in your area if you have any questions about this qualification.

Note: Some locales have health and building codes covering square foot per person. Check with your local code or health inspector if you think this might apply.

On the form, once you've decided what your qualifications for maximum occupancy will be, you will then fill in the number of bedrooms in your rental and calculate the total occupants in the space provided.

Concerning the topic of occupancy there is one more important point worth mentioning: A landlord cannot refuse occupancy based on family status. In other words, the landlord cannot legally decide who constitutes a family. For instance, just because someone doesn't have legal custody of a minor doesn't mean the person can't raise that minor, thus constituting a "family." Simply stated, one or more adults who take care of one or more minors earn family status, and this is protected by law.

7) *Acceptable Previous Landlord References*

If you can locate them, previous landlords are the absolute best source of information regarding your tenant prospect's rental history. They most likely were not friends with the tenant prospect, and probably aren't still in touch with them, so the chances of getting an honest reference often begins here. The previous landlord has already gotten rid of the tenants if they were a problem and will most likely let you know that putting that particular applicant in your place would cause nothing but headaches. They'll also tell you how much they miss the applicant if they were a wonderful tenant.

How many? Should you be fortunate enough to speak to *two* previous landlord references, that is even better. I'm always extremely pleased to have a conversation with a previous landlord. On the form, I recommend circling "Y" for yes and asking for two previous landlord references, if applicable.

Current landlord references—Y/N. Speaking to the tenant prospect's current landlord can reveal some important information but you need to exercise caution when doing so. The important thing you need to remember is that if the tenant who still resides in the building of the landlord you're calling is a problem, the current landlord may lie or at least twist the truth about the tenant and their "good" qualities in order to get the problem tenant out of his or her rental unit. Because of this possibility, extra care must be used when talking to a current landlord. What a current landlord tells you about your prospect is less important than what a previous landlord tells you. Personally, I still like to call just to hear what he or she says and *how* he/she says it, but I don't make it a required qualification.

Establishing landlord references—Y/N. And finally, you must decide if you will accept prospective tenants if they are just starting out as renters and establishing landlord references. In cases such as these, I ask, "Why not?" There are so many other avenues you will be checking into that if the prospect is a real dud, you will probably discover it by using a combination of your other qualifications.

8) *Acceptable Personal References*

Generally, personal references can be a good source of information, but understand that many, if not all of them, are friends of the prospect and will almost certainly tell you good things about him or her. Therefore, to help you get a more accurate profile of your tenant prospect, you need to talk to at least three personal references for *each* adult renter. That means if you have a married couple applying for your rental, you need to speak to a minimum of six different people. This is a good number to shoot for, but remember that immediate relatives (parents, grandparents, brothers, sisters, and so forth) don't count as personal references. I recommend always talking to personal references.

9) *Job Stability*

Previously, you figured out the income level needed to rent your unit. What you hope to discover with this requirement is that the needed income will be consistent and ongoing. Unfortunately, in this day and age with downsizing and benefit slashing, many people are dissatisfied with their jobs. They may flit from job to job looking for better pay, improved benefits, or a connection in the workforce that clicks with them. Most people know someone who fits this type of persona.

You need to be careful with job-jumpers, especially those people who leave a job without having another lined up. They often have periods between jobs where there is no money coming in, and that turns into a money problem for the landlord.

I've had job-jumpers, and their financial situation can get difficult at times, resulting in late rent payments. I recommend that tenant prospects have 6 to 12 months of job stability as a good rule of thumb.

Of course, there are always exceptions to any rule, so let me list a couple that come to mind. If you wish to use this job requirement in your tenant search and feel you need to utilize one or more of these exceptions, simply write them in the notes sections provided.

- **New move to the area.** Sometimes people leave one locale to come to another. The reason could be for love or loss of love, to help family, chase a dream, and so forth. Naturally, these people may have to re-enter the job market in their new area.

- **Just entering job market.** This covers recent college graduates or anyone who is striking out on his or her own as a wage earner. This could include people going through a divorce, previous stay-at-home moms, and so forth.

- **Higher paying or more secure job.** This is what usually causes a job-jumper to be a job-jumper, so use caution in this area. With that said, there are very legitimate occasions where this exception is okay. Generally, if their previous two or three jobs had longevity or they were downsized, I find this exception valid.

These three exceptions are solid reasons why someone may have less than 6 to 12 months of job stability, so it might be wise on your part to include one or more of them in your decision-making process. Such a decision could be written up as follows:

Notes: Exceptions—entering job force, new move to area, or better job with good previous job history.

10) *Renting Stability*

Chances are, one of the main reasons you got into the rental business is to make a profit. One of the biggest profit eaters is the empty rental unit, so naturally, the longer a paying tenant will stay in your rental, the better. If you're concerned about renting stability, item number 10 on the Tenant Qualifications form is where you'll address this issue. My guess is if you don't want a job-jumper, you probably don't want someone who switches residences every three to six months, either.

A dilemma you might face by asking for rent stability is that you could be eliminating people who are moving for a justifiable reason. These reasons can be listed as exceptions in the notes area when filling out the Tenant Qualifications form. Some reasons for this could include:

- People who are going through a divorce and need to find a new place to live.
- People who are looking for a new home so they can put their child(ren) in a better school district.
- People who have been transferred with their job.
- People who are first-time renters.

11) *Smoking*

Smoking is really hitting the news lately, what with nonsmoking restrictions in bars and restaurants, and outrageous lawsuits against the tobacco industry. The concern from a landlording standpoint is that smoke gets everywhere in a home. It gets into carpet so badly, professional cleaning doesn't guarantee the removal of the odor. Smoking also leaves a film on all the trim, walls, windows, cabinets, and so forth, which takes a lot of time and effort to remove from a rental unit when you are preparing it for the next tenant. You need to keep in mind, however, that if you eliminate smokers, you reduce a large percentage of your rental prospects, which can be a problem if you are trying to rent in a tough market.

If you do decide to rent to smokers, you need to decide whether you want to charge more rent or ask for a bigger security deposit. As discussed in the pet section, if you are going to charge extra, go for rent. You'd rather receive the extra money regularly versus at the end of the tenancy.

12) *Extra Qualifications*

The last line on the form is for making up your own qualifications to cover areas I might not have mentioned. For instance, suppose you live in an area with a lot of casinos and you worry about getting a gambler who is falling fast into debt. You could write your own qualification this way: *Gamblers accepted with good credit and cash flow.*

Let me remind you that there are many areas one could use as a reason to eliminate tenant prospects. Most of these are directly or indirectly covered on the Tenant Qualifications form. Please make a mental note of the following reasons and work your qualifications around them:

- False application
- Too many occupants
- Pets
- Lack of income to pay rent
- Doesn't pay bills
- Turned over for collection
- Record of past due rent
- Bankruptcies
- Applicant has judgment or suit liens
- Using, selling, purchasing, manufacturing, or distributing illegal drugs
- Selling or representing prostitution
- Possession of stolen property
- Possession of illegal firearms
- Negative previous landlord comments
- Damage to previous dwelling
- Heavy drinking/smoking
- Disruptive activities

In fact, you could write a qualification for any subject you think might be a problem for you or your rental area. Set your own rules here. Just remember that whatever you choose cannot violate the Fair Housing Act. (See page 46 for completed sample form.)

Final Tips On Using the Form

Before I close this chapter, let me give you a few thoughts on filling out the prospect qualification form:

- Fill out one section completely before proceeding to the next.
- As you fill out each section, ask yourself these questions:
  - Am I violating the Fair Housing Act?
  - Is this qualification necessary for my rental situation? If it isn't, simply write N/A for not applicable across the qualification and move on to the next item.

– Are my qualification expectations reasonable for my clientele and rental demographics?

– Are my standards for this guideline too rigid?

- Try to fill in this form a few days before you need it. Review it after a couple of days to make sure you're still confident in your choices.

- Remember you *are* allowed to alter qualifications at any time if you see the need. Just don't discriminate illegally and make sure you date and initial any changes as you make them. You can write your changes in the notes section provided in the appropriate categories. Never forget that once you've changed a guideline, the new standard is now the one by which all new callers will be judged. Don't judge one person on the new change and the next on the old standard. Keep it consistent.

- Please realize that the qualifications may not work for your clientele, or the current economic or rental climate. Pick and choose the guidelines you need and fill them out according to what you believe will give you the best chance of successfully renting your empty unit.

- You may discover you have more than one tenant prospect who passes your qualifications. You are under no obligation to rent to the first person who makes the grade. You can collect a couple of good candidates and then choose the most qualified—as long as you don't break any Fair Housing Laws.

The qualifications are listed in the order of importance. If you feel your guidelines are too rigid to find a tenant, start at the bottom of the form and work your way up the sheet, loosening guidelines as needed.

In Closing

In general, use the Tenant Qualifications form as little or as much as needed. If you are unsure, try using the major qualification section and just add those minor qualifications that are truly of concern to you. Even though the form seems long and drawn out, remember that if using the form saves you one unforeseen and costly problem, it will have been well worth it. (Of course, by using this system, you may never even know how many bad tenants you gave up).

Also, please remember that when you first look over and try to understand this form, it seems extremely overwhelming. In fact, the first time you fill the form out, it may take up a considerable amount of time. Don't despair. Once you've used the Tenant Qualifications form three or four times, you will breeze through it in minutes. Eventually, as you fill the form out for one unit, the next time you have to rent another unit, you may just copy everything from the previous form and adjust only the one or two areas that you think need altering.

It is also likely that once you've developed basic qualifications that work for you, you will use the same qualifications on every other rental you have by just changing addresses and dates.

Once you have completed this form, make two copies. One goes in a file marked Tenant Qualifications for future reference and the other gets stapled to the Caller Interview form (covered in an upcoming chapter). You will use these two forms when the phone starts to ring. If you are having any problems with these last two chapters, reread them and do a practice form or two. I can't emphasize the importance of this form enough. It is by far the most important one in the whole book.

Note: You can access this form at our website
www.FindThatQualityTenant.com.

CHAPTER 4

Writing the Ads

I f you've done your job in preparing the rental property and you've filled out the Tenant Qualifications form, you are now ready to have people take notice and rent your product—the dwelling. After all, you don't really own *rentals* until you rent to somebody.

Before You Begin

Before beginning the advertising process, you need to do the same thing you did in chapter one: Step into the shoes of the tenant. I can hear what you're saying: "This is the second time he's asked us to be a tenant. Is he going to do this in every chapter?" The answer is, no, not every chapter, but this mental exercise is important: As long as you own rentals, you're going to have tenants, and anytime you don't see eye to eye with them, you have the ingredients for a problem. Always be prepared to step in their shoes for a brief second because they probably will never step into yours. A quick view from their perspective will go a long way in helping you solve or avoid problems, and in general, be a more successful landlord. A detective once told me that it's easier to catch a thief if you think like a thief. If you want to solve a tenant problem, do so by thinking from a tenant's perspective.

Well, the same line of thought works for advertising for a good tenant. Be the tenant you want to attract. For a moment, imagine you are the tenant and look at your rental through the tenant's eyes as you prepare the ad.

What to Consider

Consider these basic categories when you look at your dwelling through a tenant's eyes. First, what about the general area where the house is located? Is it safe for kids? Is it a high crime area? Does it have a neighborhood watch program? Is the house remote, and therefore, easy to burglarize? If the house has any of these problems, can you correct them?

What about convenience? Is it close to shopping? Church? Schools? Highways and byways? Is it walking distance to these areas or a 10-minute drive? Is there public transportation?

When you look at the area from a tenant's perspective, you're looking for the draw of your advertised property. Basically, what convenience qualities stand out and/or what is it about the area that would cause a tenant to want to rent this particular unit? All rentals have something in these areas that could appeal to a tenant prospect. You just need to find it.

Next, look at the house through the tenant's eyes for cleanliness and value for the buck. When considering cleanliness, ask yourself these questions. Would you let *your* kids play on the carpet? Is the kitchen super clean or is there filth around the sinks and floors? Would you eat there? How about the restroom? Does it shine like a new penny or are there scum rings collecting in the tub and toilet? Think about it this way. You own the rental. You've been here before so you're somewhat accustomed to the cleanliness of the place. If the place looks unclean to *you*, how unclean does it look to tenants?

How about the value of the dwelling? Look at other comparable homes or rentals in the immediate area and compare yours to theirs. Is your rental affordable for the clientele who want this neighborhood? Is yours a better value or are you asking too much for rent? Try not to overprice your rental unit, because that mistake will quickly cost you money. For example: if you make $1,200 a year profit on your rental when it's rented ($100 per month) but you can't rent your $600 home for two months because you're asking $650 instead of $600, you've lost a year's profit. Be careful about deciding how much rent to ask for. I would advise that if you show the property and after two weeks, no one has filled out an application, either lower the rent or improve the property.

How to Advertise

When you are ready to advertise, there are many venues from which to choose. I will cover only the ones most popular, cost effective, and easy to use. Please keep an open mind so you can figure out what the best method is to find tenants for your rental. Here are some suggestions:

Real Estate Agents

Chances are, you probably won't get a lot of leads from a real estate agent, unless that agency specializes in rentals and rental-related calls. If you regularly work with an agent, however, perhaps you can make a call to him or her so the agent knows you have a vacant unit for rent. Some agents might even let you put a flyer up in their office. (Remember that if real estate agents allow you to do this, it is because they hope you'll remember them when it's time to list your rental for sale.)

Vacating Tenants

If your vacating tenant has been a valuable one and you think he or she might have good leads from work or their family and friends, ask for rental referrals. You could even offer a small finder's fee if he or she delivers a successful tenant. If the vacating tenant is breaking a lease with you, use extra care in checking out his or her recommendations, because if a tenant breaks a lease, he or she is still legally financially responsible for the lease *until* you find a new tenant, or until the lease expires, whichever comes first. So it stands to reason he or she might be inclined to recommend someone who may not be what you're looking for.

Other Tenants

They could also be a source of prospects, but a word of caution here: You shouldn't pick and choose which tenants you ask or don't ask, because if you don't ask every tenant you have in the building, complex, and so forth, you might be setting yourself up for a discrimination suit. If a tenant asks *you* if you have a vacancy for rent, that's a different story, but be careful who you ask for tenant leads when your vacant unit is part of a large complex where tenants regularly talk among themselves, comparing notes, and exchanging gossip.

Family and Friends

I don't recommend renting to family or friends because you could end up with a problem. Too often, family and friends don't understand the rental business and the need to have regular rent payments so you can keep up the mortgage and such. Add to that, the reasons family or friends need to rent from you is they are going to have a hard time renting elsewhere. In other words, they are aware they might need a helping hand: your helping hand. Such scenarios can be devastating to lifelong friendships and family holidays. Because of these reasons and the fact that I like my family as well as my friends, and want to keep it that way, I've decided not to rent to either group. On occasions, I will use family or friends as a *source* for tenants but be aware that this could lead to a touchy situation in the future if a tenant problem develops. Renting to family and friends is, of course, your option. Just tread carefully.

Neighbors

If you have quality neighbors who live close to your rental unit, they can be a good source for prospects. If they recommend someone to be their neighbor, chances are that recommendation will be of good quality since people tend to want neighbors who are like themselves. On the other hand, if the neighbor who gives the recommendation is loud, disrespectful, and dirty, his recommendation possibly could be too, since like kinds tend to hang out together. Keep these things in mind when considering asking a neighbor for tenant leads.

Signs

I used to put a sign only in my multi-units, because I believed a sign on a vacated single home was an invitation for vandalism. But I have since changed my thinking. People are smart and can easily figure out if a house is empty whether it has a sign in it or not. I soon came to the realization that if a neighborhood is prone to crime, the house will be watched by vandals and thieves with or without a sign present. Because of this reasoning, I now use "For Rent" signs in all my empty multi-units or single-family homes. If vandals are a main concern and you feel better by not displaying a sign, then by all means, forget it and use a different source of advertising.

With that said, here is the main advantage to using signs for advertising: It is said that almost 70 percent of people who buy or rent a house drive through a neighborhood they wish to live in and look for a "For Rent" or "For Sale" sign. This statistic may be a little high, but I didn't run the test, so I'll quote it as I read it. If that statistic *is* accurate, then a sign is an excellent tool for attracting tenant prospects.

If you decide to display a sign, put one in the yard anywhere it faces a street (front, side, or both) and one in the front window (in case the one in the yard gets damaged or stolen). Keep in mind that the busier the street, the more successful the sign. Just put a phone number on the signs and nothing else. By doing so, you may use the signs on other rental properties as your investing becomes more successful and your real estate empire grows. Also, leave the curtains open so people can see inside, especially the kitchen and front room, if possible. This allows people the opportunity to look in and visualize their furniture in your house. It also eliminates anyone calling who doesn't like a kitchen layout, certain carpet color, and so forth.

If the dwelling you are renting is in a multi-unit apartment building, and you put a "for rent" sign inside the building, you might want to put another sign in the front door that includes additional information. I suggest listing the number of bedrooms first and printing that information large enough to read from the street. That way, passersby can read it. Then, if there is room, you can add other pertinent facts about the rental. Finally, make sure your contact number is large enough to read from the street.

Rental Guides

Many small, medium, and large cities/towns have these free guides in the supermarket and other such stores. They often cover only larger apartment complexes, but if they have a small properties section, you might want to run an ad in these guides, constructed something along the line of your newspaper ad.

Flyers

Flyers do not cover a large area unless you distribute them yourself or pay someone else to do it for you. But if you put a few at local businesses near your rental that have good foot traffic, they can be useful. Here's a partial list of places you could put your flyer: churches, schools, dorms, hospitals, factories, drug stores, grocery stores, corner convenience stores, bowling alleys, and so forth—anywhere you think has the foot traffic to generate the kind of renter you want to attract.

Put something on the flyer that will grab people's attention. With today's technology, computers and digital cameras allow you to easily put a front view of the property on the flyer. You might even wish to add a few smaller pictures of the kitchen, living room, or some other strong amenity the dwelling has. You also need to include all information pertaining to the rental unit and you might write a whole paragraph describing the rental. This wouldn't be cost-effective in the newspaper ads but would work nicely on a flyer. Don't forget security deposit, monthly rent, and your phone number.

You should also cut the sides of the flyer into horizontal strips with your phone number listed on each strip so people can tear a tab off and take it with them. This is especially helpful if the flyer will be hung somewhere instead of distributed to individuals. Last but not least, if you use this tab method, make sure your number is displayed on the flyer just in case all the tabs get used.

Newspaper Ads

This is the one that really works for me. My guess is that it's probably the same way almost anywhere you live. For some reason, people just pick up a newspaper when it's time to rent. They go out and grab the Sunday edition, or if they're moving any real distance, they may read the local edition of their desired destination off the Internet. Other than a sign, I seriously doubt you'll get more bang for your buck than a well-written, well-placed newspaper ad. Since newspaper ads are so important, they will be discussed in two sections.

Section One: About the Ad

First, you have to figure out the best paper to run your ad in and on which days. If you doubt that ad location and timing are important, just watch television commercials for a few hours. You can bet the marketers of those commercials are making the most of their advertising dollars.

For example, what commercials air during an NFL football game? Beer commercials, car commercials, and any other commercial that caters to men between the ages of 20 and 50. Seldom will you see toy commercials or a commercial for laundry soap or waterproof mascara. But watch *Oprah* or *The View,* and you'll see a lot fewer beer commercials and many more ads for cleaning products and cosmetics. Just as in product advertising, proper timing and ad placement are important for finding good tenants. Keep in mind that ads are expensive and since you're trying to become financially independent, you need to spend your money wisely.

If you list your ad in a major city newspaper, especially on Sunday, your ad will drown along with all the other ads. Take Chicago, for instance. If you put a "For Rent" ad in one of their major papers, you'll be competing with hundreds of other ads. To better your odds for getting noticed, you must whittle down your specific area listings. Let's say your rental is in northwest Indiana, which is covered in the Chicago classifieds. In a Chicago-based paper, what is the smallest heading you could place your ad under? Would it be northwest Indiana, which includes basically two complete counties? Or could you list the city in Indiana where the rental is actually located? Let's say your property is in Hammond, Indiana. People there know Hammond as South Hammond or North Hammond. So can you list it as one of those? How about Chicago itself? Even though the Loop or Wrigleyville technically aren't suburbs, both are recognized areas of Chicago. The point I'm trying to make here is that in the bigger newspapers, go for the smallest geographical heading you can list your rental under.

On the other side of the coin, you could use the small free local papers that many areas have. They usually just reach out to the surrounding community, but this may be all you need. In the beginning of your rental experience, you'll want to experiment to see where ads work best: large paper, community paper, or something in between.

Which Days?

What day or days do you run your ad? In my experience, Sunday is the best day to run an ad because if people buy only one paper a week, it's the Sunday paper. These people could be in a hurry to rent or starting to look for next month or anything in between. This is also the ad they will probably hang on to through the week. I often get calls from my Sunday ad on the following Thursday or so.

Most newspapers have cheaper rates for the longer time period you run your ad. So you might get three days for a few dollars more than your Sunday-only ad, or a ten-day special for the price of seven days. Always ask about specials and run the ad for the longest time frame for the best rate that you can get.

Print Options

Another thing to consider is bold print versus regular print. Once you decide on the paper(s) to run your ad in, you need to choose bold or regular print for the ad. It seems to me that even if everyone else's ads are in bold print, mine gets lost if I use regular print. So I always use bold print. Some papers don't allow a mixture of print, but if yours does, try different combinations and see what grabs your attention.

Short Ad Versus Long Ad

There are two opposing views on this topic. Some say the more information in an ad, the better prospects you receive because potential tenants are eliminating themselves based on all your ad information, leaving only truly interested parties to call you about your ad. This may be true, but with the price of a line of print in an ad, it could be very easy to run up a monthly ad bill of $200 or $300 or more, especially if you run ads in two papers and for multiple days of the week.

Others say shorter ads save money and you will receive more calls because people have questions that aren't addressed in the ad. Both sides have merit but personally, I generally use a medium size ad, about three lines or so. If the phone lines are hot, I might give more ad information to slow them down, and if the phones are slow, I may take out information, hoping more people will call.

Also keep in mind that some ad wordings will work better than others. If you run the same ad week after week, people are going to label your property and you'll get fewer calls. Change and/or restructure your ad every two weeks or so. That way, it's fresh, and if you use the tracking form that is explained later in this chapter, you'll know what wording is getting the best results.

When all is said and done, be willing to try different ad wordings, lengths, and newspapers to find what works best for you. Now let's write the ad.

Section Two: Writing the Ad

Before we actually write an ad, let me remind you of a few of things:

- As you write the ad, be your tenant. I can't emphasize enough how important this is. Successful advertisers always put themselves in the consumer's shoes before they write an ad for a product. And whether you realize it or not, the tenant *is* your consumer. Write the ad from their eyes.

- Do not pull "bait and switch." That means what you advertise, you better have. Don't waste your time or their time with faulty or misleading information.

- Do not repeat information. For example, if your ad is listed in the newspaper under "Houses for Rent," there is no need for you to place the words, "For rent: single-family home" in your ad. That information would be a repeat of what the reader already knows, not to mention a waste of ad space and money for you.

- Last but not least, do not discriminate. This can happen quite by accident, because the information you advertised with the intention of being helpful, could possibly be misconstrued as discriminating. Phrases such as "close to a Catholic church" or "mature adults wanted" might cause you problems. In the first example, people could say you are looking for a tenant from a certain religious group, and in the second example, someone might say you don't want children. (In fact, never use the word "children" in your advertising; it isn't necessary.) Both of those areas are covered by the Fair Housing Act of 1968. *The absolute best way to avoid a discriminatory problem is to describe only the rental in your ad.*

Ads and Tracking Form

With all these pointers fresh in your mind, it's time to write an ad. We will use the Ad and Tracking form that is in your book. If you look at the form you will notice that the upper part of the form will be used to write

STEP ONE

Ads and Tracking Form

Address: _____

Day(s): _____ Month: _____ Date(s): _____ Year: _____

AD

(1) _____ (2) _____ (3) _____

(4) _____ (5) _____

(6) _____ (7) _____ (8) _____

TRACKING

Source	S	M	T	W	Th	F	Sa	D	O

NOTES _____
_____

Address: _____

Day(s): _____ Month: _____ Date(s): _____ Year: _____

AD

(1) _____ (2) _____ (3) _____

(4) _____ (5) _____

(6) _____ (7) _____ (8) _____

TRACKING

Source	S	M	T	W	Th	F	Sa	D	O

NOTES _____

your ad and the lower portion will be used to track the efficiency of that particular ad. Begin by taking a look at the top half of the form, which includes the address of the property and the days you plan to run the ad in your chosen media.

Importance of the Date

As you fill out this information, be sure to list the current year, because if you keep your rentals for any length of time, it could prove valuable to have the date when you write your next ad. How so? Let's say in February 2006 when you first rented your house, the local factory where half of the town worked at was up and running. People wanted to rent in this town because they worked in this town. But a year later, in February 2007, the factory laid off 4,000 people because of a sluggish economy or some other unforeseen calamity. Suddenly, with the economic downturn, no one is beating a path to rent anything in this town. Likewise, there could have been a great, but short-lived economic change for the better, such as the year the Olympics were held in a particular town. For many months before the actual Olympics are held, there are many things that need attending to. During this pre-game period, everything in town is bustling above normal, so rentals are easier to fill, and at higher rents. Even though the year is a small detail, it could remind you of certain situations pertaining to that year that might make a difference in what or how you advertise.

This information will prove useful to you should you decide somewhere down the line to analyze your advertising and evaluate how effective certain ads are compared to others. I will explain this in much greater detail at the end of this chapter. For right now, just understand what needs to be placed in what blank.

The Body of the Ad

After this basic information, the form includes eight numbers, each followed by a line. Each number represents an important ingredient in the structuring of your ad. To better explain using this form, we will write an ad for 712 Oak in the town of Miller, referring to each number one at a time and build our ad as we go.

1. Area. Start with the area the rental is located. People almost always begin looking for a dwelling in a certain area or areas, so use the area name that the majority of people will know. Remember that if the rental is in a large city, try to list the smallest popularly known area possible, as featured below. For our example, we would list "Miller."

2. Hook, snare, bait, the catch. What do the following phrases have in common?

- "Where's the beef?"
- "Help. I've fallen and I can't get up."
- "Clap on. Clap off. Clap on. Clap off. The Clapper."

They all have "sizzle" words or catchphrases that make us remember the product years after the ad that popularized the catchphrase is extinct. These simple phrases were vital to the success of the product they represented and in these examples actually helped to rocket sales past anyone's expectations.

I'm not saying you need a catchphrase so people will remember your ad for all eternity, but the first word in your ad needs to be a sizzle word or phrase that grabs the reader's attention. This word or phrase is the most important one in the whole ad because it should pique the reader's interest, causing them to look at your ad more closely than the other ads in that section—and hopefully getting them to call in response to your ad.

Basically, the word or phrase could be anything that really highlights the house or the area it's in. Examples include close to schools, cleanliness, big yard, pool, large garage, or quiet.

Remember to view this phrase from a tenant's eyes, because what you think is great may not be that hot to a tenant. For example: *Miller, large lawn, 3 acres.*

If you have a small two-bedroom house on 3 acres of lawn that will attract mostly new couples or retired elderly folks with very little money who probably can barely afford their $100 push lawnmower, do you think 3 acres is a plus or minus? Not that I wouldn't use *big yard, 3 acres* somewhere in the ad, but just remember that you want twenty calls in response to your ad, not two. So write the ad in the same way your prospective tenant base will interpret the ad.

What do you do if your house is so mundane and ordinary that you absolutely can't find a good sizzle word to describe it? Go clean it again and then advertise *extra clean* as your sizzle words. *Clean sells*, plain and simple. Always remember that fact.

Another idea you might want to try is making your sizzle word(s) the general heading of the ad. Simply spell it out in capital letters, centered on the first line of your ad to draw people's attention to it. This technique is often employed by car dealers and large apartment complexes in the classifieds. This method will probably cost you more, but it could be worth it.

One of the best phrases I used to use at the beginning of my ad was *A-1 tenant wanted*. I say "used to" because our paper had a management change in the advertising department and the new management felt this term might be discriminatory, so eventually they refused to print it. I argued that the person reading the ad would decide if they were of A-1 quality or not, so I wasn't discriminating, I was just looking for people who held themselves up to high standards. I lost the argument, but that doesn't mean you can't try this catch-phrase and see if you have success with it. Before my newspaper refused to print my ads with this phrase, I got a lot of quality tenants with that phrase.

Let's add the chosen sizzle word to our ad. We now have: *Miller, super clean.*

3. The body. Here's where you list amenities. First, always list the number of bedrooms. This is your biggest call eliminator, next to the price. People almost always have a preset bedroom standard in mind when they begin to house-hunt. Next, list bathrooms, but only if there is more than one. If you only have one, use your ink on something else. Of course, if your area still relies on outdoor facilities and an indoor bathroom is a plus, then by all means, do list the bathroom.

Then, if the house has any of these items, list them in this order: basement (bsmt), garage (gar), fenced yard (fncd yd), and central air (CA). There are many other amenities worth listing, but I find these four features are the heart and soul for most house hunters.

As far as listing other amenities, keep this rule in mind: *Whatever you put in print has to be of interest to the prospective tenant. Newer roof* or *new siding* means a lot less to a prospective *tenant* than to a prospective *home buyer*. If you run out of home amenities but still want to include more information, add another sizzle word, such as *spacious, beautiful neighborhood,* or *close to highway* to the ad.

Let's review what we have so far: *Miller, super clean, 3-bedroom, 1.5 bath, basement, central air.*

4. Closer. The closer is a word or words that tilt the caller in your favor should they have many properties to possibly call on. It is usually not about the house, but geared toward the prospect themselves, such as *Section 8 okay, available August 1,* or *no pets allowed.*

Of course, what I'm saying to you about the closer is going somewhat against the advice I gave you a few pages back; which was "the best way to avoid a discriminatory problem is to describe only the rental in your ad." If you personalize your ad with a closer, you *must* make sure you do not say anything that could be misconstrued as a violation of the Fair Housing Act. Since smokers are not covered by these laws, you can use a closer about smoking. Pets also are fair game with the exception of animals used for the aid of a handicap or disability, such as a seeing eye dog. *Section 8 okay* just shows you are willing to accept a broader range of applicants.

I never list the address of the property while I'm working on it. I don't want every unqualified Tom, Dick, and Harry stopping by. I'd hate to turn somebody away in person only to have an argument or other problem arise. Likewise, I leave out the address while my subcontractors and cleaning people are working on the dwelling. You never know who might steal their tools and such. I do often list an address after all work is complete (especially if the property is quite a drive from my house) so people can check it out on their own. If you don't want to list the exact address but would like people to know the general proximity, simply list a well-known landmark or intersection in the ad, such as *near Miller Mall* or *close to First and Taft.*

Using a closer is a good way to take an ad to a more personal level, just be sure you do not violate any Fair Housing Laws. Let's add a closer to the ad that we've structured so far: *Miller, super clean, 3 bedroom, 1.5 bath, basement, central air, pets allowed.*

5. Address. If you wish to list the address, this is the spot to do it. Never list your address first, because you want people to read your ad before they see the address. Otherwise, if they run out to look at your three-bedroom dwelling when they need four, you've wasted their time. Also, listing the address after describing amenities allows the potential tenant to get enthusiastic about your rental unit. The ad now includes the following: *Miller, super clean, 3 bedroom, 1.5 bath, basement, central air, pets allowed, 712 Oak.*

6. Rent. I always list rent. This is the greatest determining factor for people calling or not calling. With very few exceptions, people know what they want, or can afford, to pay.

Now our ad includes: *Miller, super clean, 3 bedroom, 1.5 bath, basement, central air, pets allowed, 712 Oak, $800 per month.*

7. Security deposit. Putting the security deposit in print is not as important as rent, but I still list it because I want people to know how much money they'll need to move into my unit. If you also collect last month's rent, this would be the place to list that as well: *Miller, super clean, 3 bedroom, 1.5 bath, basement, central air, pets allowed, 712 Oak, $800 per month, $750 security deposit.*

8. Phone number. Of course, you need a phone number where prospective tenants can reach you once you start advertising. I recommend having a second line installed along with an answering machine in a back room of your house. You'll get calls as early as 5:30 A.M. to as late as midnight. I don't know about you, but I prefer not to answer the phone at either of those times. What I do is check this machine upon waking, before lunch, midafternoon, after dinner, and just before bed. My machine also has remote access so I can check calls even if I'm out of town. The use of a second line also allows for a professional sounding business entity for tenant prospect calls and helps to keep your private line just that, private.

Some people I know use voicemail and/or call forwarding to cut out the ringing-phone-in-the-house syndrome, which is fine; just make sure you check your messages regularly.

One word of caution: Many prospective tenants who call about an ad and receive a machine or voice mail will simply hang up and call the next number on their list, never to call you again. So if you choose to not answer the phone each time it rings, be forewarned that you will lose at least some valuable prospective tenant calls. I'd advise mixing the two thoughts: Answer the phone when it is convenient and you can mentally handle the conversation, and let technology cover for you during the time you need a break.

Now let's add the phone number to complete the ad: *Miller, super clean, 3 bedroom, 1.5 bath, basement, central air, pets allowed, 712 Oak, $800 per month, $750 security deposit,* 555-1234.

If you use a website to further help advertise or show your rental, this is the location for saying so in your ad. Something along the lines of "additional information or photos available on our website at _____" is appropriate. Also, this is the area of your ad to include your email address if you wish to be contacted in that manner.

Now that we have finished constructing an ad, I want to remind you to customize your ad as needed. Eliminate or add sizzle words, phone numbers, and other information to make your ad work for you.

Tracking

At this point, if you've hung with me so far, you now have a list of ways to advertise and a guide for writing a complete and thorough newspaper ad. All this is well and good, but now you are faced with the question of how you really know which ad is working and which one isn't.

The answer is simple: Track your advertising. Log how many calls you get on what day from which ads. Generally, this is a pain (if you even do it at all) because you scribble on a piece of paper who called when and from what ad source, and then your notes get disorganized so you aren't able to compare one week's results to the next. To solve the problem, use the following tracking form. It's easy to use.

Reviewing the tracking part of the form. Let's take a look at the tracking section of the Ads and Tracking form. In addition to days of the week, which are listed and abbreviated below, we also have the words "drive by" and "other" included in an abbreviated form:

- S—Sunday
- M—Monday
- T—Tuesday
- W—Wednesday
- Th—Thursday
- F—Friday
- Sa—Saturday
- D—Drive by
- O—Other (tenant, neighbor, flyers) source

This tracking section is listed under the ad writing space so you have that week's tracking with the correct ad. You'll notice that there are two spaces per day for each week. There are also two spaces to the left of Sundays, tagged "source." These spaces are for you to chart two papers (or other sources) at once.

For example, in the first space you might list the big newspaper you advertised in; let's call our newspaper *The Post*. Should you decide to advertise in two papers, the second space would be for a second ad. If you need a third line, just write it under the chart. Let's take a look at a filled-out tracking form *(See page 77)*. For training purposes, we'll say we ran a newspaper ad in two papers: *The Post* and *The Miller Gazette*. The ads ran Friday, Saturday, and Sunday for *The Post* and all week for *The Miller Gazette*. We'll also say we got two calls from the sign we placed in the front yard (drive by), and we even had a third party give out our phone number to a friend of theirs who wants to rent a dwelling (other). We had no flyers put up. Every time we get an inquiry about the rental we place a tic mark in the appropriate spot. Please remember when tracking newspaper ads, the important thing is to make sure you're marking the day the prospective tenant *saw* your ad and not the day they *called* you about the ad.

Notes. Periodically, you will have a holiday or something will happen to change the ad efficiency for a certain day. Put a star or asterisk by the day and the reason below in the notes section. Also use the notes section for other thoughts you might have and wish to remember for the next time you write an ad, such as the 4,000 factory workers who got laid off in the earlier example.

Here's a look at a completed Ad and Tracking form for the Miller property we've used as our example throughout the chapter. *(See page 77.)*

In Closing

After your search is complete, you need to properly file the form. First, make two copies. One goes in a file in your file cabinet (or in your computer) under "Ads and Tracking." As you file the forms, always place newest ads on top of older ads. These will be used as reference the next time you need to write an ad for that or another of your properties.

The other copy is attached under the filled-out Tenant Qualifications form for this property. Keep this combination of forms near your phone for when it starts to ring.

Note: You can access a full-size copy of this form on our website at
www.FindThatQualityTenant.com.

STEP ONE

Ads and Tracking Form

Address: _____

Day(s): _____ Month: _____ Date(s): _____ Year: _____

AD

(1) _____ (2) _____ (3) _____

(4) _____ (5) _____

(6) _____ (7) _____ (8) _____

TRACKING

Source	S	M	T	W	Th	F	Sa	D	O

NOTES _____

Address: _____712____Oak_____

Day(s): _S - Sa_ Month: _July_ Date(s): _4 - 10_ Year: _2007_

AD

(1) _Miller_ (2) _superclean_ (3) _3 bd, 1.5 bath, basmt, CA_

(4) _pets allowed_ (5) _712 Oak_

(6) _800 rent_ (7) _350 sec._ (8) _555 - 1234_

TRACKING

Source	S	M	T	W	Th	F	Sa	D	O
Post	11	14	1			1		11	1
Gaz		1		1	11	1			

NOTES _Sun. was 4th of July_

77

Step Two: Prequalify

I n step one, you prepared yourself, your dwelling, your qualifications, and your ads to begin your tenant search. During step one, you never actually speak to any potential tenants. Step two changes all that: This is where you will learn how to prequalify all the calls you receive from any of the advertising you did in the previous step. It is at this point in the tenant selection process that you will begin to separate the wheat from the chaff. You want to find the best of the best applicants who fit your preset qualifications, which are based on the Tenant Qualifications form you filled out back in step one. By the completion of step two, you will have found qualified tenant prospects to whom you will show your rental property.

CHAPTER 5

The Caller Interview

With the completion of the first step (preparation) in the tenant selection process, you are now ready to begin step two, the prequalifying step. By completing the Tenant Qualifications form, you have set the groundwork for the rest of your tenant selection process. These preset qualifications, or standards, will be your guide and point of reference as you prequalify all interested parties about your rental unit. Keep the tenant qualification form handy during this step as you may need to refer to it often.

Interviewing Callers

The first thing you'll need to do when prequalifying tenant prospects is interview anyone who calls about your rental advertising. I dislike the interview process, as I'm sure most people do. It's something I never look forward to, and after many years of prequalifying tenant prospects, I'm still sometimes uncomfortable doing these interviews. I have come to realize the reason for the discomfort is twofold:

1. The natural fear of talking to strangers
2. Interviewing just takes time

Natural fear of talking to strangers

Because I feel these reasons effect just about everyone, let's take a moment and discuss them. First, let's look at the natural fear of talking to strangers. For some people, speaking in public is scarier than death itself. And even though there may be a phone between them and the other party during their initial interview, many people are uncomfortable with the process. Unfortunately, the interview process doesn't get easier when you must evaluate those strangers knowing that one of them could soon be a part of your life. A big part of your life. Someone you must trust to pay rent on time, keep your property in good condition, and not turn your rental into the neighborhood brothel. This causes a lot of anxiety because understandably, you wonder how to make a good choice.

As I've already mentioned, after placing tenants in units for many years, sometimes I still wish I didn't have to interview people. But it comes with the territory, so I've learned to do it, do it well, and above all, be in control.

In fact, being in control is the best thing you can do to rise above the fear and anxiety of speaking to these strangers. You need to learn to be in control of yourself and your interviewee. Having control will provide you with the upper hand and strengthen your confidence to perform the prequalifying interview to the best of your ability. By being in control, you will likely be more thorough and appear more professional.

When I speak of control I mean be *in* control, not controll*ing*. There is a difference. To be controlling means you are probably steamrolling and intimidating your caller. It means you're probably being arrogant and demeaning. It means you might be considered rude. When you are controlling, you put the caller on the defensive and therefore you probably will not get the best or most accurate answers to the information you are looking for. On the other hand, being *in* control means you know where you're headed with the interview and how to get there. It means you speak *to* your caller and not above them. It means you are pleasant and professional. And it also means *you* won't be controlled, steamrolled, or intimidated.

Interviewing takes time

We'll take a look at the fact that interviewing just takes time. Unfortunately, this too is hard to avoid. Every night after you come home from your job or other daily duties, you'll have to return calls from interested prospects, sometimes two or three times until you reach someone successfully. When you do reach someone, one call or interview may take up to twenty minutes or more.

Since time is the issue at hand, or more specifically the use of *your* time, you need to ask yourself a question. Do you really want caller interviews to last twenty minutes or more? Not each and every call, that's for sure. Think about it. If you receive ten calls a night and it takes you twenty minutes to find out each caller doesn't fit your qualifications, that means you spent three and a half hours on the phone for nothing. On top of that, when you are done returning calls, dinner is cold and you missed the latest episode of your favorite TV program. Not worth it.

But don't worry. There is a solution. Even though interviewing takes time, it doesn't have to take *a lot* of time. If you wish to run the phone interview in a timely manner, let me give you a valuable tip. Use your Tenant Qualifications form as your guide. With this form, you've already taken the time to develop on paper the desirable and acceptable tenant you wish to have. Because you have this guide, when you begin interviewing your caller, ask those questions that most likely will quickly eliminate the tenant prospect from renting your unit, based on your tenant qualifications. Questions concerning credit, income, pets, eviction, occupancy, and criminal history are best. It makes no sense to spend a lot of time talking with someone who really doesn't qualify to rent your dwelling, so use your established Tenant Qualifications to ask the necessary questions.

In fact, the first minute of your telephone conversation is geared toward trying to discover and eliminate unqualified callers as quickly as possible. In simple terms: Get your tenant prospect on the phone. Ask a few questions. Eliminate them as soon as possible. This is your first primary goal for each interview.

I know that this idea of eliminating callers goes against the philosophy of some landlords who feel one day's lost rent is borderline unacceptable. But I have always been of the belief that I would rather have an empty rental *for* 30 days than deal with unwanted tenant problems *in* 30 days. In other words, I think the best way to eliminate trouble is to eliminate the troublemakers. I do this over the phone before they're in my rental.

Then if during the eliminating questions, the caller is consistently providing answers that qualify them as per the tenant qualifications you have developed, you must change the primary goal of your conversation from eliminate to *investigate*. Eliminate, then investigate.

Once you've entered the investigation stage, here's where you want to spend time asking lots of detailed questions. At this point, find out everything you can about the caller. If he or she is willing to talk, make this the conversation that lasts twenty minutes. Spend some time on the phone in deep conversation. Learn all you can about the tenant prospect and anyone living with them. Be thorough and complete because you don't want to go rushing out to show the rental to someone until you really know they qualify to rent from you.

Think of it this way: Why drive fifteen minutes one way, only to spend five to thirty minutes discussing the same issues you could have easily discussed on the phone? This could prove to be a waste of time, especially if they don't show up, or they do show up, but find out that the unit doesn't fit their needs or they're simply not interested. When that happens, you have to drive home to begin the same procedure all over again. The sad part is, I know landlords who will use this procedure over and over again, wasting valuable time, like a hamster running in a wheel.

Or what if you are showing the rental and discover something about the prospect that disqualifies them? Now you have to eliminate that prospect in person, face-to-face, eye to eye. Are you comfortable rejecting someone in person? How about rejecting two someones? How about two someones with a sad story holding a baby? *Remember this: It is far easier to reject or eliminate someone over the phone than in person.*

So don't be afraid to ask a lot of questions in your caller interview. Spend the time on the phone.

With all that said, let me recap how I use the caller interview procedure.

First, I *eliminate.*

Then, I *investigate.*

I do both with this ultimate goal in mind: *When I decide to show a caller my rental unit, I am confident that I would rent it to them provided they did not falsify or omit any information I received from them on the phone.*

That is my ultimate goal for all caller interviews. This is a pretty lofty goal, and I will be the first to admit I don't achieve it each and every time, but I do know from comparing notes with the many other landlords with whom I associate, I have an extremely high success ratio. For that reason, I am going to ask you to make this your goal as well.

STEP TWO

Caller Interview Form

Name _____ Date _____

Phone # _____ Phone # _____

Ads_____

1) # of Occupants _____ 2) Pets _____

3) Move in Monies   Y/N   4) Eviction   Y/N   5) Felony Conviction   Y/N

6) Income 1)_____time _____   2) _____ time _____

7) Credit 1) _____   2)_____

8) Occupancy Move date _____ Reason _____   Space _____

9) Financial Information

    Car Pymt   _____ Credit Card Pymt _____

    Health Insurance _____ Student Loans _____ Other _____

NOTES: _____

Name _____ Date _____

Phone # _____ Phone # _____

Ads_____

1) # of Occupants _____ 2) Pets _____

3) Move in Monies   Y/N   4) Eviction   Y/N   5) Felony Conviction   Y/N

6) Income 1)_____time _____   2) _____ time_____

7) Credit 1) _____   2)_____

8) Occupancy Move date _____ Reason _____   Space _____

9) Financial Information

    Car Pymt   _____ Credit Card Pymt _____

    Health Insurance _____ Student Loans _____ Other _____

NOTES: _____
_____

85

The Caller Interview Form

To help you accomplish this goal, I've developed the Caller Interview form. Please take a look at it so you will better understand the form as I explain its use. Using this form will not only help keep you on track with your interviewing, but it will also serve as a future reference for caller information should you receive a large number of tenant prospect calls. Therefore, once your ad is placed, have copies of this form handy along with a copy of your Tenant Qualifications and Ads and Tracking forms for when the phone starts ringing.

Your Phone Choices

As I've already mentioned in a previous chapter, I advise keeping a phone with an answering machine in a back room so you can return calls at your convenience. If you keep your caller answer sheets near the phone, then as you check your messages, you simply fill in the first line of the form with a caller name, date you received their call, and phone number(s). Logging calls in this way helps ensure you keep track of who called and in what order.

If you are returning calls from somewhere other than your desk, it might be wise to throw some Caller Interview forms in a folder to carry with you. Or at the very least, memorize the form and keep some kind of paper handy to jot down the caller's information. You'd hate to receive that perfect call at a time when you can't record and remember all the pertinent material.

Returning Calls

After you listen to your messages and log each name and number, begin returning calls. Naturally, some people are home when you return a call and some aren't. For those who aren't home, try to keep track of how many times you've called. If you got an answering machine when you called, leave a brief message acknowledging the fact that you are returning their call. Then put an *A* (for answering machine) by the name of the person you called. If you didn't get a machine or a person, use a tic mark for each time you attempt a call. By recording your attempts to return calls, you can defend yourself if someone ever says you deliberately didn't return their phone message.

Learning the Form

Should you get the caller on the phone, be ready to begin your interview. Give your name and ask how the person is doing today. State why you called and ask when and where he or she saw the ad. Log the answer in the space marked "ads."

On the form, after the word "ads," you will notice different words with blank spaces following each word. These words are the categories you will use to eliminate then investigate your caller. Notice these categories are not in the exact order of your Tenant Qualification sheet, which was designed in order of importance, but instead are placed in an order that is more caller-friendly as far as extracting elimination-then-investigation information from your tenant prospect.

Also realize that for learning purposes we will go over the categories and related questions in the order listed on the interview sheet, although as you question your caller, feel free to skip around and ask questions in any order as they naturally come up. You may even find convenient opportunities to interject other unlisted questions as they pop up in the course of natural conversation. Just keep in mind that in the initial part of the interview, you are trying to get truthful answers to the important topics as soon as possible, so try to stay on track.

Rules for Best Performance

As you begin asking your important interview questions, you will need a few guidelines to help you do it successfully. They are as follows:

- Give and take in your phone interview. Just because you are trying to eliminate callers quickly doesn't mean you can't answer questions and have a comfortable conversation.
- Make the interview and questions seem natural, not canned. Any conversation that feels natural and pleasant will be easier to control and will provide more accurate information. Try to word your questions so they can't be answered with yes or no. Yes and no answers

provide only the surface information; you want details and facts. Complex answers will provide you with that.

- Try not to give the answer you are looking for when you ask the questions. The caller may tell you what you *want* to hear instead of the actual facts.

- One of the best rules to remember to help you keep in control of a caller is this: The person who is asking the questions is in control. This doesn't mean you cannot answer any questions, just do it sparingly—especially in the early stages of the conversation.

- Last and most importantly, listen and listen well. Active listening will help you ask the right questions at the right time, so you can unearth information quickly and easily. Silence can be your friend. Ask a question and then wait for an answer. *Listen.*

Conducting the Interview

1) *Number of Occupants*

Often, to start the eliminate/investigate process, I recommend asking the question, *How many people will be residing in the rental?* As you know, occupancy is one of the qualifications you might have filled out on your Tenant Qualification sheet and it is a good qualification with which to start the interview as it is easy to answer and nonthreatening in nature. When you receive their answer, jot it down in the space provided. If the caller passed the qualification, move on to the next topic.

If they should fail the occupancy qualification, however, you will want to end the conversation. Simply explain to the caller he or she has too many occupants for your size dwelling. Thank them for their time, then end the conversation. In fact, you should always eliminate the prospect as soon as they fail one of your preset qualifications. Do not proceed with more questions in hopes of "passing" the caller, which is a *very* common mistake. Instead, simply end the call as professionally and as quickly as you can. Be polite. Be sympathetic but be firm. The failure to instantly end a call when someone fails a qualification is probably the biggest mistake you will make as an interviewing landlord. Everyone does it. I've done it in the past and on rare occasions, still do.

2) *Pets*

The next item on the form has to do with pets. Since it is very important that you don't reveal your policy on pets until after the caller has told you what pets he or she owns, simply ask, "What pets do you have?" After the caller answers, write in one dog (abbreviated as 1D), or two cats (2C), one bird (1B), and so on, for whatever pets they have. If you do not accept their type of pet, you can end the interview at this point. If you do accept their pets, don't go into detail concerning pet questions at this point, because interviewing people about their pets can take a long time. Your main goal is to try to finish the main elimination questions first in case the caller fails one of your other important issues. You can go back and get details about their pets when they pass the main questions.

The one exception to this rule is to ask what breed of dog they own. If the caller has a dog that might be listed as dangerous and you don't accept the dogs that are in this category, this would eliminate the prospect. (The topic of dangerous dogs is addressed in depth at www.FindThatQuality Tenant.com.) Should you find yourself in a situation where you don't accept the caller's type of dog, you need to explain to the caller the dangerous dog list and your preset stance on accepting them, then end the conversation. If they fail because of a dangerous dog, add the word "dangerous" and put a slash through *1D* to help you remember why you ended the call, just in case someone should try to sue you for discrimination in the future.

Whenever I turn someone away who owns a dog I've listed as a dangerous breed, I always explain that my insurance company is unfavorable toward these dogs and has stated they may not support a claim if an attack should happen. I then state that I'm very much a dog person, but my insurance company is much wiser and more educated in this matter and therefore I will follow their lead.

3) Move-In Monies—Y/N

The next important question you need to ask about their moving is, "Will you have all the required monies before you move in?" Personally, I don't take payments on security deposits and the like because I feel if a prospect doesn't have the required money to move in, then he or she is obviously starting their residency with me "in the red." And it has been my personal experience that once a tenant is behind financially it often takes a long time to catch up.

Also around the time I'm asking if they have the move in monies, I ask these two questions: "What do you pay for rent now?" and "Is this rent amount within your budget?" When I ask these questions of course, I'm hoping to hear positive answers and a dollar figure close to or above what I'm asking for rent for my unit. This makes their "old rent" a lateral trade for their "new rent," which helps reassure me of their ability to pay.

Occasionally, you will get an answer to the previous question where their current dollar figure is considerably lower than the asking rent. If you do hear a lower rent figure than what you're asking, don't panic: instead, investigate further. The caller's income may have changed for the better (a recent promotion) or they may have a scenario (newly married, two incomes, etc.), which makes financial sense as to why they can afford a larger rent payment.

If you are happy with the answer to item three, proceed to the next area.

4) Evictions—Y/N

You'll want to broach this subject with a question such as, "Have you ever been evicted or asked to move out?" If they were asked to move out of a previous dwelling, find out if it was for an acceptable reason, which would mainly be that the landlord wanted his property back either to move into or sell. That reason doesn't eliminate them as a prospect, but do eliminate them if they weren't paying their rent, broke the house rules, or did something illegal.

5) Felony Convictions—Y/N

Next, ask your caller, "Have you or anyone who will reside in the dwelling been convicted of a felony?" Should the answer be yes, ask the follow-up question, "Was that felony drug-use related?" For the most part, you are under no obligation to rent to anyone convicted of a felony, although there is one area in this category that is protected by Fair Housing Law. Over the years, HUD investigations have placed protection on rehabilitated drug abusers by extending coverage under the part of Fair Housing protecting the disabled. This is a prime example of how case law alters an original law.

Basically, what the case law states is that people with felonies that are substance abuse felonies (using, not selling) cannot be refused rental of a premise *if that person is currently in or has completed a rehab program and is still clean.* If he or she finished a rehab program and fell back into the habit, the person is no longer protected under this act. Obviously, if the person answered yes to the previous question, you will need to ask follow-up questions to determine if you can or cannot eliminate them at this point. Should you have additional questions concerning this topic, contact your local HUD agency for further answers.

6) *Income*

Generally, by the time you've reached the point of inquiring about income, you've probably already asked ten or so questions. When you reach this point, if you're still interviewing the caller, you are now beginning to change your objective from eliminating them to investigating them. This change of objectives requires much more accurate and detailed information. You must now begin to ask more detailed questions and start to build a profile on the prospect's objectives, circumstances, and lifestyle to see if your dwelling truly fits their needs and they fit your qualifications.

When you begin this process, strive to learn about their character traits and moral standings in addition to gathering information. Look at these callers as potential long-term business associates (which they are) and see if they fit your landlording goals. Also keep in mind that although you are investigating callers, you should still eliminate anyone who fails to meet your qualifications.

As we discussed in chapter 2, the prospect's income is very important, so you will approach the subject with a series of questions to inquire about this topic. First, ask, "What is your total monthly take-home pay?" Then ask, "Is this amount verifiable through pay stubs or tax returns?" Follow up these questions by asking, "And is this figure before or after taxes are taken out?" Record all your answers in the space provided. When you record the caller's answer concerning taxes, write *AT* to designate after taxes and—yes, you guessed it—*BT* for before taxes.

Should the caller be planning on sharing the rental with someone, ask about the spouse's/roommate's/significant other's income in the same way and record it in the second space. Naturally, if there are three roommates, list the third income elsewhere.

On occasion, people will tell you about extra cash income they make on the side—under the table, so to speak. When you hear this, you have a decision to make. Do you count this cash as income or not? Let's think about that for a moment. The problem with "cash" money is you don't know if the stated figure is steady, accurate, or even truthful, so I recommend you use this general rule: *If there is no proof of income, don't list it. If there is proof, list it.*

Time. Next, ask how long the caller has been on the job. You might also inquire about their previous job while you are at it. Record the answers next to the word "time" on the caller interview form.

7) *Credit*

When you begin to ask questions about credit, you are starting to touch on a subject some callers may feel uncomfortable talking about. That is why you don't ask about credit for the first question or two. Since credit can be a delicate topic, I recommend handling the situation by telling your caller something like this: "My next question concerns the topic of credit, so excuse me if I'm getting a little personal. I just need to tell you that I run a credit check on all serious applicants. The applicant pays for this report. So I don't waste your money, could you please rate your credit for me?" Then wait for the answer. If the caller says good or no problem, ask the follow-up question, "Does this mean you are current on all your bills, not behind on anything?" By asking this question, you will uncover what good credit means to the caller. Some callers will think good credit is no bankruptcy and only 10 late pays. Others will think good credit is no credit. Then ask, "Do you know what your credit score is?" Many people have no idea what their score is but the question is worth asking. If the person gives you an answer, write it down.

For any answer less than good, ask deeper questions, along the lines of "What's wrong with your credit? Please give me some details." Or "Have you ever filed for bankruptcy or do you have any judgments against you?" Again, listen to the responses. If the person says yes, he or she has filed bankruptcy, ask how long ago. Then write a *B* for bankruptcy and the length of time in years next to that.

You may also wish to ask them a question along these lines: "Are you currently paying on a bankruptcy or judgment and if so, how much per month?" If he or she is making such payments, jot down the dollar figure for future reference. As you're interviewing, ask the credit questions as in depth as possible and jot those answers down. Try to ask questions until you are either satisfied they can live up to your standards, or until they have eliminated themselves. If for some reason after three to five questions you still are unsure where their credit really falls, proceed with the interview and come back to credit later. You may uncover your answer as you ask other types of questions.

Sometimes you will have two roommates wanting to rent your place. Ask them *both* about their credit. In fact, you should also ask about both a husband's and a wife's credit. That is why there are two spots in the credit section for answers: so you can ask two people who plan to cohabitate about their credit. List them both on the form.

A word of caution about credit and roommates: Unlike a husband and wife who generally know each other's financial situation and credit problems, often roommates have no clue as to how the other party pays his or her bills. So if you ask the calling roommate about the prospective roommate's credit issues, chances are you will only receive an optimistic guess. When you have this scenario, interview the calling roommate. If this person passes your qualifications, then you can interview the second roommate before you show them the unit.

After you've covered the first seven topics on your Caller Interview form, the elimination process is basically done and the investigation process is well under-way. If you're happy with what you've heard so far, you should continue to ask questions to dig out more information on any areas where you're cloudy about their answers. Now is the time you may wish to learn more about their pets, income, credit, or other areas you have more questions about. Remember, the more information you get on the phone, the more likely you are to show your rental home to someone who fits your goal. Let's look at that goal one more time so you don't forget it: *When you decide to show a caller your rental unit, you know that if they wish to rent the unit, you would rent it to them provided they did not falsify or omit any information that you received from them on the phone.*

8) *Occupancy*

If you're pretty satisfied with the caller's answers to questions 1 through 7, you are now deep into the investigation part of the interview, where you are working for additional information. You'll notice number 8 is listed as occupancy and is longer than the rest. This is because you'll be asking four or five questions concerning the subject of occupancy and you need to write down any information that is important to you.

When you ask about a tenant prospect's occupancy, begin with, "How soon do you want to move in?" This question is a fairly important one because you want to rent your dwelling as soon as possible, and you will receive calls from people looking to move two or three months down the road, which means your rental stands empty longer—and that is more money out of your pocket. But more importantly, this question opens the door for questions of deeper substance. For instance, if they are moving immediately, you may wish to pose the question, "Are you currently breaking or have you ever broken a lease?" This particular question can be controversial among landlords. One side of the fence frowns upon lease breaking of any kind, while others, myself included, feel it is much less an issue than other areas of concern.

I do see both sides, but as I just stated, even though I may ask the questions and will put some stock in their answers, I don't automatically disqualify a lease breaker. Here's why: Things happen in people's lives. They fall in love and decide to cohabitate; they fall out of love and split up. They get divorced, become ill, and get transferred. A constantly changing economic climate might result in people suddenly finding themselves out of a job or unable to handle their bills anymore. Any one of these could be a justifiable reason to break a lease.

Even if none of this happens, other problems can creep in. How about the new tenant in an apartment building who inconsiderately makes noise until 2:00 A.M. but unfortunately, shares a common dividing wall with another tenant who must begin the day at 5:00 A.M.? Or the neighbors who are inconsiderate to those around them with barking dogs, loud music, and other problems? These can also be sound reasons for breaking a lease.

And finally, tenants break leases because some landlords don't live up to their end of a lease. Everyone has heard of stories where a tenant calls a landlord about a legitimate problem and weeks later, it still isn't fixed, let alone looked at.

Put yourself in the tenant's shoes: You're three months into a one-year lease, but the new neighbor's dog keeps you awake, or your spouse left you, or you lost your job, or you're tired of lighting the hot water heater morning, noon, and night. When you're in any of these situations, with nine months left on your lease, each day is torture. The fact is, many people break leases and often for some very good reasons.

Because there are so many justifiable reasons for breaking a lease, I've adopted the attitude that if tenants feel they gotta go, they gotta go. After all, if they were my tenant and they stayed and were miserable because I pressured them to stay, they would probably make my life miserable as well, perhaps in hopes that I'd eventually ask them to leave. Even though my absolute first choice is to not have to deal with a broken lease, I'd rather have a broken lease than live day to day with a problem or unhappy tenant.

You may feel that if someone broke a lease in the past, then there is a good chance they will break one with you. I can appreciate that line of thought. After all, profitable landlording really boils down to keeping the rental rented with the least amount of turnover possible. If this is your line of thinking, depending on how strongly you feel about it, this question, "Have you ever broken a lease?" could be written up as a qualification on your Tenant Qualifications form. Just write it up on the form under "extra qualification."

Also keep in mind that when the time comes to follow up on the tenant prospect's application, you can ask this question to current and previous landlords and rest assured, if the landlord felt extremely burned or left holding the bag because of a broken lease, you will hear about it in their reference. If they broke a lease for a good reason, you will also hear about it (from the tenant, not the landlord).

Basically, this is a question worth asking and the answer you receive should, at the very least, be put toward building a character profile of your caller.

Reason. Another question to consider asking is, "Why are you moving?" Be forewarned: You will get all kinds of answers to this question. Pay close attention to see if you are comfortable with their answer, and if you're not, be prepared to ask more questions. An example would be, "We're living with Mom, a friend, an aunt, etc." When you hear this answer, say to the caller, "May I ask why?" Sometimes you'll hear, "Because I need a ride to work." or "I couldn't afford my bills." When you hear these types of answers, it should make you ask yourself: *How old is this person? Can he or she handle money responsibly? Is he or she mature enough to rent on his or her own?*

Other times the answer is, "My husband/wife just got transferred and we didn't want to rush a housing decision until we know the schools and area."(A job transfer generally means more money, and they are obviously mature enough to think before they leap.)

You might hear, "We lost our house to fire." Or "We had medical bills so we moved in with relatives to try and save our credit."

The answers you hear and the way people say them could reveal a lot about the caller's character and maturity, so be sure to always ask this question. If their answer makes you nervous, do not be tempted to eliminate them. Instead, ask more probing questions until you fully understand their situation. Their answers may turn out to be solid, valid, and acceptable. And besides, you should only eliminate someone because they are not up to your preset, legal standards, not because they made you nervous.

Space. Many times when you ask, "Why are you moving?" the response will be, "We need a bigger place." This is an acceptable answer, but it will need further investigation.

First of all, few people are willing to give away a lot of their accumulated material possessions. This means if they are leaving a 1,200-square-foot ranch with a basement and moving into your 1,000-

square-foot ranch without a basement, they probably are not going to have enough room. The real problem is that many times tenants don't realize how big the unit they are currently living at really is. They will take a guess but since they've probably never measured the unit, their guess could be off by 200 or 300 square feet, which is equivalent in size to one or two average bedrooms or a one-car garage.

When you ask questions concerning space, get the specifics in the following areas:

- Furniture: What big items do they have (buffet, 10-seat dining table, 8-person sectional, etc.)? Visualize and discuss where they are going to put those items in your rental to make sure they will fit.
- What kind of closet space do they have now in comparison to your rental?
- Do they really understand size? For example, let's say you ask how big their sofa is and how many people it seats. If the answer is, "The sofa is 5-feet wide with seating for four," something is wrong. Either the couch is a 5-foot loveseat seating just two or it is 10-feet plus, capable of seating four people. Anyway, in this scenario, the answer tells you that the person doesn't really grasp space as it pertains to footage. So you may have to take control and help him or her sort through the issue.

Also, be aware that sometimes you can trade space for space, meaning their basement items might go in your garage, shed, or attic. Of course, if your place is equal to or bigger than their current residence, then storage space issues are usually narrowed down to garage and shed items.

Another point concerning space is about children. When the kids are five years old, they can easily share a small room with bunk beds and a small dresser. But as they get older, each child has an adult bed, an adult dresser, a stereo, television, computer, and so forth. If these same kids are still sharing a bedroom, they may quickly run out of space. Unfortunately, many tenants fail to realize this, and once they move in, though they are good tenants, they're cramped and more prone to move when the lease is up.

Since I can vouch from experience that lack of space is one of the quickest deal breakers when showing qualified prospects your rental I'd like to give you some advice. Whenever you think your house might truly be too small for a caller, give them the address and suggest they drive by. This is with the understanding that they look at the rental in regards to how it would accommodate them sizewise. Advise them to look in the windows and visualize where their furniture and other personal items will go. Explain how people naturally accumulate things and you have seen on more than one occasion where tenants moved in only to be cramped in their living quarters. Also explain that you hate to see good tenants have to move twice because they just didn't have enough space. It is inconvenient to them and to you. Ask them to be honest with themselves and if they believe the rental could truly work for them, have them call you and make an appointment for a showing. Callers appreciate the honesty, professionalism, and thoughtfulness on this subject.

When discussing this issue about kids and space, remember that you are not to discriminate against their children. You are merely letting the caller know this could be a future problem for them, and you want them to be aware of that potential. Let the caller know it is totally at his or her discretion to decide if this is an issue that they are concerned about. The only reason you bring this up is because you want to make sure the rental has the space the potential renter thinks he or she needs.

Please don't suggest a drive-by look until you've finished interviewing them and you're pretty sure they will otherwise qualify to rent from you. You don't want to have to eliminate them later.

Also during this conversation covering occupancy, I'll ask, "What area are you living in now?" I ask this especially if I don't recognize the telephone prefix, town, or locale from which they are calling. This is important because often, the caller doesn't know the area and thinks they are ten minutes from their job (or other important area of their life) and does not realize that they are 30 to 60 minutes or more away. This question eliminates them if driving distance is a factor, which again saves me a wasted trip to the dwelling.

As I interview, I'll also ask, "How long have you been at your current dwelling?" and "How about the place before that?" If their answers prove they have the rental stability I'm looking for, I'll continue. If I discover they move every three months for poor reasons, I'll terminate the interview.

If all has gone well, I generally finish up the occupancy category with these questions. "How long are you hoping to stay in your new place?" and "How long a lease will you sign?" I generally shoot for a one-year lease minimum on any rental. That seems to be the industry standard, at least in my area of the country. You might have to take a shorter term if that is more prevalent in your area. Try for the longest commitment possible. Remember, every time the unit is empty, it *will* cost you money.

9) *Financial Information*

In this category you will try to make sense of their finances as far as spending habits and where their money really goes. You'll get more details when they fill out the rental application, but now is a good time to ask the basics on their spending habits. Also be aware if they are just squeaking by on the minimum earning requirements.

Car payment. One of the larger expenses people have is car payments, so ask, "How much is your car payment?" and "How many car payments do you have?" Most people have at least one car payment, but if they are paying a couple of them or have unusually high payments, again, that money could come from their rent fund. A new car—or any financed car for that matter—also has a much higher insurance payment. If they have a car payment, make a note of the dollar amount in the space provided.

Credit card payment. Here I just want to know the amount they pay on their credit cards each month. Most people have a good idea and will usually tell you without a fuss.

Health insurance. In addition to the aforementioned car payment, there is another big area where a person's disposable money can go, and that is health insurance costs. With high malpractice insurance, a larger population whose life expectancy is longer, and the expense of new technology, the cost of health insurance has skyrocketed. Because of these reasons, many people cannot get coverage at their jobs. Add this group of people to those who are now self-employed, and you will see that many of your callers are paying their own way when it comes to health insurance. That is, if they are covered at all.

Of course, noncoverage leads to a totally different problem. If someone renting from you gets hurt or sick and there is no coverage, you can bet in no time at all that there will probably be some financial hardship in the household, which will affect you within a short period of time.

After reading my thoughts on health insurance, you can understand why you need to ask these two questions: "Do you have health insurance through work?" If they say no but indicate they pay their own, then ask, "How much is that per month?" By now, you are probably beginning to understand that depending on what the caller's payout on these higher ticket monthly expenses is in comparison to what they earn can have a vast impact on what they can really afford in a rent payment. It is your duty to ask about and analyze their financial situation because often what they think they can afford in rent may not be realistic.

Student loans. There are two other possible high-ticket monthly expenses that could affect the rent outcome. I run into each of these occasionally, but they are not as common as the ones previously mentioned.

The first is student loans. Some callers are just starting out on their career paths. If your caller had eight years of schooling for a medical degree, there is a good chance he or she has accumulated some expensive school debts along with it. Being new to the field, he or she probably hasn't reached his income potential yet but is still obligated to pay back these loans after graduation.

If you think you have a scenario like this, it might be worthwhile to ask, "Do you have a school loan payment?" and "How much is that per month?"

Another area of concern is one that is relatively small now, but if you spend any time in the rental business, I believe you will see it grow. I have already seen it happen. That area is children caring for their parents.

The days where people retired at 65 and passed on a couple of years later have greatly changed. Nowadays, people are living 25 to 30 years past their retirement age, and unfortunately, many of those people are using up all their savings and then some in the process. This means those retirees often will need extra financial assistance, which may come from their kids. If you get a feeling about this, you might need to ask, "Are you supplementing anyone else's income from your own, such as helping your parents or paying child support?" If you ask the question in this way, not only will you cover the issue of a child supporting a parent, but you will cover any divorced or separated parent who is paying alimony or child support as well.

Other. During my interviews I ask a lot of financial questions for a couple of reasons. First, by this time in the phone call, I realize there is a good chance this person could be my next tenant so I'm trying to build a sound profile on what kind of financial responsibilities he or she has. Second, since I know I'm going to ask other financially related questions in person when I show them the dwelling, I am subconsciously preparing them for the fact that I ask a lot of questions. Third, a lot of this information will be reported on their credit report so by having the number the prospect tells me already written down, I can compare it to see if this person exaggerates or lies. Ask as many questions as you feel you need to about their financial situation. Write those answers on the line labeled "other."

In case you are skeptical about asking people about their finances, let me make a statement: *Do not be afraid to ask questions about money because the ability to pay rent is probably the most important, problematic issue you will deal with on a regular basis, so knowing a caller's ability to pay is very important.* You'll notice in that statement I said "on a regular basis." Because you will have other problems. Furnaces break down, pets might be found in a dwelling with no pet agreement in the lease, toilets leak, and general wear and tear will happen, so expect it. But when your tenant has a shortage of rent month after month, no matter how small, it becomes your problem month after month. And believe me, it seldom gets better.

Notes

The last item on the caller interview sheet is a couple of lines for notes. As you interview tenant prospects, there will always be one or two who really stand out from the crowd. When that happens, chances are you may wish to ask many more questions and record more information. These lines are where you would do that. Trust me, the more notes you have, the better prepared you'll be later on in the process.

Reading Your Caller

As you are accumulating your answers in each category on each caller and you begin to believe you may have a quality tenant prospect on the line, you must still do some further analyzing and deductive reasoning to determine if this truly is the best prospect for your rental home. Basically, you'll want to take all the information you're gathering and continually build a profile of your caller. Look for facts or clues that help you ask the best questions that will most likely pertain to the individual situation at hand.

Take a look at the following example to get an idea of the kind of deciphering skills I'm talking about: Let's say there's a caller on the phone who is a single white male, approximately 35 years old, working as a car salesman at a large Ford dealership, making $4,000 per month, taking home $3,200 per month. After his normal monthly expenses for food, clothes, phone, cell phone, cable, heat, water, sewer, garbage, entertainment, gifts and miscellaneous expenses, hobbies, and any other expenses unknown to us, you discover he has $1,400 of disposable income for the rent of your $800 house.

Let's analyze this prospect: From your initial conversation, these are the things you learned: white male, probably in his mid-thirties. Is any of this of great importance to you? It shouldn't be. This information simply states race, gender, and age, three areas we do not discriminate against. But the gender and age are nice to know because they help you ask more detailed follow-up questions. For instance, a man is less likely than a woman to stay home and raise the kids, or at age 35, he probably has little in the way of student loans. So as long as you don't discriminate, you can use any information you've acquired to ask better questions.

Anyway, so far, he can make rent with $600 to spare. Great. He also works for a large car dealership, so he probably has health insurance and there's a good chance he gets to drive a demo car, which is something you may wish to ask. Things are looking good. His age shows he probably doesn't have a student loan, but he is single. So you ask, "Are you supplementing anyone else's income or paying child support?" and discover he was married and is now divorced, leaving him with a child support payment of $387 per month, which he says he pays religiously. This $387 from his expenses still leaves him with more than $200 above his rent payment per month. He's even earned an extra brownie point because he makes his child support payment regularly. This prospect looks very good up to this point and you should be pleased.

But what happens if two simple facts about the caller are changed? Instead of 35, he is now 25, and instead of working for a Ford dealership as a salesman, he works for Ford Motor Company as an engineer. Could this affect things—and how? Remember, he's still divorced and paying child support, but now he's 25 years old, so chances are, he's only been out of school two or three years. This probably means he's making about the same money as the 35-year-old car salesman, but he still needs time to mature in his field to earn really good money. Being an engineer, he could also have a pretty stout school loan he is paying off, so you ask, "What is your monthly student loan payment?" and find out you need to add $400 to the aforementioned expenses.

The chances are also good he doesn't get a demo car to drive and since Ford Motor Company cuts his paycheck, company loyalty has this young man driving a Ford product. A new Ford product. Quite possibly a higher scale, new Ford product, thus making his new car payment above average along with high car insurance. So as you can see, with just two fact changes in our scenario, our second prospect doesn't look as good as the first. The second prospect is one with much greater risk, proving the point that you can have two very strong prospects, both working at good paying, respectable, stable jobs, but with a few minor changes, one of them would be hard-pressed to make the monthly rent. Of course, you will have to thoroughly analyze both prospects to know who really is more qualified.

I gave you this scenario to make you think. You don't need to ask every question available as you perform your phone interview, but you do need to observe the scenario and ask the right questions. You also need to ask enough of them to help you build a sound profile of the caller to see if they truly have the qualifications you require. It's your house and you have to make the final decision. Since good tenants and the ability to pay rent are your landlording lifeblood, you must get comfortable asking questions in all the important and sometimes delicate categories. Failing to follow through and learn this information could cost you a lot of money.

Here are a few pointers to help you get the most out of your prospect interviews:

- Try to get answers to the first seven major questions in the caller interview sheet as quickly as possible. I find I get my seven major questions answered best when I intersperse three to five other minor questions to help smooth out the conversation. Your goal is to eliminate, then investigate.

- As things progress, ask a lot of follow-up questions, all of which begin with why, where, what, who, when, and how. Asking these questions, especially during the investigation part of your interview, in an open-ended way can provide a wealth of information.

- Make the conversation flow. Control without being controlling.

- The chance of someone needing to be asked every question is minimal. Ask what you need for any and all areas you want answers to. Don't waste your time asking questions that have little relevance to qualifying that particular caller.

- Follow and lead the conversation (yes, at the same time) to get the information you need.

- Converse with the caller on his or her level. Don't use fancy vocabulary if you are dealing with someone who might not be comfortable with that. Try to mirror the way they talk. If the caller speaks rather slowly, don't you talk a mile a minute and confuse him or her. Work to build a rapport not only through words but also through voice inflection and dialect.

- If during any of these major questions the caller gets upset or feels you're prying or asking things that aren't your business, apologize and end the conversation (unless you did get off track and crossed a line; then you apologize immediately). You don't want to spend time on a caller who develops an attitude and feels you haven't a right to learn about people who want to rent your dwelling.

Remember, your major goal is to get a *highly qualified prospect to your house*.

Let me add one more thought: The phone interview skills to unearth that quality tenant may very well be the hardest part to learn about landlording. It takes time and practice. But with a little effort and patience, you can acquire the interview skills necessary to find the best possible tenant. Take it from me: If you really take the time to listen and get more detailed information from your caller, you will be conducting quality, in-depth phone interviews quicker than you might think.

In Closing

If you feel confident in your understanding of the caller interview chapter and its related form, please continue with step two (prequalify) in your tenant selection process. Do so by studying the questions and mock conversations in the next chapter and try to pick up on the major and minor questions. As you read them, build a concept of the tenant prospects in your mind.

Note: You can access this form on our website at
www.FindThatQualityTenant.com.

The title of this book is not *How to Find That Quality Tenant in 48 Hours*. Often finding a quality tenant who fits your landlording needs will take some extra effort and some extra time. Things run in spurts: periods of good and not so good. Uncovering a quality tenant is the same way. You may only receive three calls one weekend and then 20 the next, all from the same ad. Or you might go two weeks without one prospect who passes your qualifications and then suddenly you have three or four. It happens. Learn to roll with it. Things will work out and the rewards will be worth it.

CHAPTER 6

Questions and Conversation

I know much of the last chapter dealt with interviewing, but that was first and foremost about introducing to you the elimination and investigation concept and process, as well as correctly using the Caller Interview form. With this chapter, I hope to give you some additional guidance to help you improve your interviewing skills from a landlord's point of view.

List of Questions

Let's start with the following, which is a partial list of additional questions you may wish to ask during the phone interview. I didn't provide you with this list in the previous chapter because I wanted you to concentrate on the main questions of importance in each category. But now that you are coming to grips with the interview process, it is time to expand your list of questions. These questions are listed by category for convenience. Of course, there are many more questions you can ask in each area and naturally, different ways in which to ask them. I compiled this list to give you something to work with. Use what you need, feeling free to add or delete when necessary.

Occupancy:
• Who will be living with you?
• How many adults and how many children?
• Any part-time occupants?

Pets:
- What are the names of your pets?
- Are they inside or outside pets?
- Are they housebroken?
- Are they spayed/neutered?
- Are they licensed?
- Are they caged indoors?
- Are shots updated?
- Are they declawed?

 Credit:
- How's your credit?
- Please rate your credit.
- Have you ever filed bankruptcy?
- Was your bankruptcy a Chapter 7 or Chapter 13?
- Was your bankruptcy medical?
- How long has it been since you filed for bankruptcy?
- How much are you paying on a judgment or garnishment?
- How much longer are you paying that judgment or garnishment?
- Are your wages currently being garnished? If so, for what reason?

Eviction:
- Have you ever been evicted?
- For what reason?
- Have you even been asked to move out? Why?
- Have you ever refused or held back rent? Why?

Income:
- What do you take home per week? What about your spouse?
- Do you receive any regular bonuses?
- Do you have any other source of regular income?
- What is your occupation?
- How long have you been on the job?
- Will you have all the monies when you move in?
- Do you have verification of all income?
- Is all income documented?

Expenses:
- How much rent do you currently pay?
- How much is your car payment(s)?
- How much are your total credit card payments?
- Are you supplementing anyone else's income, alimony, etc? If so, how much?
- Do you pay any other loan payments? How much?
- Do you have health insurance?
- Do you pay your own health insurance? How much per month?
- Do you have any expensive hobbies?
- Is this rent payment affordable for you?

Move in:
- How soon do you want to move?
- Why are you moving?
- Where are you at now?
- How long have you been at your current residence?
- How long were you at your previous residence?
- How big is your current residence?
- How long are you hoping to stay?
- How long of a lease will you sign?
- Do you have any extremely large furniture?
- Do you own a waterbed?
- Tell me what bothers you about your current residence.

Miscellaneous:
- Have you ever been convicted of a crime?
- Was it related to drug usage?
- Are you a garage mechanic?
- Are there any smokers in the household?
- Are you in a garage band?
- Are/do you...? (Include here anything else you've developed as a tenant guideline.)

The previous list isn't necessarily complete. In actuality, if you doubled the number of questions, you would still have room for more. It's quite possible the list would never end. I'm offering this list to get you started and help those creative conversational juices start to flow. Only you know what you really need and want from your prospective tenant and with so many possible scenarios that you might encounter, only you can truly develop the questions that will work best for your rental situation.

Asking Better Questions

When you ask these questions, try putting them in your own words so you feel comfortable with them. Make them sound and feel like they are a natural part of your vocabulary. If need be, write your own questions down and keep them handy. The reporters and professional interviewers do it all the time, whether you realize it or not. And do not be afraid to add, delete, or alter questions at any time.

In the following pages, you will find excerpts of conversation to help you understand how to handle some delicate situations that come up. They cover questions or topics that some people might find hard to approach and give you answers that might help you when you have to give the caller a rejection.

Before we look at the excerpts of conversation, let's review the main goal of the phone interview: *first eliminate, then investigate.* Let's also quickly review the basic steps you'll take in your phone conversation:

- Get his or her name and number. Engage in a couple pleasantries.
- Mix major and minor questions, trying to cover the major questions as soon as possible.
- Find any potential problem tenants using the major questions or forms of the major questions.
- If the caller passes the major questions, use more minor ones to start building an accurate portrait of him or her.
- If things develop in a positive fashion, make arrangements to show them the residence.

110

With all that said and done, let's go over excerpts of conversation. For the sake of continuity, we will use the tenant qualifications we established for 712 Oak back in Chapters 2 and 3.

The Professional Tenant

You: Hello

Caller: Yes, hello. I'm calling about your three-bedroom in Miller.

Y: Yes. Hi, my name is Don, and yours?

C: Tina.

Y: Hi, Tina. (Got the name) How are you doing today? (Starting with the basic pleasantries)

C: Fine, and you?

Y: I'm fine, thanks for asking. Tina, do you mind giving me your phone number in case we should get disconnected?

C: It's 555-1001. (Got the phone number)

Y: Tina, can you tell me where you saw the ad for the house?

C: In Sunday's *Post*. (Got the day and paper)

Y: Would you object to me asking you some basic questions?

C: No, go right ahead.

Y: Thanks. Tina, when are you looking to move and how many people will be living with you? (One minor question leading into one major question)

C: As soon as possible. There are five of us. Two adults and three kids.

Y: What kind of pets do you have?

C: No pets. When can we see the place? We're ready to move. We have cash.

Y: That's fine. I always prequalify people over the phone so I don't waste people's time running to the unit for nothing. You know, making sure the house is what you need for size, location, and so forth.

C: We're not picky; we believe it's a nice place. In fact, I don't need to see it. I trust you. Like I said, we are ready to move and can pay up to three months rent in cash.

Y: Why the hurry to move?

C: We're tired of this place.

Y: Can you be more specific?

C: No, not really. We just have issues that make us want to move quickly.

Y: Tina, you seem like a nice lady. I'm a professional landlord. I *always* thoroughly prequalify all callers before I show a rental unit. Then I require the complete filling out of a rental application, employment verification, credit check with a score of 600 or better, two good past landlord references, three quality personal references, and a criminal background check, among other things. Everything is evaluated before I turn keys over to anyone. The process can take two to five days and if things don't check out you could be denied the rental. Being in a hurry, do you want to chance the process?

C: No, I think you want too much information. I just want a place to rent.

Y: And I want to rent it to you if everything checks out. And that means for each adult signing the lease.

C: We're in too big of a hurry. I'll keep looking. 'Bye.

Y: Thank you. Good luck and goodbye.

I wrote the above scenario for two reasons. First, a lot of people will tell you they need to move as soon as possible. To some, ASAP means tomorrow and to others, it mean as soon as they find a place that will work for them, generally within 30 days. It is your duty, as a landlord, to find out what ASAP means to each caller. The second reason I wrote this particular sce-

I have noticed that almost every time I interview someone who needs a place "tomorrow," I find that with a little more investigation, he or she turns out to be someone I will not accept as a tenant. Unless their current residence burned to the ground or flooded, most quality tenant prospects can wait a week while you do your due diligence process on their information.

nario was because even though there are really good quality people who want to rent from you, there will also be a few who are what I call "professional tenants." Professional tenants know the game. They know how hard it is to evict someone once they are in a unit, and once in will obey no one. They also know cash is king and very enticing to the struggling small-time landlord. Those professionals often prey on the single-family or small-rental landlord. They do this because they know that larger complexes have much more sophisticated (until now) systems for weeding them out, so they shy away from such places.

You can often tell a pro by clues such as offering to pay a few month's rent in advance (which often never fully materializes), doesn't care or need to see the place, always tries to steer the interview back to their goal and priority, and in general, will not want or be able to pass your scrutinizing standards. Although not every person who fits this scenario is trying to pull a fast one, many are, so be careful.

Let's continue with the next interview, beginning after all the pleasantries.

Pets, Rent, and Security Deposit

You: John, when are you moving and where are you at now?

Caller: Well, whenever we find something. We just got married and we're staying with my in-laws.

Y: Say no more. I can understand. So there's just you two?

C: Yeah. (Here you got the answer to the major qualification occupancy guidelines without even trying.)

Y: What do you have for pets? (He has no idea if I accept pets or not.)

C: She has a cat she calls "Lonestar." I call him "Pain." Do you accept pets?

Y: Yes, but I charge $25 more per month for rent, and I collect $300 more for the security deposit.

C: So you collect extra rent and extra security deposit? I don't think that's very fair.

Y: Why's that?

C: Well, I can understand extra security deposit, but why rent? The cat isn't going to take up much space or drink much water. It just doesn't seem right.

Y: John, at one time, I might have agreed with you, but it has been my experience that most dogs and cats, no matter how good they are, have bad days in which they chew, claw, or have accidents on the carpet. In one "bad day," a lot of damage can be done—sometimes hundreds of dollars worth, especially to carpet. Truth be told, I'd rather just collect a much larger security deposit and no extra rent, but generally such a large sum would be a burden to any new tenant. That's why I collect a smaller deposit and extra rent instead.

C: The problem is, I just won't have the extra $300. Can I pay $40 extra rent but not the extra security deposit?

Y: I can appreciate your honesty, but herein lies the problem: If you move in and after only two months you move out, I've only collected $80 toward any damage a pet might have done. The risk is too great.

The above conversation was written to help you deal with this topic, should you accept pets and decide to collect both extra rent and extra security deposit. Even though I went to great lengths to explain my policy to this caller, you are under no obligation to do so, although a small explanation is nice.

Dangerous Dogs

Caller: Hi. I'm calling about your three-bedroom house. I just have one question. Do you accept pets?

You: What do you have?

C: I have two dogs.

Y: I love dogs. What kind are they? (You'll notice I didn't reveal my answer. Instead I "answered" the question by responding with a positive, personal opinion about dogs, hoping the caller will be more apt to answer truthfully.)

C: I have a pit bull and a rottweiler.

Y: I'm sorry. I do accept pets, including dogs, but both of your dogs are on the dangerous dog list that my insurance company now uses against homeowners. If I allowed that kind of dog into the house and one of them bit or attacked someone, I could be held responsible—maybe even lose my house. My insurance company probably wouldn't defend me, either.

C: But they're both good dogs and have never even snapped at anyone.

Y: Oh, I believe you, but to keep my liability down, I'll continue to comply with the insurance list.

C: I'll get rid of the dogs.

Y: I would never ask that of a pet owner. That would be unfair to you and your dogs. Goodbye and I wish you good luck.

Some people do "get rid of" pets, but it has been my experience that when they do, the pet comes back in a few days or weeks. (The new owner couldn't control him, didn't like him, and so forth.) Also, if they get rid of one pet, they often get another. I *never* make a rental decision based on the promise of giving away a pet. Never. Most people who promise to give a pet away mean well, but giving a pet away is very hard to do, so don't bank on it.

Also, if the dog in question is part dangerous dog and part not, I still have to eliminate them. If the dog is a true mutt and even the owners don't know its species, and I can't tell what it is, I can't disqualify the dog. This is a gray area you will run into. Be fair and use your best judgment.

Breaking a Lease

You: Have you ever been evicted or asked to move out?

Caller: No, sir.

Y: Have you ever broken a lease?

C: Uh...yes...yes, I have.

Y: Can you tell me about it?

C: Sure. We were living in the upstairs apartment of a four-unit building. It was a no-dogs-allowed building, but the people below us snuck in a small dog. You know, the little ones that yip when they bark. Well, this dog barked constantly—sometimes hours on end. Days, nights, weekends. He was an equal opportunity yipper! Anyway, I complained to the management company a couple of times, but the dog was still there two months later. I got fed up and moved out.

If you've read the book up to this point, you are aware of my feelings about breaking a lease. Since I do believe there are good reasons to do so, I would always recommend that you hear the story of why the lease was broken. As you listen to the story, try to figure out if it is truthful and sincere. Listen to see if it fits the personality you've determined of your caller. Above all, listen to see if *you* think it is legit. Then you can make your decision about the lease breaking. Of course, it goes without saying you will ask the previous landlord about the situation in your processing step.

For the record, let me state that I've had tenants break their leases and most, if not all, did so for pretty good reasons. I'm aware that some landlords will disagree with me and never look at a tenant prospect who has previously broken a lease. If you are one of those people, I don't want to change your mind. I can understand your reasoning.

Felony Convictions

You: Now that I've asked you about evictions, I must ask my next question. Have you or anyone who will be residing in the residence ever been convicted of a felony?

Caller: Yes, many years ago. I served my time. Is that a problem?

Y: Maybe. What was the crime?

C: As I said, I served my time. I don't wish to reveal that. It's none of your business.

Y: Actually, you're wrong. The laws says I can deny to rent to anyone convicted of a felony, but the law also states that if that felony was related to substance abuse and the offender is in or has successfully completed rehab and is still clean, I cannot refuse them rent based on that conviction. Let's try again. Was the felony related to substance abuse? Not dealing, but usage?

C: No.

Y: I'm sorry, I'm going to end this call based on that information. Nothing personal, just business. Good luck.

As you can see by this situation, this can be a loaded topic. Personally, I've never had anyone say they were convicted of substance abuse (other things, just not abuse) so I can't say how I've handled such an issue. My recommendation is if you have such a prospect and that prospect has passed all other qualifications and they honestly are the best candidate you have for the dwelling, proceed with the five tenant selection steps. Show them the unit and let them fill out the paperwork. Over the next couple days as you process their information, call your local HUD agency and your lawyer if necessary to find out how to best handle the situation.

> Remember, being arrested or acquitted is not the same as convicted. If you have any concerns about this topic, I recommend talking to your lawyer about them.

Below Required Income

You: The rent is $800 per month. How will you pay the rent?

Caller: I have a job where I take home about $410 per week.

Y: So you're saying you take home about $1,640 per month. Do you have pay stubs to verify this?

C: Yes, I do.

Y: And your wife?

C: She's planning on getting a job.

Let's pause and discuss this caller's income. We'll pretend we have been receiving very good answers to our questions thus far. The caller is starting to look acceptable but is just a little bit short of income. Take a look at his and his wife's situation: At this time, they are taking home about $1,640 per month, which is $160 short of your $1,800 take-home standard (remember what you filled out on your income standard back on your Tenant Qualifications form). At this point, you might end the conversation because you have no proof the caller's wife will get a job, and you don't want to bank on their future hope for income. I recommend the job actually be theirs when they talk to you.

But maybe all is not lost for this couple. Since they are $160 short per month, they might make it. If there is one thing I have learned in this business, it is that some people can live on $24,000 a year while others have trouble getting by on $60,000. This couple might be those $24,000-a-year people.

To figure that out, we need to look at a couple of issues. The first is the fact that this couple is living with in-laws and therefore probably have not established themselves financially. Or if they have established some credit, it should be a fairly clean record because they don't pay market rent so hopefully they pay their other bills on time. Either way, you don't really know if they have money saved or if they can live within their means even though they are close on the required income.

The second issue is that you require a minimum of $1,800 a month income, and they only have $1,640 per month that they can document. How do you handle this problem? I suppose you could overlook the $160, but you could be setting yourself up for an eviction later down the road if they still can't make the rent. You'd also be disregarding the tenant qualifications you established earlier, which is not a good habit to get into.

The best way to handle this problem is to have a little financial leeway in place before the phone starts to ring. Let's look back at the Tenant Qualifications form under the income category. See the line labeled "notes"? If you had used that area to write an exception—"Allow 10 percent less take-home if they pass cash flow and credit check forms"—this would give you a little leeway in your decision process while still keeping strong income boundaries established. An exception such as this is not out of line and can prove to be quite valuable, so keep this thought for the future.

I did not make this exception a standard qualification on the form because I felt if you use a lower ratio for figuring income and then write this exception as a crutch to support that lower income, you may have above average rent collection problems from your tenants. I am trying not to set you up for failure. If you believe you have a strong income-to-rent ratio, you may want to add this exception.

Credit Checks

You: I run a credit check on everyone.

Caller: I don't want to waste my money on a credit check. If I don't pass, I lose my money.

Y: I'm sorry. I treat everyone the same, and I always run a credit check.

C: Will you refund my money if I fail?

Every once in a while, you will have somebody on the phone who will say it's unfair for him or her to have to pay for a credit check. When I hear this, I give the following response: "When I bought this rental, the bank ran a credit report to show I was a good risk. I paid for this report out of my own pocket. I paid to prove I was creditworthy of the keys to this dwelling. Likewise, I feel since you want me to pass those very same keys on to you, you need to prove your creditworthiness to me. In other words, it is your turn to pay for the report."

Generally, after I've had this conversation, I tell the tenant prospect if we're not able to see eye to eye on this point, he or she should look for a rental elsewhere. I believe if people are arguing about a small credit reporting fee before they are even on the premises, this attitude is a sure sign of things to come.

Bankruptcy Call

You: I run a credit check on everyone, which the tenant pays for. How is your credit?

Caller: Well, I have some problems, but I'm working on it.

Y: What kind of problems?

C: I hurt my back at work about 18 months ago, and it's still in litigation. Because I was out of work for a while I've had some late pays on my credit cards and car payments. I always paid rent on time, though it was tough. I hope to get all the medical bills cleared through work, but they're dragging their feet.

Y: How much back money do you owe?

C: Well, I was behind about $4,000, but I've whittled it down to $2,300 or so.

Y: Are you back to work?

C: Oh yeah. I've been back for a year now, and like I said, I'm digging out financially. I just can't believe the insurance company isn't paying yet.

Depending on your qualification involving other credit problems, this caller might be okay. His financial problem was medical, and he cares enough to keep fighting to pay his bills as he fends off bankruptcy. He has also cut his previous debt to almost half. You can't know for sure, but his conversation makes sense and seems honest. I would keep interviewing him to see if he really has the income and other standards you need. Also ask him how recent his late pays were and if they are caught up yet. If he is an otherwise good prospect, you could get extra security deposit from him.

Another Bankruptcy Call

Caller: We filed bankruptcy about two years ago. We've been good since.

You: What do you mean by "good"?

C: Well, we ran up my credit cards a few years back. You know, buying adult toys and vacations. I lost my job and it caught up to us. We lost the house and everything. Never again.

Y: Bankruptcies scare me a little because I need to know my rent is going to come in on time so I can pay my mortgage, taxes, and insurance. I have rented to folks with bankruptcies, and here is my policy: If your bankruptcy is a year or older and your income, current credit, references, and so forth look acceptable, I am generally willing to rent to you with additional security deposit.

Even though this caller had a bankruptcy, this prospect could be a very favorable one, provided they currently earn enough money to cover their expenses. The reason I say this—beside the fact the bankruptcy is two years old—is the caller's attitude. Without any help on my part, the caller took full responsibility and blame and admitted the bankruptcy was caused by their own immature actions. They were not passing the buck. It sounds as if they have learned to be more financially responsible since the bankruptcy. If they have a good, proven track record in the last two years, they could possibly qualify as a stable tenant.

As you are probably beginning to see, you will encounter many different scenarios and conflicts when it comes to credit and earnings. Find out the cause of any conflict (especially financial). Try to figure out if the problem is solved, getting better, or likely to happen again. *Keep in mind that any caller with a credit problem has a sad story. It's his or her sad story. Leave it there. Don't get emotionally involved. You want to know facts and future stability. Make your decision primarily based on current cash flow, income, and recent financial history.*

Rental Size

You: How much do you take home a week?

Caller: About $1,000 a week.

Y: Not bad. How big of a place do you need and how many people will live with you?

C: I'm divorced, but I get my two boys every other weekend, so I would like three bedrooms.

Y: Where are you at now and why are you leaving?

C: I'm in Miller also. I've been here three years but the landlord wants to sell. I think he want too much for it. Otherwise, I'd buy it.

Let's pause for a second and review the answer to the last question. This caller gave you some good insight about himself when he said, "Otherwise, I'd buy it." These were just four words in one sentence, but this tidbit of information could be a great advantage or disadvantage to you, depending on *your* plans in the future for your rental.

If you are in the mindset of keeping and paying off your property, it's possible this caller is wrong for you. He can handle a good-sized mortgage and is willing and possibly wanting to buy a house for himself. He might move out after a few months of renting if he finds a good buy, thus leaving you with an empty rental again. Don't think that if he finds an excellent deal, your lease will stop him. It won't.

On the other hand, if he is serious about buying and you would possibly sell your rental house, then having him there might work out for both of you. I give you this scenario because I want you to keep in mind that as you ask your questions, you need to be open to what you hear. Let's continue the conversation as if you were interested in selling your rental house.

You: I see. How many square feet are there where you live now?

Caller: I'd say 1,200 plus a basement.

Y: Mine is about 1,400, but I don't have a basement, only a crawl space. Do you see yourself cramped in this house? I mean, essentially, you are losing about 1,000 square feet of storage. (Here we cover that downsize issue. Remember, space is a big killer of prospective tenants. Unfortunately, unless you ask this question in conversation, you won't find out it's a problem until you've shown the unit. At that point, you've wasted a trip.)

C: Well, I need to get rid of some accumulation, but I've turned about half of this basement into a woodworking area. Maybe I could move the woodshop to that garage. How big is the garage again?

Y: It's a two-and-a-half car garage but has only one electric circuit. Will that be enough electric?

C: I doubt that is enough to run all my tools. I'm sorry. I don't think renting from you will work out.

This conversation proves how quickly a good caller can get even better or suddenly fizzle out. In the beginning, he was average, then when he wanted to buy, he suddenly became more appealing. But because of his hobby and the unit's lack of space to accommodate that hobby, he lost interest. I've labeled this up-and-down cycle "caller roller coastering." Emotionally, the caller's answers take you up and you think you found your dream tenant, but then suddenly with the next questions and answers, they drop you to square one. This happens all the time, so get used to it. (Actually, you will if you stay in this business long enough.) Let me say though, if it's going to drop and fizzle, it's preferable to find out in a 5- or 10-minute phone conversation with a caller, instead of driving to the property and finding out there.

Discrimination

Let's finish our sample conversations with this new and delicate situation.

Caller: I might be interested in your three-bedroom. But if you don't mind, I gotta ask a question. Are any of the neighbors the "unpopular" kind?

You: Well, I'm sure some are more popular than others, but if you're hinting about race or nationality issues, I must say I won't answer that question. I am a fair and professional landlord and will not discriminate on any of the legal issues including the ones you've hinted at. Thank you for your time.

This could be a loaded question for two reasons. First, some people are prejudiced and think you automatically are, too. You don't need these kinds of people living in your rentals. They cause trouble and headaches.

Second, there are people who call landlords and "test" them to see if they discriminate. Often, they throw a little bait at you to see if you say anything discriminating. To avoid these situations, do not ask or answer questions concerning race, religion, gender, age, marital status, or disabilities. If they offer this information, fine, but never, ever take the bait and ask these questions yourself. *Do not ask questions about race, religion, gender, age, marital status, or disabilities. Ever!*

In Closing

With that said, you have reached the point where you are wrapping up the questions and conversation chapter. Of course, I could write dialogue for this chapter until it made *War and Peace* look like a Cliffs Notes. Since you will find yourself involved in all kinds of conversations, my goal was just to get your wheels spinning and better prepare you for certain situations. Keep in mind, the interviewing process is not an easy one. It takes effort and some skills, most of which you can acquire with practice. A few of those important skills are listed below:

- **Communicate.** Keep the conversation alive and flowing. Conversation is just that: conversing. Both parties need to talk in full, lengthy sentences. The words yes and no should be few and far between.

- **Be a super sleuth.** Dig, pry, evaluate, guesstimate, figure, predict, and analyze. You're not solving a murder mystery, but you *are* problem solving: hopefully, before they get to be your problem.
- **Be patient.** Sometimes, people need time to open up and start to talk. A little patience and trust will go a long way toward providing that openness you desire. And again, control the conversation. Try to do this without being rude or overbearing. Remember, you will catch more flies with honey than you will with vinegar.

Also, you need to know your qualifications and boundaries. Repeat your set goal and work to achieve it. Do you remember that goal?

When you decide to show a caller your rental unit, you know that you would rent it to them provided they did not falsify or omit any information that you received from them on the phone.

In addition, don't waste time with people who are belligerent, argumentative, manipulative, controlling, trying to "wheel and deal," or defiantly refuse information. They'll waste your time, and you don't want these types of prospects living in your rental.

Last but not least, realize that no matter how hard you try, you will run into gray areas when interviewing callers. It just happens. The problem with gray areas is they can undermine your tenant qualifications, resulting in a potential future landlord problem. Look at gray areas closely, because sometimes you might easily be able to solve them. I'm not saying to break, bend, or cheat on your qualifications. What I am saying is if you come to a gray area, ask enough questions until you know the caller has truly met or failed to meet your standards.

Practice

If you are still uncomfortable with the interviewing process, role-play some interviews with someone close to you, or tape a mock conversation of you asking the questions and any follow-up questions you might have with a family member or friend. Then listen to yourself and evaluate your strong and weak points. If you worked a few minutes a day for only one or two weeks, you'd be surprised how much your interviewing skills will improve.

If you have a good lead or two, get them to the house for a showing!

CHAPTER 7

What Do They Need?

Landlords living in the same building or in very close proximity to their tenants is not unusual. Maybe they own a duplex and rent out the other side. Maybe they got a great deal on a house a few blocks down from them so they thought they would enter the rental business. Sometimes this close proximity is a plus. One such occasion is when it comes time to show the dwelling to qualified tenant prospects. Being in the same building or just around the corner is such a convenience in those circumstances.

But other landlords aren't so lucky. They may live 5, 10, or more miles from their rental. How do these landlords handle showings? If you are one of those landlords, there are two good ways to show a rental dwelling.

Showing Your Property

The first is to run out and show a prospect the rental unit as soon as you are able to set up a time that works for both of you. The advantage to this method really depends on the prospect. If he or she seems to be of the highest quality, an answer-to-your-prayers prospect, you want him or her at the house as soon as possible. You don't want this good prospect to make another call or lose the excitement for your rental. When you have a great prospect, don't lose him or her. You need the prospect, and the prospect needs you. Of course, the disadvantage of individual showings is, if you run out each time you have a prospect, you could be wasting precious time and gas.

Holding an Open House

The second way is to hold an open house. Basically, you tell each prospect that you will be at the house during certain hours on a certain day. It is their duty to show up between those hours. Some landlords like this idea best because it gives an impression that many people are interested in the rental unit, which is a definite advantage. The other advantage is that it saves time and shoe leather.

I've used both ways, but generally, I like the individual showings. By showing prospects the house one at a time, you'll get to know them a little better. You'll have extra time to ask more personal questions—questions they might not answer (at least truthfully) if there were other strangers mingling around. The quality time also allows you to answer their questions more thoroughly and will make your rental unit more appealing to the prospective tenant.

One of the problems with the open house is that if you make a terrific prospect who called on Wednesday wait until Saturday to see your dwelling, he or she very well might have found another place to rent before Saturday arrives. I've lost more good prospects than I'm willing to count by wasting a day or two to show someone the rental unit. Nowadays, I figure that since I'm doing such good pre-showing interviews, my odds of a successful showing are pretty high, so it makes little sense to lose a terrific prospect by making him or her wait a couple of days.

Another problem with open houses is that you may end up with two or three good prospects who qualify, but there is always one that stands out above the rest. They may have better qualifications than the rest. It could be a prospect's personality or just your gut feeling about them.

Here's a gentle reminder: Your gut feeling can't be like Archie Bunker's gut feeling. It can't be based on anything illegally discriminatory, but on your fair requirements. Here's an example: You will allow smokers and dogs. One good prospect smokes and owns a dog. The second prospect doesn't smoke or own a dog. All other things are equal. You don't mind smokers or dogs, but deep down, you know the chance of less wear and tear on the rental is with the nonsmoking, no-dog prospect. By conducting individual showings, you can try to show the best prospect first, and then schedule the others shortly after that.

Another way of avoiding the problems that can come up with an open house is to collect applications until a predetermined date. Again, you could lose a good prospect because he or she may not want to wait the allotted time. And you'd also have to meet with the chosen prospect again to collect applications and/or credit check fees because most people aren't going to give you that money up front until they have been chosen as a tenant. Naturally, two trips to the rental take up more time. As you can see, there are advantages to each way of handling showings. Try them both to see what works for you.

My suggestion is to try to line up the prospects back-to-back with your best prospects first, then second best, and so on. Leave ample time between them (30 to 40 minutes or so is good) so that if the first prospect wants to fill out the paperwork for the unit, you have time to do so. If the second prospect wants the place too, you could always take that application as a backup. This idea works well, especially if your rental unit is a distance from your house. An added note: Bring something to do if you line up more than one prospect in case someone doesn't show up.

What Tenants Should Bring When Seeing Your Property

Once you've decided how you're going to show the house, you need to make sure the prospect meets you at the rental with as much of their needed information as possible. You don't want to make unnecessary trips showing the property if you can help it, and having all needed paperwork and information required by you at the time of the showing will go a long way toward preventing these extra trips.

When you have the prospect on the phone, either from your initial interview or when you call back to schedule a showing, you need to tell him or her this: "I'm going to ask you to bring some in-

> If you believe you have a tenant prospect who is what you are looking for, you should briefly go over your rules and regulations before you get off the phone. You want to make sure he or she is comfortable with your rules and can live by them.

127

formation to make the showing a success should you be interested in the unit. Please grab a pen and paper and write down the following..."

Tell them you'll need five personal references from each adult who will sign the lease, including names and phone numbers (I want to speak to at least three references, so I always ask for five. Parents, grandparents, and other relatives don't count.) Ask them to bring the following:

- Past landlords' names, addresses, and phone numbers
- Copy of their Social Security number or card
- Copy of current driver's license or photo ID
- Recent pay stubs (I recommend asking for two months' worth.)
- Solid verification of other income source, such as alimony check stubs, regular pension, or government support check stubs, and so forth. (You want concrete proof that they have solid, reliable income. Have them show you proof for at least two recent, consecutive months. This is a must, because you don't want to be chasing government agencies on the phone trying to verify this information.)
- If self-employed, a copy of last two years' tax returns and three to six months of bank statements.
- One or two current utility bills with their present address on it (optional)
- One other source of ID or credit card (optional)
- Bank name and phone number (You might want this to verify they have an active account. This may also be optional. Some landlords want bank account numbers, but with the increased identity theft, tenant prospects are more reluctant to give that out. I don't blame them. I wouldn't give out any account information, either, but you can ask.)
- Cash for their credit check (If you are charging a deposit to hold the property, at the showing would be the time to collect that. If your rental market is extremely hot, I would think about collecting a healthy deposit to hold a unit.)
- Any other bits of information you require that are not mentioned here

Last but not least, let prospective tenants know they will need *all* parties present who will be making the decision on renting. Also let them know to plan for about 45 minutes for the showing and to fill out paperwork if they like the rental.

Once this list is given and verified as understood by the prospect, set the appointment time. Give precise directions, including north, south, east, and west, notable streets, and easy-to-locate landmarks on how to get there. Remember that not all people are good with compass-type of directions, so include left and right turns, number of stoplights or signs, and approximate mileage between these streets and landmarks. If you can't do this properly, drive to your unit from *all* possible

Besides seeing proof of Social Security number and driver's license you should make it a practice of having the applicant bring you a copy of these items to submit with their rental application as these two pieces of information can prove valuable if a tenant problem arises. Unfortunately, many tenants won't be able to get them photocopied before the showing. If this is the case, you simply have the tenant fax you these copies ASAP after the showing.

directions and write a complete set of directions down. (You could get your directions off MapQuest, although it may not have the designated landmarks.) You should keep this set of directions in your file of paperwork on that rental so you have them for future reference. Don't lose a great prospect because *you* gave poor directions.

Before You End the Call

As you conclude your call, again give prospects a precise meeting time and your cell phone number. Have them repeat what they need to bring, the complete directions, the time of your appointment, and your cell number. Ask them to call you 30 minutes ahead of their scheduled time—or whatever time you need before you leave your house—if they are going to be late or not show up at all. Also, be sure to thank them for their time.

Unless you live within walking distance of the rental you are showing, I advise you to use these techniques. You'll be glad you did.

Step Three: Paperwork

After completion of steps one and two, the chances are you have a couple of good potential tenant prospects that are interested in your rental, and who you believe fit your tenant qualifications. When you get to this point you are ready for step three, which is where you accumulate all the tenant prospect's information on the required paperwork. This paperwork will be used to double-check and verify all the information you collected over the phone. Should the tenant prospect actually become your tenant, the paperwork will become a part of their file for future reference or problem solving for the duration of the lease. Even though this information may seem mundane, read it completely, as I'm sure you will find valuable information within.

CHAPTER 8

The Rental Application

Congratulations! If you are using this system and things are going correctly, you should have completed step one (prepare) and step two (prequalify) and now have at least one very qualified person to show your rental to. In step three, you will actually meet with your tenant prospects, show them the rental unit, and fill out all the required paperwork. Before I explain the details of step three (paperwork) to you, I would like to tell you a story.

The year 1971 was a very pivotal year for me in terms of growing up and viewing the world differently. I was 10 years old and was getting a look at life around me without rose-colored glasses. For starters, that was the first year I experienced death in my short life—well, at least a death I could remember. My first grandfather passed away when I was three or four years old, leaving me with very faint memories of him. In 1971, when my second grandfather passed away, I was old enough to be affected by his death, and even though I wasn't extremely close to him, I had enough memories and understood how his passing would impact me.

It was also during this year that I was introduced to Archie Bunker. My newly widowed grandmother suddenly had a lot of extra time on her hands, and to occupy that time, she began watching more television. *All in the Family* was introduced in 1971 and it quickly became one of her favorite shows. Since she lived almost directly across the street from us as I grew up, and because kids love to go to Grandma's house, it only made sense that I was at her place quite a bit. So consequently, I was exposed to Archie Bunker and his views on life.

For those of you who don't know Archie Bunker, let me describe him for you: Archie believed himself to be America's most patriotic and vocal citizen. He had an opinion or explanation about anything and everything. Unfortunately, he couldn't communicate those thoughts without yelling, arguing, labeling, discriminating, or showing his true ignorance and lack of education on whatever topic was at hand. Of course, to make matters worse, he never saw these faults in himself and didn't want them acknowledged by anybody else.

All in the Family was a great show because it covered topics that had never been previously addressed on primetime TV. By touching on these issues, the cast helped to show all of America something we didn't really want to admit: There may be a little of Archie Bunker in all of us.

This brings me to the point of the story and why I am beginning this chapter with it. Perhaps we all possess some of Archie Bunker's negative character traits but just don't want to fess up to it. Some traits are worse than others and some can land you in trouble if you're not careful, which is why the main traits I want you to be aware of are prejudice and discrimination.

I believe prejudice and discrimination are born of a combination of things. They often begin in the home environment and/or the area and time in which we each live. They continue to thrive through ignorance and lack of education, resulting in an unfounded fear that often deadens one's sensitivity to the human connection. As stated previously, prejudice and discrimination are against the Fair Housing Act, and the reason I bring them up again is because every being on earth has things they are prejudiced about. It may not be race, color, religion, or creed, but it could be height, hair color, weight, clothing, or a number of other things. If you're like most people, you probably aren't aware that you have prejudice in your psyche. But you do. We all do.

Step three covers the topic of having all the necessary paperwork filled out by your tenant prospect, and it is in this step that you will actually meet the applicant. Therefore, I want you to realize something of importance, which is this: Sight is typically the first of the five senses used when making a prejudiced judgment. Since you are meeting a prospect at your rental unit to see them for the first time, I want you to remember not to label or pass judgment on your tenant applicant when you first lay eyes on them. I guarantee that often what you expect to see and what you actually do see are not the same thing. Even though your prospect was polite, courteous, and passed all qualifications with flying colors on the phone, it doesn't mean when he or she shows up at the rental this person won't have green spiked hair or body piercings or numerous tattoos—or drive a beat-up Chevy when you like BMWs. He or she might wear thick glasses or sloppy clothes, or be fighting a weight problem. None of this matters. Keep in mind that this person initially passed your qualifications over the phone, so treat him or her as if they were a picture-perfect, Ivy league college grad dressed for a modeling spot in *GQ* magazine.

Do not discriminate based on sight; discriminate based on qualifications.

Late Applicants

When you show up for an appointment, try to be early. Five minutes is more than enough time. Most people will be on time but a few will show up 5 to 15 minutes late. By arriving just a few minutes ahead of schedule, your wait time will be kept to a minimum for the latecomers.

If you remember some advice from the last chapter, you should have given the prospect your cell phone number and asked him or her to call you if they are running late or can't show up at all. This is good advice, but it doesn't always work, so as an added measure of security, I will often place a call to the prospect a couple hours before the showing to remind them of our appointment. If they are not at the showing within 15 minutes of the appointed time, I don't wait around any longer. I have waited in the past, and I have learned that almost without exception, when the terribly late did show up, they were not worth the wait.

I also seldom give a no-call, no-show prospect a second chance at a showing unless there was an emergency or unforeseen circumstance that kept them from being able to contact me. You can allot as much time as you want, but my experience has shown me that latecomers or no-shows are generally not the quality tenants I'm seeking.

When You Arrive

Should you arrive before your scheduled appointment, use this extra time wisely. I suggest you keep a few plastic, recyclable shopping bags in the glove box of your car. That way, when you get to the dwelling, you can make a quick check of the property grounds and pick up any debris that is lying around. While you're at it, pull a few weeds and put them in the bag as well. Check the mailbox for any junk mail. Once you're done checking the property, all you do is tie the bag handles together and toss the bag out when you get back home. As you're policing the dwelling, take the time to make sure that all gutter extensions are in place and that there are no broken windows or anything else on the property vying for your attention before the prospect arrives.

There are two kinds of rental dwellings that you could be showing: occupied and unoccupied. Each is handled differently. Let's discuss occupied units first.

Occupied Rentals

If the current tenant still lives there, don't show the property unless you have an outstanding prospect who is *highly* interested. Before showing an occupied house, have the prospect drive by and take a good look at the property. Explain that there are still people living there and that you must protect their privacy, especially since they trust you enough to allow you to walk people through their home.

When I show an occupied unit, I ask that everyone stay together and not touch anything. I lead a quick tour of the dwelling, then after the tour, I will answer any questions. I always try to do the questions-and-answer session outside, weather permitting. If I can't do that, I suggest driving to a local restaurant or back to the prospect's home (you get to see how they live with this method) to continue our discussion and to fill out any necessary paperwork. Remember, the longer everyone stays at your current tenant's home (even though it is for rent, if they still live there, technically, it's still their home) the more likely the chance that something gets dirty, damaged, or stolen.

Showing an occupied dwelling can be bothersome and inconvenient to the current tenant so try to make these occasions rare.

Here are a few tips to help you decide when to show an occupied dwelling:

- Only show the dwelling to someone highly qualified who has driven by and who you believe will almost certainly rent the unit once he or she has seen the inside.

- Only show a dwelling that is clean and uncluttered. If the place will not make a good first impression, wait until the unit is empty, cleaned, and painted.

- Get permission from the current tenants and let them know what time you'll be at their home and assure them you'll only be there for a few minutes.

Unoccupied Rentals

Even though showing an occupied dwelling can save you money because the time between the old tenant leaving and the new tenant arriving can be greatly reduced, you'll probably find that many of your showings will be at empty rental units.

When you show an empty rental, the precautions change. You no longer have to worry about someone causing damage to anything your current tenant owns, but the issue of personal safety now enters the picture. If you are a female, use extra caution when showing a rental unit by yourself. I recommend the following safety rules:

- Let someone know where you are going, the names of who you are meeting, the time of the meeting, and the approximate time you'll be back.

- Try to take someone with you if possible.

- Carry a charged cell phone. By the time you read this, a large part of the country will have a satellite tracking system for cell phone emergencies. With this system sending an emergency callout, you can still be tracked down even if you are unable to give your location. You just have to leave the phone on.

- Carry a loud shrill whistle or an obnoxious noisemaker and can of mace with you, ready at all times, and know how to use it.

- Try to stay between the applicant and an unlocked exit so you don't find yourself trapped with nowhere to go.

- When you get to the house, ask for a photo ID. Then call your answering machine or a trusted friend and give this information. Give the name of person you are meeting, including ID number, address, birth date, and the time of the call. Do this outside in view of everyone before entering the rental.
- Above all, trust your instincts; these are your best natural source of survival. I highly recommend a book called *The Gift of Fear* by Gavin DeBecker. It is a book about listening to one's instincts when it comes to personal safety.

As long as you make safety a top priority, showing an empty unit can have many advantages.

The Showing

At this time, let's proceed with the showing. Once your prospects arrive, greet everyone with a handshake and ask for their names. This approach shows professionalism and will help establish a comfortable, relaxed atmosphere, which will yield a more productive showing. Open the door and as everyone steps in, ask them to remove their shoes or wipe their feet, whatever is your protocol. Then begin your tour. Lead everyone through the living and private quarters, one room at a time. Give them time to look things over and ask questions. This personal one-on-one time between you and the prospect is often crucial in addressing issues they might have. You want this walk-through to be leisurely and informational, but don't talk forever and don't use all the obvious amenities as a sales pitch.

Just as you asked a lot of questions earlier in the process, be prepared to answer a lot of questions at the showing. These questions will cover topics about the dwelling itself, the neighborhood, your policies, what-if questions, and anything in between. Be patient. And be honest.

Practice Your ABCs

In addition to addressing any concerns or issues your prospect might have, you also want to work on the ABCs of sales (Especially if you really like the prospect and think they live up to your qualifications). The ABCs of sales stand for *Always Be Closing*. Of course, this refers to you as the salesman working to get someone to purchase your product, which, in this case is the rental unit.

In other words, as you show the rental unit, you need to add in a few questions that force people to visualize themselves living at this home. Ask questions such as, "Where would you place your couch or TV or bed in this room?" or "You said you liked to cook. Did you notice the kitchen has a lazy Susan right next to the dishwasher?" Also, general comments such as the following will go a long way in helping them picture the house as their home: "If you are the outdoors type, those old oaks in back offer outstanding shade to the property." Or: "On the phone you mentioned your concern about high utility bills. Just so you are aware, all the windows in the house are only three years old." Whatever ABCs you use, they

On occasion, you will show a rental to prospects you thought passed your qualifications but you become unsure at the showing. Unfortunately they want to fill out the application. When this happens, you may wish to simply say something along these lines, "I'm not sure if you will be accepted for the rental based on such and such criteria; however, you are more than welcome to fill out all paperwork and give it a try if you would like." You will then need to take the application with you and if they truly did not pass, reject them from home. You also may choose to say nothing and just let them fill out the paperwork. Whatever way you choose, your main goal at this time is not to upset the prospects for your own safety. A good, safe, nondiscriminating habit to get into is, offer everyone to whom you show the rental an application. You believed they were qualified before you showed it to them; collect all the paperwork and analyze it at home. You never know.

need to sound natural and spontaneous, because even though you are trying to sell your rental, you don't want to appear pushy or desperate.

Once you've shown everyone the unit and have answered all their questions, ask them if they're ready to fill out an application. If they say they need time to talk things over, don't part ways and go home. Instead, offer to step outside for a few moments. This might be enough time for their discussion and any controversial areas they may have about the rental might be worked out at that time. When potential tenants are unsure about renting from you, give them ample time to think about it before actually leaving the unit. Once they leave, there is a good chance the applicants may decide against renting your dwelling simply because of the old adage, "Out of sight, out of mind."

Filling Out the Rental Application

If you have a clean dwelling and it is correctly priced, I guarantee that eventually, someone will want to rent it. When they do, it is time to begin filling out the rental application. Here's how I recommend you handle this process.

Keep a folder in your briefcase, labeled "Step Three" (or something to that effect). Place all the forms you need for the tenant prospect to fill out at the showing in this folder. Keep plenty of each form paper clipped together in this easy-to-identify folder. I put a large rubber band around each folder to keep things in order in case I drop the file. Also make sure you have a couple of pens handy.

I suggest you have a copy of your rules and regulations handy at the showing (visit www.FindThatQualityTenant.com for a free copy). Should your tenant prospects really like the dwelling, let them review the rules and regulations before they begin filling out the paperwork. You'd hate to go over the rules the day of the lease signing and find a rule the tenant couldn't live with, possibly deciding not to sign the lease. If he or she agrees to your rules and regulations, give him or her the application.

140

STEP THREE

Rental Application

(If applicant intentionally lies, falsifies, omits or hides pertinent information during any stage of the tenant selection process, applicant can be denied rental of said property. If applicant is not of legal age, or does not have a Social Security number or other form of government issued I.D., applicant can be denied rental of said unit.)

Personal Information (Please Print Clearly)

Name _____ Date _____

Home Phone _____ Work Phone _____ Cell Phone _____

Date of Birth _____ Maiden Name (if applicable) _____

Driver's License # and State _____ Social Security # _____

Names and relationship of every person to live with you even if only temporarily (include ages of minors)

_____

_____

Names, breeds and descriptions of all pets _____

Present Address _____

How long at this address? _____ Rent $ _____

Reason for moving _____

Owner/manager _____ Phone # _____

Previous Address _____

How long at that address? _____ Rent $ _____

Reason for moving _____

Owner/manager _____ Phone # _____

Previous Address _____

How long at that address? _____ Rent $ _____

Reason for moving _____

Owner/manager _____ Phone # _____

copyright 2007 Blue Collar Publishers

The Rental Application

If you look at the rental application provided in this book, you will notice that each rental application is designed for one person, so you need to give one rental application to every adult who plans to rent from you. This means one per husband and one per wife. I like each adult applicant to fill out their own applications. Should one person's handwriting be illegible or mostly incomplete, I have another to fall back on. I can also cross-reference a couple applications to double-check the accuracy of their information.

Likewise, if there are two people who want to be roommates, each roommate should fill out an application. Roommates have no ties to each other, so there is no real reason for them to stay together for eternity. Consequently, one of them will probably move on during their tenancy. When that happens, you want separate paperwork on each person so you can keep better files on who is living in your rental. And remember, any new roommate who moves in to replace an old roommate has to go through the same interviewing process. Otherwise, you lose track of who is renting from you.

Remember to have enough applications and pens on hand to accommodate everyone who will be filling out paperwork, including yourself.

Let's go over the application and discuss some of its finer points.

Personal Information

Home/work/cell phone. The rental application is basically self-explanatory, but let's take a look at it bit by bit in more detail. After the name and date, you will notice that your form has three lines for three phone numbers. Have them fill in as many as possible. More is better, because if the applicants become your tenants, then the rental application will be your source of information on that tenant. If this happens, you'll want the work and cell numbers so you have multiple ways to keep track of them.

Date of birth/driver's license/Social Security number. The date of birth, driver's license number, and Social Security number are important because they are the key to accessing the prospect's personal information and crucial to tracking tenants down if they should cause you problems or disappear owing you money. In fact, it is so important to have these three items listed on the application correctly, that once the rental application is filled out, you will ask to see everyone's Social Security card and driver's license (or some other form of ID) to verify that the written information (names, birth date, and all numbers) actually match what is on these cards. At that same time, you should take a peek at any picture on those cards to see if it looks like the applicant. This is important information, so don't be afraid to ask for those ID cards.

If they can't show you one of these necessary cards, you can still proceed with the application process. If they pass all the necessary stops, at lease signing time, you need to see proof or receive copies of these items. No excuses.

I can't emphasize enough the importance of seeing a photo ID when you receive a filled-out application. You must know that the person represented on the application is the same person in front of you. In particular, make sure the Social Security number is verified. Your applicant could have a terrible credit record and provide you with a family member's or friend's record that is superb, possibly resulting in putting an unworthy tenant in your rental.

Maiden name. Also listed among these numbers is a space for maiden name. This line will obviously not apply to everyone, but if it does, be sure to get this information. It will be an additional aid in tracking someone down if it becomes necessary later on down the road.

Name and relationship. The application also includes a spot for names and relationships of every person to live with the tenant, even if only temporarily. It also requests the ages of all minors. This information helps you determine if the prospective tenants meet your occupancy requirements. Temporary minors are included because even though a child who visits every other weekend does not count as actually living there, knowing about the situation will keep you from surprises in the future and might give you extra insight on lifestyle and space requirements for the prospects.

Pets. Following the names of all the people in the house is a spot for names, breeds, and descriptions of all pets. Of course, you want to know what kind of animals they have and a little bit about them. If you neglected to find out their pet status before you showed them the rental, you are doing them and yourself a disservice. It's unfair to wait until you show the rental to reveal what pets you allow in the dwelling because if you won't allow their pet and must turn them down, you've wasted everyone's time. Find out about pets on the phone.

You might be asking yourself why you are bothering with pets and number of occupants on the rental application when you should already know this information from the phone interview. Here's why:

- When they fill out the information you should already know, such as pets, or how many occupants, you are getting the applicant's answers in their handwriting. If there are problems in the future, you'll have a little more evidence to pull from that paper trail.

- Asking again helps ensure there was not a communication problem or information breakdown during the phone interview. If there was, now is the time you'll discover it.

- If they become your newest tenants and are as good as you prayed for, knowing all the kids and pets goes a long way toward giving the tenants the respect they deserve. And as we all know, if you give respect, you often get respect.

Rental History

Present address. You can't go wrong by having this much written information. After they fill out the occupants and pet information, you ask for their current address and related information.

Previous address. Although current landlord information is useful, I'm personally most interested in previous landlord information, and I recommend you try to get as many previous landlord phone numbers as

STEP THREE

Rental Application

Income Information

Current employer _____

Supervisor's Name _____ Supervisor's Phone # _____

Dates employed ____/____ to ____/____   Occupation _____

Hours worked per week _____   Current Pay $ _____

Second OR Previous Employer_____

Supervisor's Name _____ Supervisor's Phone # _____

Dates employed ____/___to___/____   Occupation _____

Hours worked per week _____   Current OR Ending Pay $_____

Previous Employer _____

Supervisor's Name _____ Supervisor's Phone # _____

Dates employed ___/___to___/____   Occupation _____

Hours worked per week _____   Ending Pay $ _____

List other sources of income and amount (steady bonuses, government checks, alimony, child support, etc.)

_____

Nearest Relatives (2 total)

_____

_____

Personal References
(Minimum 3 PER adult, excluding parents, grandparents, siblings and relatives)

Name _____ Home Phone # _____ Other Phone # _____

Name _____ Home Phone # _____ Other Phone # _____

Name _____ Home Phone # _____ Other Phone # _____

Name _____ Home Phone # _____ Other Phone # _____

Name _____ Home Phone # _____ Other Phone # _____

possible. As I mentioned earlier, it is these previous landlords that you really want to talk to. It will be from these landlords you will get the most honest answers about your prospect's tenancy habits.

Income Information

Current employer. Next on the application, you need to find out about the prospect's employment. Naturally, you want to know who the tenant applicant works for and how long they have been employed there. Proof of job stability is crucial. Of course, if the prospect is a married couple and both work, you want information on both husband and wife, which will be pulled from both applications. Actually, you want employment information on any person in the house who is helping to pay rent. You never know who will be splitting up with who or losing their job, therefore changing the household income. Knowing everyone's income will help you understand what to expect from the tenants should one person move on or lose a job. For income information, begin with present occupation and include present employer, phone number, supervisor's name, supervisor's phone number, dates employed, hours worked per week, and current pay.

Second or previous employer. In your landlording career, you will discover that some renters work two jobs. When they do, you need to know the information pertaining to that second job as well. You are looking for the same information as previously stated for their first job. If they don't have a second job, then simply use this section to fill in previous job information.

Previous employer. Immediately following the second or previous employer is an area dedicated to just a previous employer. If previous employment applies, get this information. If at all possible, you want to talk to at least one previous employer. The reasons for this are the same reasons you want to talk to a previous landlord: You are more apt to get the truth out of a previous employer rather than a current one. I have received some outstanding information and references from previous employers, so if the previous employer or supervisor will answer your questions, you can learn a lot about your applicant's personality.

Although a landlord probably spends less than one hour per month or even per year with one of his tenants, a supervisor or coworker often spends 40 or more hours per week with the applicant. Chances are, a supervisor will know much more about your applicant's true character traits.

Other income. After asking all of the applicant's employment history, you want to know about any other sources of income. Here you want to know about steady bonuses, alimony, government assistance, or anything that reveals to you that there are other sources of income streaming into this occupant's hands.

Personal References

After finishing with work and income information, the applicants need to list their personal references. I ask for a minimum of three, and these exclude parents, grandparents, siblings, and other relatives. The ideal situation is to acquire five personal references per adult who will be living in the household. Make sure each reference has at least one current phone number as well.

You'll notice there are spaces for personal reference names and phone numbers only. Knowing their address probably won't do you any good. The only possible reason you would need reference addresses is if your tenant skips out owing you money and you want to track them down.

In almost every circumstance, I do not bother to track down a fleeing, deadbeat tenant. I feel that no matter how much they owe me, it is much wiser to spend my time and energy trying to reestablish tenancy in my empty dwelling than pursuing a deadbeat. Chasing people you can't find only elevates your blood pressure and takes up your time. If the tenant did move on and owed you a lot of money or did something illegal, use the police and court system to do your tracking work. That's what they are there for.

STEP THREE

Rental Application

Other Information

Major credit card _____ Exp. Date _____ Mo. Pymt. $ _____

Other credit reference_____ Exp. Date _____ Mo. Pymt. $ _____

Other credit reference_____ Exp. Date _____ Mo. Pymt. $ _____

Other credit reference_____ Exp. Date _____ Mo. Pymt. $ _____

Have you ever filed bankruptcy?   Y/N   7 or 13?   How long ago?_____

How much is judgment payment? $_____

Have you ever been convicted of a felony?   Y/N   Was that conviction for drug use?   Y/N

Have you ever been evicted or asked to vacate?   Y/N   Have you ever broken a lease?   Y/N

If so, give reason _____

Vehicle Make _____ Model _____ Year _____

License Plate # _____ Mo. Car Payment $ _____

Vehicle Make _____ Model _____ Year _____

License Plate # _____ Mo. Car Payment $ _____

Vehicle Make _____ Model _____ Year _____

License Plate # _____ Mo. Car Payment $ _____

Emergency Contact _____ Phone # _____

Address _____ Phone # _____

Emergency Contact _____ Phone # _____

Address _____ Phone # _____

I declare that the above statements are true and correct. With my signature, I authorize verification of my references, employment and credit as they relate to my tenancy and future rent collection. I also authorize a criminal background check to be done by the owner, manager or representative of said property listed on this application.

Date _____ Signature _____

Date _____ Signature _____

148

Other Information

At this point in the application, you've reached the section that covers miscellaneous items.

Credit reference. Knowing credit card information is good should you decide to accept credit cards for payment now or in the future. As an added plus, if someone is late with their rent, you can ask them to borrow from their credit card to fulfill their financial obligation to you. You'll also note that there's a place to ask what the payment is for each card. This is so that you can transfer that information to another form later in the investigative process.

Other credit reference. Following major credit card information is other credit reference. Again, in all likelihood, these will be more credit cards, but they could also be student loans or other sources of credit. As on the credit cards, ask for an expiration date. With credit cards, this is useless information because a credit card will always reissue a new card. But with other sources of credit (car loans, student loans, personal loans, and so forth), this expiration date allows you to find out when that loan is paid off. If a loan is within a few months of being paid off, that could be a plus for their cash flow situation.

Filed bankruptcy? Now it's time to find out about bankruptcy. This issue has pretty much been covered in previous chapters, at least how it would pertain to landlording. Why, you ask, is it here? Just like everything else, you get their answers put down in their own handwriting. If they filed bankruptcy, you want to know if it was a chapter 7 (liquidation of debt) or a 13 (reorganization of debt)—these will be discussed in a later chapter. You also need to know how long ago they filed. You want a written record of the fact that they are paying a judgment, and you need to know how big that payment is so you know for sure how it affects the money they have left for rent. You also want to verify that the length of time since they filed for bankruptcy falls within your guidelines. Unless their bankruptcy was filed recently or there was a glitch in the recording of the bankruptcy, this information should also show up on their credit report allowing you to cross-reference information.

149

Convicted of a felony? The next area addresses whether the applicant has ever been convicted of a felony and if it was related to drug use. There will be some more details on this particular question in the next section that leads you through analyzing the rental application. I spoke on this topic previously, but feel it is worth mentioning again. As of this writing, under certain guidelines, a drug use conviction is protected by the amendment to the Fair Housing Act in 1989. Because of this protection, you need to know if an applicant's conviction was connected to drug use.

Evicted/broken a lease? Finally, there are two more questions: Have you ever been evicted or asked to vacate? Have you ever broken a lease? These are two questions you should have already discussed on the phone and know the answers to. You ask again so you have their response in their own handwriting. It is also possible you have decided to accept some people who have been evicted or asked to vacate. With the reason for their eviction now in writing, you can double-check to verify that it is acceptable to you. This answer can also be a source of questions for your present and previous landlord references, so pay attention.

Vehicle information. Vehicle information is required so you can keep track of all vehicles parked at the rental, and it could serve to help track a tenant down if the need arises.

Emergency contact. This is an important area. There are two spots here, and you should get both completed with full, first and last names, address including city, and as many phone numbers as possible. You never know when you might need these contacts, emergency or otherwise.

With the completion of the emergency contact numbers, you are ready to have the tenant prospect read the application's closing statement. I've listed it here for your convenience: *I declare that the above statements are true and correct. With my signature, I authorize verification of my references, employment and credit as they relate to my tenancy and future rent collection. I also authorize a criminal background check to be done by the owner, manager or representative of said property listed on this application.*

With the first half of that statement, the applicant is giving permission for you to follow up on all the information filled out on the application. The second half of the statement gives you permission to run a criminal background check on the applicant. *You must have the date and the applicant's signature to perform these checks. It is illegal to do so otherwise.*

In Closing

Well, there you have it: a complete breakdown of the rental application I currently use for my rentals. I say "currently" because I still add or delete information as I feel it is needed. I recommend you do this, too.

If something is overlooked that you wish to add, please do so.

If you wish to totally skip a section, so be it. Make the application work for your rental situation. And it goes without saying, you can use any application you have as long as it has the correct information on it. My application is not the only one out there, so feel free to look around. Find one you're comfortable with that will suit your needs. You could even design your own if you wish. Now that we've covered the basics of the application, let's go over some of the other required paperwork.

Remember, all the information the tenant applicant gives you on the paperwork is given with the trust that you will use that information correctly. This means you do not give out any important names or numbers to anyone who is not directly related to the task at hand. When the time comes to destroy these records, it is advisable to shred them before you discard them.

Note: You can obtain this rental application for your use at our website www.FindThatQualityTenant.com.

151

CHAPTER 9

The Credit Report

A hundred years or so ago, the world of credit was much different than it is today. Mom-and-pop businesses extended credit to the families in the neighborhood and banks or savings and loans provided mortgages and business financing to those in the surrounding community. Most of the time, all you needed was a job, a good reputation, and an honest intention to pay back the borrowed capital, and you had a loan.

Sometime during the 1950s and 60s, however, mortgages and loans began to be financed by larger out-of-town lending institutions. Couple this with the increasing popularity of the credit card, and the result is that more credit was extended to more people. The need arose to keep track of who had credit, how much credit they had, and if they paid that credit back as promised. Decades later, the result was a billion-dollar industry of credit reporting overseen by credit bureaus and regulated by government agencies.

Why a Credit Report?

As a professional landlord, you absolutely need to know if your tenant prospect is paying their bills and paying them on time. Running a credit report on these prospects, using one of the established credit agencies, is the easiest, most accurate way to achieve this goal. I highly recommend you check the credit of anyone who will be living in your rental and who is going to be responsible for paying the bills. To help you understand credit reporting, I will need to pass on some information to clarify this subject and some of its intricate workings.

The Credit Industry

The credit reporting industry has a dozen or so credit bureaus, many of which are designed to do specialty types of reporting. As a landlord, you are probably most interested in working with one of the "big three" national companies that are the leaders in the field of consumer spending. Those three leaders are Equifax, Trans Union, and Experion (formerly TRW).

The computer systems of these three companies contain credit information on almost every adult in America. In fact, billions of bits of information are added to these files each and every month. These credit bureaus do different things with this information, but as a landlord, you are only concerned with how they compile and report an individual's credit history and how fast and accurately that report gets to you.

The credit reports you get on your prospects will have information from four primary sources, as follows:

1. Subscribers—companies that extend credit to consumers.

2. Collection agencies—agencies chasing delinquent accounts.

3. Public record—tax liens, bankruptcy filings, judgments, garnishments, and in some states, evictions made available to the public.

4. The person the report is about—every time someone fills out an application for credit, it can be entered into the credit bureau's system for updating.

The collective information from these sources should, properly prepared, give you a firm idea of your tenant applicant's spending habits in regard to credit, including who they owe, how much they owe, and if they are behind on any payments, both past and present. You will also discover judgments or bankruptcies and see the extent of credit damage these judgments have caused. It is exactly this type of information you are looking for to help you make a decision about renting to a particular applicant.

This chapter is the first chapter in step three (paperwork) dedicated to a subject for which I haven't provided you a form. The reason for this is that there are many credit bureaus whose services you can employ. Unfortunately, some of these agencies have procedures and applications that are unique to that bureau. Under these circumstances, it would be virtually impossible for me to give you a standard form to use since many of these agencies would not use any form but their own.

Finding a Credit Report

After you've completely read this chapter, pull out your phone book or get on the Internet, and look up "credit agency," "credit bureau," and/or "credit reporting." Call the listed companies and explain that you are a landlord and wish to start running credit checks on tenant applicants. Ask them to send you one of their current applications and any information they have regarding credit reports and how to read them. Do this with more than one agency so you can find the one that best suits your needs.

A point you will need to remember when looking for a credit bureau is that not all collection agencies or subscribers work with each of the national big three, but might only work with one of them, therefore making it probable you will receive an incomplete report. For instance, sometimes subscribers such as mortgage companies, auto dealers, small retail, medical, or utility providers possibly do not report to a credit bureau *unless* you've had late pays or a history of problems. Other providers such as bank cards, major credit cards, and federally issued loans will usually report monthly. This doesn't necessarily make the credit reporting industry bad, just confusing—especially if you read your own report and can't figure out why your mortgage isn't listed, but your 200-dollar Visa debt is.

To ease this problem, try getting your reports from a credit bureau that pools their information from all three of the big companies, which is slowly becoming popular but still somewhat difficult to find. You should also look for a company with helpful employees who will answer your questions completely and quickly, especially as you are learning to read and analyze credit reports.

Pulling Your Own Report

While you are calling around looking for a credit bureau to run your credit reports, I suggest you call TransUnion, Experion, and Equifax to order a report on yourself. The total cost of all three reports should equal about $20 to $25 and take four or five days to receive.

The advantage of ordering your own report is twofold: First, you will get to verify that your personal credit information is correct, and second, you will get a little practice learning how each agency lists their information.

Getting in some practice will be a huge plus when it comes time to reading other people's reports. Learning to read credit reports is much easier to do when there is little pressure to do so. Trying to learn to read them the night you must make your tenant selection is difficult to do and could be hazardous to your financial situation if you happen to read the credit report incorrectly. To order your report from the big three, you may call their toll-free numbers or use their websites, which I have listed below:

- TransUnion, PO Box 1000, Chester, PA 19022; 800-888-4213; www.transunion.com
- Experian, PO Box 9530, Allen TX 75013; 888-397-3742; www.experian.com
- Equifax, PO Box 740241, Atlanta, GA 30374; 800-685-1111; www.equifax.com

Pulling Reports Online

In the past few years, the credit industry has made it easy for people to pull up their own credit reports off the Internet. The best known of these sites is www.MyFico.com. The problem for you, as a landlord, is that these sites are designed for people to pull their own reports and not for one party to pull a report on another party. For you to get a credit report on a prospective tenant using this method, you would need them to pull up their own report. This has drawbacks.

Most tenant applicants will not pay for a report until after they have seen the rental. This means that if they do want the property, they will have to then pull the report and send it to you via fax or email, or drop it off in person. This adds time to the whole processing step, especially if they take a few days to perform this task or if they totally mess it up.

They could also obtain the online report from somewhere you know nothing about. If this report doesn't come with a score or has a score that isn't in line with your qualifications, the report may not do the job you intended it to do.

I'd rather not take these chances. I prefer prospective tenants to pay me the credit check money when they fill out the application because it gives them a financial commitment to the rental process. I also like to control the timetable of the processing step by ordering the report on my tenant myself. And I want to analyze the same type of report every time I have a new tenant applicant. I want the same format and credit score so as not to get confused by the unknown. Ultimately, of course, you need to do what is best for you.

Credit Application

Now that you understand a little about ordering credit reports, you need a credit application for your tenant prospect to fill out. I've already explained why I can't effectively give you a good, universal credit application, but what I can do is provide you with the next best thing.

Basically, a credit report application will have the same general information as your rental application. It will consist of the applicant's name, phone number, Social Security number, birth date, maiden name, and possibly requests for other information such as driver's license number, current and past addresses, employment history, and so forth. Of course, the credit application will also have a statement that gives the agency the right to run a credit check on the person whose signature is on the bottom of the application.

National Association of Independent Landlords

Since you already have a filled-out rental application, wouldn't it be nice if you could find a source to run a credit report off of the rental application you currently use? Well, there is such a source: the National Association of Independent Landlords, Inc. (NAIL). This association is designed specifically to unite, educate, and help landlords in what they do. For a modest annual fee, you may join this organization and receive their many benefits (criminal background checks and tenant monitoring to name a few). Let me explain how NAIL can help in your credit search.

First, understand that you do not have to be a member to run a credit report, although I recommend joining the organization for the information and support provided.

Second, NAIL gets its credit reports done through Equifax. Equifax, being one of the big three, does an outstanding job of reporting credit, but like any of the three national names, it doesn't have 100 percent complete information on any given credit report. In fairness to Equifax, Experian, and TransUnion would have the same problem. As I've already stated, the only way to combat this issue is to find an affiliated credit bureau that gathers reports from all three national names, but that can prove hard to do.

Third, the credit reports issued by NAIL provide a credit risk score, which, if you remember back in the tenant qualification chapter, is one guideline I highly recommend you use to weed out potential problem tenants. This is a huge convenience and one of the main reasons I use NAIL. (I will explain credit risk score in the chapter on analyzing credit.)

I suggest you use the services of NAIL because they will run credit reports right off the rental application provided in this book. This is one less form for your tenant applicant to fill out and simplifies your rental showing. To use this rental application for a credit check through NAIL, simply fax it to them (1-800-352-4588). Remember that there will be two applications to fax if a spouse or roommate is involved. Indicate the number of applicants on your cover page (which is included at the end of this chapter). Be sure to include the fax number where they can reach you.

NAIL will then run a credit report and probably get it back to you the same day or at least within 24 hours. They will then bill your credit card accordingly for the number of reports you ordered. Joint reports are for couples with the same last name, and individual reports are for people with different last names. The whole process is quick and simple. If you are a member, NAIL can also set you up with an account to retrieve these reports online. This is a time-saving process, but it has to be handled correctly so you are not accused of credit fraud.

For more information on using NAIL for credit checks, call them at 1-800-352-3395 or get on their website at www.Nail-USA.com.

If you choose to use a local credit reporting agency to run credit checks instead of NAIL, keep this thought in mind: Back on the Tenant Qualifications form I suggested you use a credit risk score to provide you with a definite cut-off point between good and bad credit. Many credit bureaus will not provide this score, so if you wish to use the credit risk score as a qualification, you'll need to find an agency that can provide it for you. Remember, NAIL provides this score automatically if you find you have problems in this area.

At the Showing

Once you have chosen which credit bureau you will use for your credit reports (other than NAIL), you'll want to make plenty of copies of their application to have on hand for the tenant applicants to fill out at the showing. Since each agency is different, you may need one per applicant or roommate, and you might even have to have one per spouse in the case of a married couple. If your credit application is different from your rental application, have the prospective tenant fill out a credit report application after the rental application is done. This should not be surprising to your prospect since you explained over the phone that you would run a credit check and that they should to be prepared to pay for that report at the showing. Then, once they've filled out the credit application, check all pertinent information to verify it was filled out correctly—just like you did on the rental application. Double-check to make sure they signed and dated the application, then collect the necessary money from the prospective tenant.

The Fax Cover Sheet

Whether you choose to use NAIL or an independent credit bureau to run your credit checks, you will probably fax your reports to them as it is the easiest and quickest way to transfer this paperwork. (You can download a fax cover sheet at www.FindThatQualityTenant.com.)

Take a quick look at the form. Make sure you include your daytime phone number as well as your fax number so someone from the credit agency can call you if there are any questions. I've also included a spot for

STEP THREE

Fax Cover Sheet

TO: _____

FROM: _____

Client I.D. Number   _____

Daytime Phone Number _____

Fax Number   _____

Number of Applicants Requested _____

Paying   Single _____ or   Joint _____

_____ Credit check

_____ Rental history check

_____ Criminal Background Check

Page _____ of _____ (including cover)

NOTES

a client ID number since most credit agencies will provide you with a tracking number for their convenience.

Number of applicants requested. Make sure you state how many applicants you want a report on. This is necessary if you use one application for two people but only need a report on one of them. If this is the case, be sure to write the name of the applicant you want reported somewhere on the fax sheet.

Paying single or joint. Each different last name is regarded as a single charge, while couples sharing the same last name may receive a joint charge. Your individual credit bureau will let you know what their costs are for single or joint applicants.

On occasions you will have a tenant applicant who will want to save the money of a credit report by asking you to review one they recently had pulled. If this report is less than 30 days old, this request could be a valid one, although you might ask why that report was pulled because he or she may have just been turned down by another landlord. Also, remember you probably won't have the credit score you may require from this report.

Credit check/ rental history check/criminal background check. Some agencies can and will run all three of these checks for you. All you need to do is check those you want. Keep in mind that there are different costs for each item you order and different lengths of time for the agency to respond back to you. Rental history and criminal background checks take longer than credit checks and will be discussed in more detail in the appropriate chapters.

Note: You can obtain a copy of the fax cover sheet at our website www.FindThatQualityTenant.com.

CHAPTER 10

The Employment Verification Form

If you've completed the rental and credit applications, then you're almost home free in filling out the applicant's paperwork. This next form, employment verification, is extremely easy to fill out and will only take about two minutes of your time to do so. In fact, there is a good chance you won't need this form at all, but I always fill it out at the showing when I have the applicant standing in front of me. I do this because occasionally, an employer will not verify the information I need without their employee's signature, so it makes sense to get that signature for the employer while I'm with the tenant applicant. I recommend you also develop this habit. It will save you time in the long run.

The Employment Verification Form

I like using this form often and would fax this page to every employer if I possibly could. It would save me time, and I would have written signatures on yet another form, which continually builds my paper trail on a particular prospect.

Part One

Filling out the form is simple. The first part of the form is for the tenant prospect to fill out. The first four lines identify everyone involved.

STEP THREE

Employment Verification

PART ONE

TO EMPLOYER: _____ PHONE # _____

ATTN: _____

FROM: _____

CONCERNING: _____

EMPLOYEE SS# _____ EMPLOYEE BIRTH DATE _____

I have filled out a residential rental application and I give permission for my employer to verify employment and answer the following questions.

Signature _____ Date _____

PART TWO

Because time is a factor in our approving this employee's application, we would appreciate you completing this form and faxing it back to us as soon as possible, with supervisor's signature and date filled out. Our fax number is _____ . If you cannot fax us, please call _____ and verify the information, then mail this entire letter back to us (for our records) at your earliest convenience to the address below.

Send to: _____

_____

_____

PART THREE

START DATE   _____

OF HOURS WORKED PER WEEK   _____

PAY RECEIVED (LIST HOURLY/SALARY)   _____

EMPLOYEE'S CURRENT OCCUPATION?   _____

EMPLOYEE COVERED BY HEALTH INS?   Y/N

IS POSITION PERMANENT?   Y/N

IS POSITION STABLE?   Y/N

Information provided by: _____

Name _____ Title _____

Signature _____ Date _____

copyright 2007 Blue Collar Publishers

To employer. This refers to the employer or company for whom the applicant works and the employer's phone number.

Attention. The supervisor or person who can verify employment.

From. The sender (you).

Concerning. The name of the employee you are checking.

After line four, there is a request for the employee's Social Security number and birth date. This information strengthens the paper trail and eases any confusion for the employer if there happen to be two Joe Renters working in the same company. And of course, it goes without saying that you should have already verified the Social Security number at the showing before you send the form to the employer. It shouldn't happen, but it is possible people might fudge the Social Security number because they don't remember the number, don't have one, or have something to hide.

Following the Social Security number and birth date is a statement that reads, *"I have filled out a residential rental application and I give permission for my employer to verify employment and answer the following questions."* The employee *must sign and date* this statement, which legally allows you to look into the applicant's job security. Without their signature, you will probably receive zilch for information from their employer. So make sure they sign this designated area.

The employee signature and date is the last area the prospect fills out. Now *you* need to fill in the next portion of the form.

Part Two

After the employee signature is a paragraph that gives instructions to whoever is verifying employment. The paragraph says: *Because time is a factor in our approving this employee's application, we would appreciate you completing this form and faxing it back to us as soon as possible, with supervisor's signature and date filled out. Our fax number is _____. If you cannot fax us, please call _____ and verify the information, then mail this entire letter back to us (for our records) at your earliest convenience to the address below.*

You will notice there are two blanks in the above paragraph. These spaces are for you to fill in your fax number and telephone number so you may be contacted somehow with the requested information. Please remember to fill in these spaces.

Following the paragraph are three lines for you to fill in your address. Once you've done that, the form can be faxed or sent to the employer, who will fill in the third and last part of the Employment Verification form.

Part Three

Let's review the information you are requesting the employer to fill out.

Start date. Start date means just that. You want to know when the applicant started this particular job.

Hours worked per week. Here you are asking for actual hours *worked*, not scheduled. Remember, some businesses over-schedule to cover their needed shifts but send people home early, which can drastically reduce their hours. So you want to know how many hours this employee actually works per week.

Pay received. Here is where you verify what they earn at their job, and whether it is an hourly, monthly, or weekly salary.

Employee's current occupation. On more than one occasion, I have had applicants tell me that they have a higher position job than what they really do. Here you get to double-check the accuracy of that information.

Employee covered by health insurance? Some employers offer health insurance and now is your chance to verify that.

Is position permanent/stable? You want to know if the job will be phased out soon or is good for years into the future. You want to know that the applicant's job is permanent.

Information provided by. The previous questions are simple to answer and should only take an employer a few minutes of their time. Once they have answered the questions, they need to fill in their name, title, signature, and date they completed the form.

At the Showing

When the potential tenant is filling out the rental application and associated paperwork, I explain that I might need this form to verify employment information, especially if his or her employer requests an employee signature before he or she will release any information. The prospective tenant needs to understand that with that signature, he or she is giving you permission to verify all employment information.

Many times, you will not need to use this form, although I always have the tenant applicant sign one for each job they work just so I know I have the form if needed. I do this even when the applicant tells me his employer will verify information over the phone. I recommend you do the same. I guarantee that in doing so you will save a trip back to the applicant at some point in your landlording career.

Note: The Employment Verification form can be accessed on our website at www.FindThatQualityTenant.com.

CHAPTER 11

The Cash Flow Statement

C ash flow is defined by Webster's dictionary as follows: cash—ready money; coin; paper money; flow—to circulate; to proceed from. So what cash flow means is "ready money for circulation." In the world of real estate investing, cash flow is an extremely important concept. For in our world, having cash flow means that the rents received from that rental will cover all the expenses associated with the rental and leave a little something left over for us to use as we please. Not having enough cash flow to cover the rental's bills every month means not only is there no money for you to keep, but you will dig in your pocket monthly just to keep the rental alive if there is a problem. But this book is about tenant selection, so how does the term cash flow fit in with your new tenant?

Everybody receives ready money (cash) that is theirs to spend, invest, save, or give away however they choose. Almost everyone has financial obligations or commitments that they must pay to sustain their quality of life. In addition to these obligations, most people choose to spend some money on life's "extras."

When people receive money, whether it comes from a job, government assistance, or any combination of different sources, this receiving of money represents cash flowing or circulating *to* your tenant prospect. From there, that money gets broken up into chunks and distributed for that individual's necessities and extras. This distribution represents cash flowing *away* from the tenant prospect. Out of all the areas a tenant's cash could flow to, you will be mainly concerned with rent. That is what the Cash Flow form is all about; proving there is enough cash to flow toward rent.

Why Use This Form?

A generation or two ago, this form probably wouldn't have been very valuable because people were much better at living within their means. But sometime during the 1980s, we as a society began to strive for bigger jumps in our perceived prosperity. It became culturally evident by the TV shows and movies of the time. Shows such as *Dallas, Dynasty, Falcon Crest,* and *Flamingo Road* only added to our thirst for material things. Movies like *Trading Places* and *Wall Street* perpetuated the "gotta have it now" mentality. Twenty years later, this mentality is more prevalent than ever. Unfortunately, the main problem with the "gotta have it now" mentality is these types of people, including renters, are often hanging on by a thread. A thin thread.

You need the Cash Flow form to help you decide what the chances are that thread is going to break. This form is a pretty simple form that *you* actually fill out. My recommendation is that when you begin to have applicants fill out their paperwork, pull out all the forms you will need. Hand the applicants the rental application and a pen. Keep all the other forms in a pile with the Cash Flow form on top. As they fill out their application, you begin filling out the Cash Flow form.

The Cash Flow Form

Before looking at and analyzing this form, let me give you some insight on how to go about using it.

Tips for Better Performance

First, keep in mind that most tenant prospects you talk to have never heard of or seen this kind of form when they want to rent a dwelling. Therefore, they could be a little suspicious, apprehensive, or defensive with the idea of revealing all their personal financial information to you, even though you probably discussed much of this information on the phone when you first interviewed them. If you sense this will be a problem, to put them at ease, you might say this to your prospects: "I've got a form here you've probably never seen. It's called a Cash Flow form. I use it because I have seen people who rent a dwelling only to realize that the rent for that unit was more than their budget could really afford. I'd hate to see a repeat of that situation, so now I double-check everyone's financial situation before I rent to them. So please be patient with me as I ask you a few financial questions throughout our meeting here. I promise it won't be too painful." In my years of using this form, I've never run into heavy resistance when I introduce it this way.

The next tip on proper use of this form is that its application begins during the phone interview. During that conversation, you should have uncovered some useful and important information to transfer to the Cash Flow form. If you have these figures handy (I recommend bringing along the caller's phone interview sheet for just this purpose), simply transfer them to the Cash Flow form at this time. Be aware of areas or topics you briefly talked about in the initial phone interview that need more detail so you can ask more questions if need be.

Also, keep in mind that some of the information on the Cash Flow form will be directly transferred off the application or credit check forms. These areas generally involve their car payments and credit cards. Therefore, you probably don't need to ask questions concerning any of these areas unless you do not understand something from these forms or are receiving two different answers to the same question.

The fourth tip is to watch for clues to a prospect's financial habits, from the moment you first show them the rental unit. You need to train your ear to pick up on the important words of their conversation that relate to how they spend their money. These clues are as simple as second grade English.

Active Listening

By keeping an active ear ready and picking up on certain types of grammar school words, you will receive clues that lead you to ask more detailed follow-up questions. These grammar school words fall into two categories: "nouns" and "action verbs." By training your ear to recognize and respond to nouns and action verbs, you'll pick up little hints about the prospect's lifestyle that can drastically affect their cash flow.

For instance, if during your conversation with a husband and wife you find that one drives west (drives—action verb, west—noun) to a job and one travels east, (travels—action verb, east—noun), then you know there are two cars so there could be two car payments. If someone mentions they bowl on three separate bowling leagues, then you'll need to ask a question about bowling. Maybe you hear your applicant mention he or she is trying to be a professional bodybuilder; you might wish to ask more detailed questions concerning food and bodybuilding supplements. In a nutshell, when you conduct your phone interview and in-person interview, keep your mind and ears open so you pick up seemingly small details that may provide clues for quality questions concerning a person's financial habits.

In fact, you should begin developing financial questions in your mind the moment a potential tenant pulls into the driveway. Look at their vehicle. Is it a brand-new expensive model or an economy model that has some years on it? The difference could be hundreds in car and insurance payments.

Continue the attentive listening as you begin to show the unit. If they walk in the garage and say "Good, plenty of room for my motorcycle," or "We can hang all our camping/skiing/other hobby equipment here," then you know where some of their cash flows. So eventually, you want to find out how much that motorcycle or camping or ski vacation or other hobby costs each month.

You might hear clues inside the house like, "Oh good, there's enough space in the living room so I can buy that big screen TV" or "We can put our piano here so the kids can continue their music lessons." Once you develop the ear

> You shouldn't need tons of questions if your applicants state they have an above-average rent-to-income ratio and a good credit score. This form becomes more valuable if their financial thread is a thin one, and they appear to be only one or two paychecks away from a financial catastrophe. In other words, not everyone will need to be asked the same questions or quantity of questions. Also, learn to sense when you need to tone the Q & A time down. You don't want to overdo it.

for picking up nouns and actions verbs, your skills with the Cash Flow sheet will open up immensely. Filling the form out will be easier, more accurate, and quicker once you've fine-tuned this skill.

Be Discreet

The last tip for filling out the Cash Flow form is to make it discreet and casual. Pick a category or two and ask a few questions leading up to the financial questions you really want to ask. You may get enough information to eliminate other questions.

For instance, let's follow up on the motorcycle comment heard in the garage:

Tenant Prospect (looking in the garage): Excellent. Plenty of room for my motorcycle.

You: What kind of bike do you ride?

TP: I've got an '89 Harley.

Y: Good bike. How long have you owned it?

TP: I bought it new in '90, so about 17 years, I guess.

Because of the casual questions and the corresponding answers, you probably don't need to ask any questions regarding a motorcycle payment since he has owned it for 17 years. What the prospect perceived as pleasant conversation was actually a ploy to pull further information from him. He doesn't know you were sizing him up and still got answers without being pushy. But if the conversation revealed that the motorcycle was purchased less than five years ago, you might want to ask about the monthly payment and insurance.

This type of casual conversation, backed with a genuinely curious or interested attitude, will go a long way toward helping you achieve the answers you are seeking. To keep from offending or shutting down a prospect, remember to make the question you want to ask sound more like an afterthought or a natural response to the conversation already in progress. This detective work disguised as casual conversation is an extremely useful skill, although tough to master. If you are not much of a conversationalist, I recommend polishing this skill on your friends and family, unbeknownst to them. I guarantee the effort will be worth it.

The Cash Flow Statement

With that in mind, let's look at the form. Of course, you want to keep your paper trail strong and consistent so this form begins like the other forms with their name and the date. After the name and date, you will see spaces for number of adults, children, and pets who will reside in the house. This information will help you keep on track with important questions and will also guide you on any category answer you might have to guess on.

STEP THREE

Cash Flow
(All figures monthly)

Page 1 of 2

Name_____ Date _____

#of adults _____ #of children _____ # of pets _____

INCOME

	Source	Amount
Job 1	_____	$ _____
Job 2	_____	$ _____
Job 3	_____	$ _____
Gov't Assistance	_____	$ _____
Other Income	_____	$ _____
Misc.Income	_____	$ _____
	TOTAL	$ _____

Income

After listing who will reside in the dwelling, you come to the income part of the sheet. Remember, income is where cash flows to the applicant, and you want to come up with a total of all *consistent, documented* income flowing into the applicant's hands. A lucky night of poker is neither consistent nor documented. Neither are one-time financial gifts, bingo, or lottery winnings, or a quick sale of the family's third car. Consistent and documented means *consistent* and *documented*. Take a look at the income part of the form.

174

On the left is a "Source" column, which lists the different areas of income. On the right is the amount column, where you will list the *monthly* amount of income. Whenever you can, convert all figures to a *monthly* figure. Failing to do so could lead you to an inaccurate decision about the applicant's total income, so you might fail a good applicant or conversely, put a tenant in your rental who can't afford it. In the following example, a husband and wife each work a job. The wife receives child support and the husband works an additional part-time job. Take a look at the form to see how you would fill out the income portion.

INCOME

		Source		Amount
Job 1	Joe	mail carrier	$	$3100 B.T
Job 2	June	clerk	$	750 2 wk $1500
Job 3	—	_____	$	_____
Gov't Assistance		_____	$	_____
Other Income		_____	$	_____
Misc. Income		1350 3 mo.	$	$450 mo.
		TOTAL	$	$5050 B.T

Job 1/Job 2/Job 3. Be sure the sources of income you list with jobs one, two, and three are steady sources and can be verified with regular pay stubs or tax returns. I suggest that any dollar figure you put in the job spaces be an after-tax figure, if possible. That is the reason you ask for at least two months of recent pay stubs. You want to see what average dollar amount they actually take home. This will save you from having to compute or guess at the amount they pay in taxes. Just make a note next to the listed figure of either before taxes (BT) or after taxes (AT). If the dollar amount you write down is a before-tax figure, simply put the letters BT next to the income amount so you remember to deal with the taxes later.

Example:

Job 1: mail carrier (Joe) $3,100 BT

You will also want to record how often that figure is received if for some reason you don't have a monthly figure to work with. Some people might give you a weekly or biweekly figure. Others might even give you an hourly figure. Whatever they tell you, make a quick note next to the appropriate job source for your future reference.

Example:

Job 2: Grocery store clerk (Jane) $750 every two weeks

If a husband and wife or boyfriend and girlfriend are both employed, you must use the combined incomes to figure out if they can handle rent, so put them on the same Cash Flow form. If you have a roommate situation and are asking both roommates to be able to support the rental on their own in case they decide to part ways, then each roommate should fill out a separate form.

Government assistance. This is where you list any monies received by the applicant from the government. It could be Section 8 for the family, social security for a child, disability, or a number of the other available government programs. Whenever you fill out the government assistance line on this form, make sure you see some kind of solid proof that this money is received in the applicant's home on a regular basis. As stated in a previous chapter, it is best to see this proof when he or she fills out the application, otherwise, you will have to meet with these people again so they can show you their proof. The chances of you verifying any government assistance on the phone are slim. See it when they fill out the paperwork. This rule applies to the next line as well.

Other income. If the applicant receives alimony, child support, assistance from Grandma, and so forth, you want to see solid proof. They must prove that money comes in on a regular monthly basis and that the person who *says* he or she receives the money actually *does*. If they can't provide proof, don't count that income as a reliable source: You'll be setting yourself up for a problem in the future.

Miscellaneous income. This line is the last space to be filled out in the income section. It is for money that is received quarterly, every six months, or at odd pay periods. Bonuses, regular stock dividends, and so forth fit in this category. Let's say the applicant takes home about $1,350 in bonuses every three months; take that bonus amount and divide by three months to get an average of $450 monthly income. (Please remember to always convert all numbers to a monthly figure). Record on the line provided.

Let me give you one last important reminder before finishing up the income section of the Cash Flow form: *Only list consistent, documented sources of income.* If it looks like your applicants don't make enough money to pay all their bills, do not be persuaded into believing and using their undocumented income. It could turn out to be phantom income (income that doesn't exist) and then the tenants will have money problems on their hands, which will turn out to be *your* money problems in no time at all. You will run into this situation quite frequently when you rent to people who work in the service industry (e.g., tips and gratuities). If you decide to use this type of income, be prepared to put a little more effort in analyzing the applicant's creditworthiness.

Expenses

In this section of the Cash Flow form, you will try as closely as you can to figure out where the applicants spend their hard-earned dollars. Since there are so many ways people can spend their money, filling out the expense column accurately is harder than filling in the income. It is not an impossible task, but it does require more questions, guesswork, and deductive reasoning to fill out the form correctly.

Let's analyze the expense section one line at a time.

Taxes. If you are adamant about seeing at least two months of recent pay stubs when the tenant applicant fills out their paperwork, you will be able to use an after-tax figure for their income figure. Chances are, if you develop and practice this habit, 95 percent of the time you will not have to fill in the tax amount on the line reserved for taxes at all.

On occasion, you will have a self-employed applicant apply for your rental. When this happen, you may want to get a better understanding on how to determine how much of their income goes to taxes, and how much they really get to keep. Visit my website, and you will find a page under the links key titled "extras," which will help explain how to determine those amounts.

All vehicle payments. A large majority of the people you ask will have a car, truck, or motorcycle payment. Many will have two payments, some even three. To fill in the line for vehicle payments, just ask how many monthly payments the prospect has and how much each one is. Motorcycles, boats, and recreational vehicles all count as vehicles. Add them up and write the total in the line provided.

All credit card payments. This is probably the single biggest reason people have money problems in our society. Credit card usage and the interest charged for that usage is slowly devouring most Americans in a mountain of debt. Just ask Suze Orman, who hosts a call-in show on MSNBC that deals strictly with money and finances. She doles out advice on how to stop being gobbled up by the credit card demons and gives honest insight into controlling one's personal finances.

EXPENSES

Taxes	$ _____
All vehicle payments	$ _____
All credit card payments	$ _____
All other loan payments (student loan, boat, personal, etc.)	$ _____
Judgments/garnishments	$ _____
Alimony/child support/other dependent	$ _____
All telephone bills	$ _____
Gas/electric area average	$ _____
Sewer/water area average	$ _____
Garbage area average	$ _____

178

STEP THREE

Cash Flow
(All figures monthly)

Page 2 of 2

EXPENSES (continued)

Cable TV area average	$ _____
All food/dining in & out	$ _____
Paid health care/prescriptions	$ _____
Auto expenses	$
Day care	$ _____
All entertainment/hobbies (movies, vacations)	$ _____
Pet care (vet & food)	$ _____
All miscellaneous (clothes, toys, holidays, mad $)	$ _____
TOTAL	$ _____

On her show she has stated that the average American family has $8,500 of credit card debt. That is *only* credit card debt and doesn't include car loans, school loans, personal loans, or mortgages. This is just the debt contained on those silly little plastic cards that you have in your wallet or purse.

This is a staggering amount and you must consider that since some people don't have credit card debt, someone else has $17,000 or more in credit card debt to make the average figure average.

As a landlord, I've seen some folks with an outrageous number of credit cards. One prospective tenant had 13. Yes, you read that correctly—13 credit cards. He used them to pay everything and after a little bit of prodding, admitted he pretty much just paid the minimum due each month. I can't recall what he said his monthly total was to pay those minimums, but I do remember he told me he wrote a lot of checks each month. Unfortunately, I unearthed this information at the showing, and it should come as no shock to you that he failed the Cash Flow form. Of course, he could have saved both of us travel time if he had just revealed his true answers on the phone! So be sure to ask how many credit cards each applicant carries and how much they pay on them every month. Get a monthly total of all their credit card payments. You most definitely want this total in your expenses column. Not asking about credit cards could be a disastrous mistake on your part. Ask. Ask. Ask.

All other loan payments. In addition to car and credit card payments, some people have other loans they are responsible for: student loans, personal loans, and so forth. If they have other loans, you need to record the monthly payment in the space provided.

Judgments/garnishments. As previously mentioned, many people have claimed bankruptcy and/or are supposed to pay child support but fail to do so. The "judgments/garnishments" line is for listing those payments that are automatically removed via their paycheck or associated with their bankruptcy.

Alimony/child support/ other dependents. Not only will you want to know if they have these out-of-pocket expenses, but you would like to find out if they really pay them, since alimony and child support are often not paid

In October 2005, the laws regarding bankruptcy changed. For the most part, these changes won't drastically affect how you search for quality tenants. What it will change is how you analyze the prospect's cash. The new laws can up the payments and the totals the filers are responsible for. Under the old laws, it was easier for someone to file a Chapter 7 bankruptcy, which basically eliminated unsecured debt with no payment from the debtor. The new laws now require a means test that determines if a filer can have a Chapter 7 or 13. The Chapter 13 bankruptcy requires some payback of debt. These payments will now be higher than before the law changed. Because of the means testing, a lot fewer people will be eligible for Chapter 7, which requires no debt payback. How all this computes to the landlord is bankruptcy filers who filed under the new laws will have higher repayment, therefore have less money available for rent.

on time. The regularity with which someone pays in this category can show a lot about a person's priorities. For instance, timely child support or alimony payments prove that a person's priorities are set straight. They know they have a moral and financial responsibility and they live up to it. This is a definite positive trait you wish to see in tenants who rent your dwellings and one trait I put a lot of stock in. I instantly feel a little more at ease with a prospect when I discover child support and/or alimony are paid regularly.

On the other hand, if payments are behind, you might see the prospect in a slightly different light, especially if child support payments are behind but the boat payment isn't. I think you get the picture. There is a direct correlation between how a person prioritizes their moral obligations to others and their financial obligations to you. To put it another way, if someone is failing to give financial support to those they supposedly care about, then the odds of you getting paid might someday follow the same path.

After finding out about all of the applicant's loan, garnishments, and support obligations, it's time to ask some other questions. These next few items are bills everyone has so you're not really prying when you inquire about their amounts.

All telephone bills. Leading off is the telephone bill. This includes all family cell phones, regular telephone lines, and computer connections. If your applicant doesn't know the answer to this question, then you have to make an educated guess, using your phone usage as a basis. Figure at least one cell, one house line (although nowadays many people use their cell phones instead of a land line, thereby eliminating one bill), and one Internet bill per month. If you have a couple applying, you can almost bet on two cell phones. Once you have come up with a guess, say it to the prospect. The conversation may go like this:

You: Do you think you pay more than $150 per month?

Tenant Prospect: Oh no, I'm sure much lower.

You: Remember, we are talking about cell number, Internet connections, and your house line. How about $100 a month?

TP: Yeah, that's probably close.

Should you have to estimate their monthly phone bill, guess on the high end. You're better off that way.

The next four lines are easy ones to fill in because all four are based on an "area average."

Gas, electric/sewer and water/garbage/cable TV. Any of these bills could be determined by calling the appropriate utility company and finding out the average rate or usage for your specific area. Most times you can call the utility company yourself and give them a specific address. They will then tell you what the average is for that particular unit. In fact, when renting a dwelling, you should know this information before showing the rental unit because many people will ask about prices on utility usage, garbage, etc. and a professional landlord should be able to tell them.

The four lines pertaining to gas/electric, sewer/water, garbage and cable TV are lines you yourself fill in. If for some reason you are unsure of those averages at the showing, leave these lines blank and fill them in when you get back home.

Once you've completed the expenses up to cable TV, you've gotten answers to all the questions that are pretty easy for a prospective tenant or for you to figure out. Since these bills are paid once a month, with the payment usually

Often you get to this point in the form and you have reason to believe there is no real reason to proceed. All the major expenses of the applicant, such as car payments, credit cards, extra loans, or other support are in line with the income the applicant shows. The applicant seems to be under control with their finances and seems to make more than enough money to cover their bills. At this point, you may wish to stop filling out the Cash Flow form, although, you might want to complete it at home just to double-check that your decision is correct.

182

about the same amount each and every time, it is fairly easy to remember what is paid for these services.

In the next half of the expenses column, the task of figuring an appropriate dollar amount begins to change, because now you need to figure out or ask about expenses that are spread out over the course of 30 days, instead of paid on a monthly basis. Items like food are ongoing, and entertainment or school clothes purchases could happen anytime, with the prices and amounts varying greatly among each prospect. It's hard to know what is spent in some of these categories unless one keeps track or adheres to a budget. Since most people don't bother budgeting or tracking these expenses, they often truly don't know what they spend in these categories.

Consequently, many times when you ask questions in these areas, your applicant will not have the slightest clue about the answers. You will have to ask more personal questions in these categories to lead both you and the applicant to a dollar figure that is realistic.

This is where you'll be glad you remembered to log how many adults and how many children are in the family at the top of the page, because what you'll do is use what your family average is for these areas and adjust up or down accordingly. Therefore I recommend that you sit down one day and figure out what you or your family spend per month in the following categories. Divide by the number of people these expenses cover, and you will have a per person average for you family. This exercise will also prepare you for executing this form. Let's look at some of these areas and I will give you clues toward figuring out an average you can make reference to, just in case your applicant can not give you a solid answer to one of the questions.

All food/dining in/out. If you ask for a monthly total on the grocery bill, you can be fairly confident that whoever does the grocery shopping will have a good idea of the month's food total. This answer is easy enough to figure out, but the grocery bill only covers dining done at home. What a family spends on dining *out* is trickier to compute.

Dining out slowly hacks a 10-dollar bill here and a 20-dollar bill there. People get conditioned to this process and lose track of what is spent over time. How this translates to you, dear landlord, is this: Some people will eat out two meals a day, five days a week, and others will eat out once every four weeks. This financial difference in dining style could mean a hundred dollars or several hundred dollars a month, depending on how many people are being fed restaurant food and how often. So how do you figure out the prospect's dining habits? You'll need to ask them.

Try to make your questions seem like a natural response to already established conversation. Expense questions that are harder for a prospect to know need to be entered in tactfully so as you dig for answers, you don't want to sound like a lawyer questioning a witness. Instead, you'll get better answers if you sound like a bartender conversing with his patrons.

After you get a rough idea of how often they dine out and how much they spend each time, then you can do the math to get a monthly figure. This figure may startle you the first couple times you analyze it.

Health care/prescriptions. Even though some people have health care and prescriptions covered through work, many others pay for at least some, if not all health care and pharmaceutical needs on their own. This can be very expensive, so try to find out what they pay each month so you're not caught off guard. I try to get this answer on the phone when I first interview them.

Auto expenses. At the beginning of the expense part of the Cash Flow form, you asked the tenant prospect about his or her vehicle payments. In this area, you are trying to figure out an average for expenses such as gas, parking, insurance, and regular maintenance and repairs. Depending on the number of vehicles and the type and age of the vehicles and how they are driven, this monthly expense will vary. Pop the question, "What is the monthly total of gas, insurance, maintenance, and expenses for all your vehicles?" You can use your own personal vehicle monthly expenses as a guideline on which to base their answers.

Daycare. Any time there are kids listed on the application, ask about daycare, especially if both parents work. Chances are, even if the kids are in school, they might have someone watching them for a couple hours after school until one of the parents gets home. And don't forget to ask about summer, when the kids are off from school. Daycare is usually a higher expense during these months.

Unless the kids are latchkey kids when the parents work, someone watches the children at least periodically. Find out who watches them and how much it costs. If you ask the question and discover that a grandparent, friend, neighbor, or someone else watches the kids after school, you still need to find out if they pay these sitters something. Many will.

All hobbies/entertainment. Everybody has some form of entertainment or hobbies, be it movies at home or movies at the theater, bowling, golf, Gameboy, weekend trips, etc. Some people spend a lot in this category and some spend very little. This is another category that is difficult to compute. Ask what they spend as a family and then record the answer on your Cash Flow form. If they cannot answer the question with confidence, figure at least $20 a month per person minimum, no matter what.

Pet care. This covers monthly food, medicine, toys, grooming, and medical care. For the average homeowner, this figure is pretty reasonable. If you have pets, you can gauge the average cost per pet. Depending on the size of the pet and extra care they need, $30 to $50 a month should be more than enough to cover a cat or dog.

There are a couple of hobbies that can really throw a person's finances out of whack, and unfortunately, they can be difficult to detect. Gambling can be a big financial drain, as can recreational drug use. Realize people do have these vices and be prepared to respond to these problems in the future if they get past your early radar. Your first warning of these problems will probably be financial.

All miscellaneous. This last category should cover any expense you didn't ask about: clothes, diapers, holidays, beer, cigarettes, mad money, gifts, and any spontaneous purchases. Basically, any item that someone might spend their money on that is not covered in one of your previous categories should be listed here.

I recommend you pick an average per person figure for the miscellaneous category and use that as your basis. I use $50 as a bare minimum, covering both adults and kids, although you may wish to use a higher figure for adults. My personal suggestion is to use $100 per adult and $50 per child for monthly miscellaneous expenses. If you feel this figure is too high or too low an average for the economic climate in which you live, adjust it for your tastes.

Even though I believe this form is valuable, it is very hard to make it complete enough for optimum results because a lot of landlords aren't comfortable prying into people's finances and even fewer tenants want their finances pried into. However, you can greatly reduce the unpleasantness associated with this process by taking some precautions.

Plan for this Form During the Interview

First, ask some of the cash flow questions during your investigation part of the phone interview that you did back in step two. Ask directly if they have insurance, high car expenses, go to the casinos, love to shop, etc. Just mix the questions in with your conversation. Make it sound like you are interested in them for who they are. When you get an answer, laugh a little, or respond by saying something like, "Me too!" "Been there." "Wow." If they tell you about a hobby, ask if it is fun or "What that's like?" Word the conversation so it sounds like you are just a person who likes to chat, maybe even a person who gets off the main topic on occasions. With a little practice, your caller will never know it was intentional. To really get good at this idea, memorize the harder categories on the Cash Flow form and make it a priority to cover a few of them before you end your phone interview.

Second, once you have extracted some of this information, write it down on the caller interview sheet as you talk to the caller. At the very least, jot the stuff down before you proceed to the next call. After all, if you are talking on the phone to them in step two, the preparation step, log that information down in preparation for this form.

Third, when you go to show your rental you know who you are meeting. Pull out their interview form and acquaint yourself with their information. Now you will be fresh to fill out some of the categories yourself without asking as many questions.

You could also adjust the figure as you see fit for each applicant's scenario. For instance, if you have two adults and three kids and use an average figure of $100 per adult and $50 per child, then you'd have an estimate of $350 per month on your miscellaneous line. But suppose you hear Mom make a general comment that she loves to clothes shop and goes at least twice a week. Hearing this, you might wish to raise your figure on miscellaneous spending.

The miscellaneous category is the last category to be filled out and therefore wraps up this form as far as the tenant applicant is concerned. Even though there is still more for you to do before you are completely finished with this form, all that will be addressed in the next step of the five simple steps of tenant selection.

In Closing

Before I wrap up this chapter, let me remind you of a few helpful hints:

- It is your responsibility to fill out this form. Do not give this form to your applicant to complete, because in most cases, they will not take the time to give thorough estimates for each figure.

- Also, even though you may try to fill in all areas of the Cash Flow form, unforeseen situations can prevent that. At the very least, try to collect the information, figures, and estimates for the spending in the categories that are hardest to prove because of lack of paper evidence.

- You will have some applicants who have a lot of extra money left after paying their regular bills. In these cases, you will not need to ask many questions in the topics that concern food, hobbies, and so forth—especially if their credit seems fine.

The Cash Flow form may seem overwhelming at first sight, but remember, you want cash flowing *to* you each and every month on a regular basis. Using this form will help you find that high quality tenant who can pay you on time without fail, and isn't that the name of the game?

Note: The Cash Flow form is available on our website at
www.FindThatQualityTenant.com.

CHAPTER 12

The Checklist—Part One

T he final form I recommend always using in step three (paperwork) is the checklist. I'm a big believer in checklists because they keep you organized and on track. Even though putting a tenant in a rental unit is a lot easier than, say, sending a man to the moon, it can still be stressful if required information gets overlooked. Using the checklist will help you avoid such undue stress.

The checklist is divided into three parts. These three parts coordinate with steps three, four, and five of the tenant selection process. You will complete each part in its entirety before moving on to the next one. This chapter deals with part one of the checklist, which is the final overview of step three, the paperwork step.

The first part of the checklist (step 3) is completed by you when you meet with the applicant to fill out the rental application, initial credit report, and employment verification form. Your goal is to get a checkmark or N/A (not applicable) on every line in part one before you leave the showing. A checkmark means the task is done and N/A means the item doesn't apply in this case. On occasion, you can't get a piece of information you want, so circle the space provided to remind you to follow up on that particular item at a later date.

Unlike the other forms in this book, you will be shown only the part of the checklist that applies to the step you are studying. A complete checklist will be available at the end of the book.

STEP 3

1) ____ Verify driver's license number and picture
2) ____ Verify social security number
3) ____ Landlord information complete
4) ____ Employment information complete
5) ____ Reference names and phone numbers complete
6) ____ Rental application signed and dated
7) ____ Credit application filled out completely
8) ____ Credit application signed and dated
9) ____ Credit monies received
10) ____ Employment verification signed and dated
11) ____ Cashflow form filled out
12) ____ Co-signer credit check completed, signed and dated
13) ____ Co-signer credit check monies received
14) ____ Co-signer cashflow filled out

Signature _____ Date _____

The Checklist—Step 3

Following is the first part of the checklist:

1. *Verify driver's license number and picture.* You need to see a picture ID of your applicant, and starting off the checklist this way gives you that opportunity. The main purpose of the ID check is to prove that the person on the photo ID is the same person who is in front of you. Up to this point, you really have no idea if the applicant really is who he or she says. You could have a situation where the tenant prospect is filling out paperwork fraudulently as another person for a number of reasons. Possibly, a friend is trying to help a soon-to-be-released convict re-enter society or perhaps a relative is trying to find residence for a mentally ill family member. These instances are very rare indeed, but people will try anything, so be sure to check identification.

2. *Verify Social Security number.* I approach the subject of ID by saying to the applicant, "Please show me your driver's license or photo ID and Social Security card so that I may verify those numbers on your rental application. If I, or someone else, can't correctly read your numbers, then the whole rental process could be slowed down for a

week or so. I'd hate to see that happen to you." When I ask in this way, I've never been turned down. People agree with me and show me what ID they have. I then compare those numbers to the ones on the form and quickly match their photo to their face before I give those cards back to the applicant.

3. *Ensure landlord information is complete.*

4. *Ensure employment information is complete.*

5. *Check that reference names and phone numbers are complete.*

6. *Make sure the Rental Application is signed and dated.* Applicants *must* sign and date the rental application. If they fail to do so, it is technically illegal to pry into their personal life even though they filled out the information on the application and handed it to you. *Do not follow up on any information if your application is not signed and dated.*

7. *Ensure the credit application is filled out completely.* The credit application must be filled out completely if you use a credit application form other than your rental application to run your credit checks. Of course, if you are using a local credit bureau to check the applicant's credit and you are using their form, you want all the pertinent information spelled out correctly on the credit check form. Make sure landlord and employment information, as well as driver's license and Social Security numbers are accurate on this form. Then double-check to see if it's signed by all parties who need to sign it. Verify the date and again, remember to collect the needed monies to run the credit check. Neither the Rental Application nor another credit check form will do you any good unless you collect the money to run the credit check from your tenant applicant.

8. *Make sure the credit application is signed and dated.*

9. *Make sure credit monies have been received.*

10. *Check that the Employment Verification is signed and dated.* Verify that the applicant filled out the top of the Employment Verification form correctly. Remember, if you're checking into more than one job, you'll need their signature on more than one employment verification form. Make sure they signed and dated it correctly.

11. *Ensure the Cash Flow form is filled out.* Some of the Cash Flow sheet will be filled out by you at home when you go over all the critical information. But what you need to verify now are all the numbers you can't get from the Rental Application or any of the figures you can't come up with on your own. It is very important to give the Cash Flow form a quick glance over before marking line 11.

12. *Make sure cosigner credit check completed, signed, and dated.*

13. *Ensure cosigner credit check monies received.*

14. *Ensure cosigner cash flow filled out.*

Glance over all these areas on the rental application and make sure everything is legible and complete. Make sure that you can read each and every phone number and they are complete. Stumbling on an incomplete phone number makes that source of information useless. Make sure all names and other pieces of information in these areas are correct and then check them off the list.

You may use N/A quite frequently on lines 12 through 14. Those lines pertain to cosigners, which many of your tenants may not have. Once you've filled out line 14, you are done using the checklist for now. This part of the checklist is the last thing you fill out at the showing of your rental unit. When you have reached this stage of the game, it will be time to part ways with the applicant. Thank them for their time and let them know you'll call them after you've thoroughly researched this information. I find I usually need about two to five business days for everyone to return phone calls and for the credit report and criminal background check to come through. Therefore, I let the applicant know this research process takes a few days, just so they understand the time constraints. I recommend you tell them this also. It is only fair and professional of you.

Once every item in the first part of the checklist is complete, you are ready to head back home and begin analyzing and verifying all the information you collected. The next step, step four (process), of the book will go into detail on how to do that.

The Checklist form is available on our website at
www.FindThatQualityTenant.com

Step Four: Process

A After you collect all the filled out paperwork from your tenant applicant, you need to go home where you can review and analyze all the information you've collected. We call this step four, or the "process" step. It will be the final step in your decision to accept or deny a tenant applicant. Study step four to improve your analytical skills for reaching that decision.

CHAPTER 13

Analyzing the Rental Application

One day as I was developing this book, my brother called me to tell me with great enthusiasm about a movie he had just watched. Since my brother is generally pretty laid back about most things in his life, I had to stand up and take notice about the subject at hand. It seems the movie that had him so stoked was the Tom Cruise film *Minority Report*.

Following his much pressured advice, I decided to watch the movie to see what was so fascinating. The movie takes us ahead 50 years into the future, and we see the country has the highest rate of murder and bloodshed in its entire history. It seems murders happen hourly in almost every city and town in every state. No one is immune. Everyone knows someone who has been murdered. Washington, D.C., in an effort to curb the murder rate, has developed a law enforcement agency called "Pre-Crime." Basically how Pre-Crime works is there is an acute combination of modern technology mixed with good old-fashioned human visions or imagery that alerts the pre-crime police on when and where a murder is going to take place. Once the "who, when, and where" are established, the pre-crime police sweep in and arrest the soon-to-be villain seconds before a murder actually happens.

It was a very intense and interesting movie and if you like futuristic crime thrillers, *Minority Report* is for you! I ended up thinking about this movie on and off for days afterward. I just couldn't get over the cool concept of predetermining a crime before it happened.

Naturally, being a full-time landlord, I started to fantasize about how great it would be to have something like that to help me "watch" over my tenants. I mean, think about it: Wouldn't you love to have "pre-late rent" police or "pre-broken pet policy" police or even just a general "pre-tenant problem" police unit in place to solve all those pesky tenant problems before they actually surfaced? I know I would. In fact, I found myself enjoying my daydreams of no unwarranted phone calls or unpleasant and expensive surprises. I was envisioning landlord utopia.

But of course, eventually I came back to earth and realized it wasn't to be, at least not in my lifetime! So I decided that I, and consequently you, will have to be our own "pre-tenant problem" police, which in a roundabout way is what this whole book is about. Therefore, I'd like to introduce you to step four in the search for a quality tenant. That step is the processing step. This step is designed to help you analyze, follow up, and confirm all the written information and paperwork you gathered in step three. If you are actually using the system and forms outlined in this book, step four is where things get a lot easier in the tenant selection process because you used the Tenant Qualifications form, and you used the Caller Interview form.

Because of all the preliminary work you did, the actual review of your applicant's paperwork is not so difficult. In other words, if you are truly trying to achieve the original goal, which is *When you decide to show a caller your rental unit, you know you would rent it to them provided they did not falsify or omit any information that you received from them on the phone,* the confirming of information is more of a formality and double-checking step than anything else.

Selection Skills

The way you use and analyze the rental application will determine if you are using professional or merely average landlord skills.

The landlord with average tenant selection skills makes decisions regarding tenants using the following process:

- Prepares the dwelling to whatever they feel defines "prepared"
- Advertises
- Shows the rental to almost anyone who calls on the ad
- Possibly takes applications, *then* begins to decide if that applicant is worth renting to

Only *after* the average landlord enters step three, and receives an application does he begin the search to see what kind of applicant he has. Such a landlord goes to the rental dwelling, takes information on people he knows very little about, then drives home to begin the investigation process he *hopes* will reveal a worthwhile tenant. If that applicant fails the process, the landlord goes back to step one and begins again.

It is of my opinion that a professional landlord, on the other hand, will have all the important guidelines outlined before the phone rings and won't even leave his home to show the dwelling until he is extremely sure the prospect on the phone can probably meet his qualifications.

Ask yourself which landlord sounds more knowledgeable and profitable. Which landlord are you? Which landlord do you want to be?

Let me repeat: If you are reading this book and using the forms and system outlined, then once you begin to go over the information on your rental application, it is more of a formality and a double-check on all things you probably already learned about this prospect.

This doesn't make analyzing any of the paperwork less important or give anyone the reason to skip over it all together. No matter how secure and content you are in your applicant's ability to meet your qualifications, you *must* still verify all recorded information. As a professional, it is in your best interest to do so because there will be times you will uncover hidden information that will change your outlook on a prospect, or at the very least, raise a caution flag.

Achieving the Best Results

Before we begin to review the application, let me give you a couple clues on how to best extract information from it.

Plan on approximately three business days to put everything together—more if you don't own a fax machine or computer and have to rely on snail mail for things such as your credit report. If you can verify all reports using the computer, that is fine as long as you keep a printed paper trail in the tenant's file. Even if you can accomplish everything by computer, I would still plan for three days to compile all needed information, not because you will spend very much time actually working on analyzing information, but because it will take about three days for most of the applicant's personal and work references to return your calls. In fact, your actual total time spent on completing all of step four should only take you about one hour unless you uncover information that confuses you or has the potential to make you nervous. In those instances, you'll definitely want to spend more time investigating that particular circumstance so you can eventually make the best decision regarding that prospect.

Accurate information

I feel now is as good a time as any to mention this final tidbit: *Keep in mind that generally, the more* accurately *the application is filled out, the better tenants they always seem to be.* I haven't done an official study, but I've evaluated enough applications and had enough tenants to know this rings true, for whatever reason.

In my previous statement, you'll notice I emphasized "accurately" but not "completely." Sometimes, an application will have less information on it because less information applies. Let's say you have an applicant who got divorced after 15 years of marriage and 13 years of homeownership. They probably can't remember who their last landlord was or what the phone number was. Incomplete or lack of information such as this may be okay and even beneficial in your search for knowledge. For example, in the previous scenario, the tenant prospect owned a house for 13 years before divorce. Because of this 13-year homeownership, you can safely assume things about them that you would have asked a previous landlord anyway, such as:

- Can the prospect pay the rent? If he or she still owned a home after 13 years, the chances are he or she was making the house payment.
- Will the prospect take care of the house? Again, chances are after 13 years of homeownership, this person probably has maintenance,

fix-up, and cleaning skills that are at least equal to if not better than the average tenant.

Sometimes good tenant selection involves reading between the lines. Often, the information you *don't* receive is better than what you *do* receive.

Let's quickly review the basics of the application, and as we do so, I will cover any areas that might need a little more clarifying.

Personal information

The information that begins the application doesn't really reveal anything about the applicant's work ethic, spending habits, or rental history. What it does do is provide all the important numbers pertaining to that applicant. Those numbers include home, work, and cell phone numbers so you can locate the prospect if you need to now or in the future. Also included are birth dates, Social Security, and driver's license numbers. You need these numbers to ensure that you can locate, verify, and connect the correct information with the correct applicant. For this reason, the last three numbers are extremely important. They are so important that I feel it's necessary to mention some previously stated advice. *Double-check these numbers directly off their driver's license and Social Security cards with their rental application to verify the numbers are legible, complete, and correct.* Failure to do so could cause you delays in follow-up on the applicant's given information and/or could cause you to gather information on the wrong applicant. Of course, you need to use this procedure on any and all rental applications you accept. Make this a regular habit.

Names and relationship. Once you have verified names and numbers, you want to look at how many people will be living in the unit. There should be a list of all minors' names and their ages. Count the number of people to see if that number is the same as what you were told on the phone, and if the number falls within your qualifications. Having a list of the children's names also helps you call people by their correct names when you interact with them. Knowing everyone's name makes you more professional and respectful.

Pets. Next are the names, breeds, and descriptions of pets. Look at this area and verify it is what you were told over the phone. Then make a mental note of what is listed. Remember this information so you can ask about the pet(s) when you speak to the current landlord. You also want to make sure you accept the pet(s) and that none of them are dangerous.

Rental History

Current landlord. Checking out the applicant's rental history is next on the application. Beginning with present address, call the landlords listed on the application. There are a couple of important points to remember when reviewing the present address.

Landlords who are family. The first item to look for is the owner/manager. Check out the name the applicant filled in on this spot. By checking the name of the owner/manager, sometimes you will discover that the owner/manager and applicant have the same last name, indicating the tenant prospect might be living with family. If the last names are different, check the "emergency contact" section of the application to see if the emergency contact's phone numbers and addresses are the same as the applicant's home phone number and address. These are clues as to whether the applicant actually lives on his or her own or is perhaps living with a relative. Of course, you may already know this information, but the process will help verify it one way or another and may help prepare you for better questions you will eventually ask.

Receiving outside financial assistance from a relative is not necessarily a bad thing, but when you know the applicant is living in this kind of situation, the amount of rent they say they currently pay becomes a gray area because there will be absolutely no way you can verify that the prospect pays the amount regularly. You can ask their current friend or parent, but your only real proof will be in the form of a cancelled check. Usually if they are paying rent to family or friends, it is in cash and not a check. When you have this situation, don't panic. Make a mental note of it, keep an open and fair mind, and continue verifying the rest of the information.

Landlord imposters. The second thing to be aware of is when you begin your follow-up phone calls to verify information on the rental application and call the present landlord, you could be talking to a friend or someone else posing as the applicant's current landlord. Friends do this sort of thing for each other: Someone needs a letter or name forged or a buddy makes a phone call with the intent of impersonating someone of authority.

One way to detect this potential problem is when you have the current landlord on the phone, begin your questions by asking them to verify the applicant's rent. The key is to ask the landlord to verify a rent that is significantly higher or lower than what the applicant states he pays. Let's say the applicant states he pays 600 dollars per month in rent. You will ask the current landlord, "Can you verify that Joe Renter is paying 700 dollars in rent?"

Most of the time (not necessarily all), the true landlord will know how much rent is being paid and will correct you on the amount, whereas the friend who is masquerading as a landlord probably will agree to whatever rent you state. This is not a foolproof scheme, therefore, it should not solely make or break your decision to rent, but it will give you a clue as to who you might be dealing with and if you need to proceed with caution.

If you contact a larger apartment complex, chances are the people fielding your call won't know the applicant's rent without looking it up. These people might answer your request for verification along these lines: "I'm sorry, I don't know that answer directly, but most of our tenants pay between $575 and $650 for rent, so that figure could be wrong."

Whatever answer you get, listen for clues and use your gut feeling to decide if the landlord you are talking to is indeed who they say they are.

When you do get their landlord on the phone, here is a short list of questions you might ask regarding applicants:

> If you really suspect you have an "impostor" on the phone, call back the next day at a different time from a different phone and ask the basic questions again. You might even have someone of the opposite sex call to help throw off the impostor.

- How much is rent?
- Is rent usually paid on time?
- How long have they rented?
- Do they abide by the house rules?
- Are they clean?
- Are they breaking a lease at this time?
- Do they have any pets?
- Would you rent to them again?

Of course, there are many more questions you could ask the current landlord, and please feel free to do so. Just remember, if the tenant is of poor quality, and the current landlord wishes to remove him or her from the premises, the answers you receive could be false. The last thing you may wish to check on a current tenant's address is to call the police department that would respond to calls at that address and see what kind of history that address might have for the duration of the tenant applicant's tenancy. You'd hate to move someone into your rental only to find out your neighbors will have to call the police constantly.

Previous landlords. Once you have called the current landlord, start calling previous landlords, which will be a better source of information in regard to the worthiness of your prospect. Keep in mind that all rules that applied for the current landlord should apply here as well. Previous landlords will fall into one of two categories: large complexes or small investors.

Large complexes. There are different advantages with both types of landlords when trying to verify past rental history. The large complexes are usually run by good, quality, professional managers who can be reached quickly and easily during normal business hours. These managers probably will not answer a lot of personal questions about the applicant, but they will verify most if not all of the important issues. These managers will almost always be able to give quick, precise answers to the same questions you asked the current landlord.

Sometimes you'll ask a question and the person on the other end of the phone will answer, "No comment," or will hesitate as he or she figures out how best to answer the question. When you come across this type of situation, ask one more of your standard questions and see if the manager can answer that one. If he or she again cannot, ask the final question, "Would you rent to this applicant again?" Legally, the manager can answer "Yes" or "No" to that question without fear of backlash. Even evasive answers topped with this final question will give you good insight in making your rental decision.

Small-time investors. Small-time investors should be asked the same questions as big complex managers. The advantage with small investors is that there is a good chance they will reveal a lot more personal information about your applicant. Because small-time investor landlords are more willing to talk, you can usually ask additional questions as long as you are not discriminating or violating any tenant privacy laws.

A word of caution: Small-time landlords often get to know their tenants on a friendlier basis, so they might not reveal negative answers to your questions as readily as a complex manager. They might even have been friends before they had a landlord/tenant relationship. Whenever I run into a small-time investor landlord in the previous landlord space on the application, I double-check the applicant's personal references to see if the landlord is listed as a friend, reference, or emergency contact. If the person is, I will put less significance on any information that particular landlord gives me, and I urge you to do the same.

The list of questions in this chapter should be asked of any landlord. When you get the landlord on the phone, begin by introducing yourself and then say: "Joe Renter has listed your address as a previous place of residence. May I ask a couple questions to verify that information?" You will notice that although I named the tenant applicant, I didn't reveal Joe Renter was trying to rent from me. For all the person on the other end of the phone knows, I may be a new landlord, credit agency, police, or some other type of business acquiring information. This approach should help.

Once you have the previous landlord's undivided attention, ask him or her any or all of the following questions in addition to those stated previously:

- Did Joe Renter have any pets?
- Were they cooperative/quiet/demanding?
- How many people lived in the household?

- Why did they move?
- Did they leave on good terms?
- Did they give proper notice?
- How much rent were they paying?
- Were they clean, especially where roaches/mice control is concerned?
- Did you have any particular problems with them?

You can also make up your own questions to ask. Some landlords will answer them and some will not. Either way, you have nothing to lose by asking, and much to gain if they do answer. In general, ask as many questions as you can to verify what you want to know.

Signs for Caution

Before moving on, let me suggest some things that should "yellow" or "red flag" your applicant regarding rent history:

- An eviction that is filed or completed
- Missing or erratic rental history
- A series of frequent moves
- Looking for residence and a job at the same time
- Past landlords are listed but are not reachable

Any of these areas should probably stop the rental process unless there was a good, believable, *provable* story behind the problem *and* all other areas of the application proved to be spectacular. For your information, in my years of renting houses and apartments these situations have never occurred for me because these people were generally weeded out over the phone during the prequalifying step.

Income Information

Current employer. Once you've concluded the applicant's rental history, it is time to verify income and employment. Even though you may have verified recent pay stubs of the tenant applicant you should still call their place of employment so you can ask the employer questions about your applicant. First, try to accomplish this over the phone. Unfortunately, many companies no longer will handle employment verification in this manner because of employee privacy laws, so often you will have to use the Employment Verification form. Its use will be covered in a brief chapter later on.

For now, let's assume someone at the workplace will verify employment. When you call a place of employment, ask for the supervisor by name. Again, if possible, do not reveal why you are calling until you actually get that supervisor on the phone. Supervisors get many calls during a day, so when you ask for them by name, you are more likely to be put in contact with that person. If you clue in whoever answers the phone what you are calling about, you may end up being passed to an applicant's buddy at work who is pretending to be said supervisor. You definitely want to talk to the real deal.

Once you have the correct person on the phone, say, "I'm calling to verify Joe Renter's employment. Could you answer a couple of questions for me?"

If the person is willing to answer, ask these questions:

- What is the applicant's occupation?
- What is the applicant's current pay?
- How many hours do they work each week?
- How long have they been employed there?
- Do they receive any overtime?
- How much is overtime pay?
- Is this position secure and long-term?
- Does the employee receive health insurance through work?

I also like to ask the employer this final question: If you had a dwelling to rent, would you rent to said employee? (Actually, I end every call I make to the applicant's employment, references, and emergency contacts—and anybody else who knows the applicant—with this question.)

A good combination of these questions should verify what you need to know, which is the income and job stability your applicant says he or she has. This is the primary goal when dealing with employers.

One word of caution concerning the line "hours worked": Nowadays, many companies keep employees less than 40 hours a week because of insurance costs and other reasons. You'll find this to be particularly true in the service and retail industries. So anytime you see someone in either of these industries, be sure to ask how many hours the applicant actually *works* per week, and not how many they are *scheduled* for.

This question is very useful for clarifying misleading information. For example, I spent many years working weekends as a deejay at weddings and parties. I was paid well for about six hours of work a week during the seasonal months. I made $50 or more per hour. If you assumed I worked full-time, it would appear I made about $100,000 a year. Dream income for a tenant! But because I worked only six hours a week, that income would be more like $12,000 a year—not such a dream. Hours worked per week is a small question, but definitely one worth knowing as soon as possible.

If the employer is friendly and easily giving information, you might wish to ask a couple more questions, such as:

- Is the employee punctual/responsible?
- Does the employee have a good, positive attitude?
- Does the employee get along well with fellow employees?
- Does the employee have a good work ethic?
- Is the employee trustworthy?

Some employers might answer these types of questions, but remember to stay away from questions that violate the Fair Housing Act of 1968.

Asking these questions from the last list are geared more toward the personality of the applicant. Keep in mind, if you ask these questions to an employer about an employee who has major character flaws, that employer might not tell you the truth for fear of employee retaliation. So beware!

Previous employers. If you have information on any previous employers it could be worth your time to give them a call. Since previous employers have no current, direct connection to your applicant, they might offer more truthful answers. I have gotten some outstanding reviews from previous employers.

A combination of properly used current and previous employers can be a good source of information, although here are a couple of areas that you should watch out for: First, almost every place of employment will be some kind of professional business. So the background sounds you pick up on during your phone conversation should correlate to that type of business. For instance, if you call a machine shop and as you're speaking to the supervisor you hear *Sesame Street* playing in the background along with a child yelling "Uno!" there's a good chance you're being bamboozled. If you think you've stumbled upon a situation like that, look up the applicant's listed employer in the phone book or call information to verify that the name of the company and phone number are legit (a good idea, anyway). You could even take a drive by the place if you felt the need.

Also when dealing with employment, use a little extra care if you run into any of the following situations:

- New job
- Short, sporadic job changes
- Lack of income verification

In fact, this last item, lack of income verification, should be a definite precaution when looking at other sources of income, your next area on the Rental Application.

These sources of income include steady bonuses, alimony, child support, government assistance, and the like. As I mentioned in an earlier chapter, if at all possible, you should have seen proof of these sources of income when the prospect filled out the application. Doing so makes your life easier at this point in time because it is often very difficult to verify many of these income sources over the phone. If you find a listed source of income that you have not seen solid proof of, call the applicant and ask for it. Do this only after everything else is verified in step four, just in case you should need any further information from your applicant.

Personal References

After you verify the applicant's income, begin calling the personal references they listed. When it comes to personal references, I recommend asking for five from each adult, in hopes of talking to at least three. *Remember that immediate family doesn't count. This includes parents, brothers, sisters, and grandparents*. An occasional aunt, uncle, or cousin is fine, but you really want to talk to co-workers, friends, and associates.

As I suggested when contacting a current employment supervisor, when you call personal references, don't reveal that you might be renting a house to the applicant. Instead, begin the conversation along these lines: "Hi, I'm calling in regard to Joe Renter. He has listed you as a personal reference. May I ask how you know this person and how long have you known him?" I am always interested in the length of time of the applicant's friendship to the reference. A short acquaintance time from each reference I call could mean a new start on life by the applicant, possibly hiding something worth knowing. What I really hope for are references who fit into different time periods of the applicant's life. For instance, one reference worked with the applicant two jobs ago and can answer work history and work ethic questions. The next reference may have roomed with the applicant so I ask them about cleanliness, rent payment, pet, and rule obedience questions.

Many references will not be home when you first call. If you leave a voice message, simply state your name and that Joe Renter used him or her as a personal reference. Say your phone number slowly and clearly twice, and ask for a return call as soon as possible. Do not state that you're thinking of renting to Joe Renter. You don't want to tip off the reference about the reason for your call. I also suggest calling these references within minutes of the tenant applicant filling out the paperwork. By doing so, the applicant has less time to call their references to tip them off that you will be calling. I would much rather speak to a reference who doesn't know my call is coming.

You will notice this area is titled *personal* references. That means once you have established how the applicant and reference are connected, you will be asking nondiscriminating personal questions about the applicant.

There are many questions you can ask, but here is a sample:

- How long have you known the applicant?
- What kind of pets do they have? Are they clean?
- Do they pay bills on time?
- Are they quiet?
- Do they work steadily?
- If you had a rental, would you rent to them and why? (Save this for the last question. I always ask this question and then listen for how quickly they respond and how believable their answer is.)

You get the picture. Ask questions about any of the issues you wish to cover, including income, jobs, pets, rental history, and so forth. Use the reference to double-check things you verified from other sources. Ask questions to build a character profile of these people. By asking three to five different people questions, you can gather a wealth of personal information about the applicant. If you have applicants who are husband and wife, you should even ask her references questions about him and vice versa. In effect, you broaden your sources of information.

Remember, the personal references applicants list on the rental application are people they handpicked, knowing or hoping those people would speak highly of them. Expect this. Just ask your questions and keep your ears open for consistency among the answers you get and caution flags on stories that contradict each other.

Another thing to be aware of is the way the references answer your questions. They may say good and positive things about the applicant, but as they say them, there may be hesitation, pauses, floundering, or a change of answers. In other words, you hear one thing coming from the reference's mouth, but pick up a different vibe about their answers.

If you get one reference out of five that falls into this category, you might dismiss the reference as being tired, not a good phone conversationalist, or just a personal character trait of the reference, and so forth.

The red flag should pop up if you get this feeling from many or most of the references.

When I run into this situation, I try to ask an abundance of questions, because I want to figure out if the bad vibe I'm feeling is the fault of the personal reference or due to the character of the applicant.

After speaking to all references, you probably will have interviewed most everyone you'll need to in order to correctly verify the applicant's information. If applicable, you should have talked to one current landlord, one or two previous landlords, one or two employers or past employers, and several personal references. This could be a total of 7 to 10 people you've interviewed in addition to the initial lengthy phone conversation you had with the applicant. Most of the time, this will be enough interviewing to aid you in your decision.

Periodically, you'll have an unusual situation that may not stop you from renting to the applicant but which warrants more investigation. If it needs investigating, investigate it. Call the applicant. Ask more questions. Get a couple more phone number to follow up on. Remember, it's your house and you need to be comfortable with any tenant you choose. Never be afraid to investigate further.

Let's analyze the rest of the application. After the personal references are a few bits of information you may or may not use. Even though you may not use them now, they could prove valuable during the applicant's tenancy.

Other information

Major credit cards/other credit references. If you run credit checks, you may not need this section, but I still recommend the applicant fill out the credit source and payment. That way, you'll have his or her payment amount for easy reference to fill in on your Cash Flow form.

You should know the answers to questions about bankruptcy and judgments from your phone conversation with the applicant, but since you want that answer in their handwriting for your paper trail and possible future reference, you ask the questions on the Rental Application.

This information should also show up on the credit report you run on the prospect, but sometimes that is not the case. Occasionally, the credit bureau will miss one of these items or more likely, the bankruptcy or judgment is so new, it hasn't had time to be recorded properly and therefore goes undetected. Since you will be reviewing the credit report and will have more accurate information about the bankruptcy from that report, the only thing I recommend is to cross-reference the Rental Application information with that on the report. Compare the applicant's stated information to the credit report to see the truthfulness and accuracy of the applicant.

Felony convictions. This is a delicate topic, and I have three points to make concerning this issue:

1. You need to realize that if they were ever convicted of a crime and they do not think you'll be checking into their criminal background, there is real good chance they might lie on this question. I mean, look at it this way: If someone did spend time in prison for a felony and is now re-entering society, that person needs a

On occasion, you have a tenant applicant who for some reason gives you a bad feeling that you can't shake. Their employment, references, income and even credit seem acceptable, but you still don't think things are right. One last avenue for possibly eliminating a candidate is to run your own background check. Simply call your county courthouse (and neighboring courthouses if need be) and check the public records of the individual. Public records are just that: public. See if your applicant has drug arrests or other disturbances in his background. You can also check local police department records.

place to live. They may now be living a very straight path, but they know anytime they reveal "yes" to this question, they will probably get rejected at most decent dwellings. If you were this person, would you lie and try to rent the place with the hopes of proving you're an outstanding tenant before anyone found out about your past? I am not condoning the behavior, but be aware it could very well happen this way. Whenever possible, run a criminal background check on your applicants.

2. Another concern has to do with the word "convicted." Convicted means actually found guilty. For every conviction, there are dozens of "accused" and "acquitted" persons. They can answer "no" to these questions and still not be lying or misleading. So why even ask the question? Well, do it in hopes of possibly filtering out some problems. That is worthwhile in and of itself. People are talkers and even though someone circles "no," he or she just might tell you something you need to know.

3. "Convicted" does not mean arrested. Never ask if anyone has been arrested, because it could be misconstrued as discrimination. The good old US of A says you are innocent until proven guilty. You can only ask if they have been *convicted*.

Was that conviction related to drug use? This topic was somewhat covered back in step three when you filled out the rental application, although the topic warrants a little more information. To begin with, you can refuse to rent to anyone who has been convicted of any felony with one small exception: drug use. (Yes, alcohol is considered a drug.) Provided they are currently enrolled in a rehab program or have graduated from such a program and are currently free from any drug activity, they can still be a candidate for your residence. Naturally, you can refuse to rent to anyone who is currently using drugs.

Have you ever been evicted/asked to vacate? This question, of course, is directed toward applicants, but you may get a more correct answer by asking their previous and current landlords. Also, some states report this information on credit reports, but others do not.

During your investigation process, you may develop a notion that the applicant might have been evicted and has not revealed such information. Should you think this is the case, call the city circuit and the county small claims court and ask them to check to see if there is an eviction record on your applicant. Most courts will do this for a small fee. Be aware that the court you call will only have records of those claims in their court. This means if you call court A, but the tenant applicant was evicted from a residence in court C, you probably will not uncover it. Of course, there is nothing stopping you from following up with every district court for every address listed on your applicant's application. Also on your credit report will be a list of previous addresses, which you may wish to follow up on.

Vehicle information. This is where the applicant needs to list the model and year of the car(s) they drive as well as license plate numbers and car payments. You also will want to make note of any car payments on your Cash Flow form.

Emergency contact. Just like Social Security numbers and other pertinent information, you should call these numbers to verify the contact person, address, and phone number. You'd hate to have to use the emergency number in the future and find out it was in-

In the course of your landlording career, you will have to reject an applicant for reasons you uncover in the processing step. When you do, you should send them a very brief letter—the shorter the better—stating why you are turning them away. A copy of this letter should also be held with their rejected application. All that is needed in the letter is the date rejected, the address to the denied rental and a brief (very brief) explanation of the legal reason you are rejecting them. You should do this even if you reject by phone. One last thought: If you reject by phone, be *very* brief. The more you say, the bigger the chance of a discriminatory lawsuit.

correct. While you are checking the validity of these contacts, feel free to use these people as further sources of personal references.

It is great to have all this information about an applicant to investigate. Unfortunately, until all legal age parties involved in renting the dwelling have signed and dated the statement at the end of the form, verifying such information is illegal.

Make sure the rental application is signed when they fill out the application and double-check the signature before you begin your phone calls. It only takes a few seconds and could save you a potential lawsuit.

There is a lot of information to follow up on and quite a few people to talk to in step four. You are doing all of this because you want to build an accurate profile on your tenant applicant. This takes a skill that can be developed and polished. This chapter was written to give you clues on what to look for as you build your profile.

CHAPTER 14

Analyzing the Credit Report

T his chapter details how to read and analyze credit reports. Before you begin, I believe it is only fair to warn you that when you first begin to analyze all these reports, you may feel overwhelmed as you read them. I'm warning you of this not to scare you off, but to assure you it's natural to feel intimidated when you first review credit reports.

In fact, I must admit that writing this chapter was intimidating for me because although I feel confident in my personal ability to decipher these reports, I'm far from a credit expert and was pulling my hair out trying to come up with what I felt was the proper way to explain this process to the general public (at least, from a landlord perspective). Truth be told, this was the last chapter I wrote, and in preparation for writing it, I interviewed mortgage brokers, credit reporting agencies, and other landlords in addition to reading books and reports on the subject of personal credit. All this preparation led me to the conclusion that understanding credit report analysis requires that basic terms are discussed beforehand. I will do my best to explain those. Please keep in mind that I am trying to cover only the basics. Complete books have been written to discuss the topic of credit. I advise you to read one of these books to better understand the world of credit and credit reporting.

What Constitutes a Credit Report

When lending institutions decide to grant or deny credit to someone, they look at a variety of things to help with the process, including the following:

- Character—defined as pay history with past creditors, in addition to residency and employment history
- Capacity—living expenses plus current debts and open credit limits
- Collateral—what the loan is secured with

The Credit Risk Score

These items are important for a lender to review, but proper in-depth reviewing could take days and since these lending institutions are making hundreds of credit gathering decisions a day, the task would be overwhelming. So most of these larger institutions will use a decision-making tool called the *credit risk score* to speed up the decision-making process. A credit risk score can best be described as a statistical summary of the information on your credit report at the time it is pulled and reviewed. The use of the credit risk score is considered faster, more accurate, and more objective than many other decision-making tools.

Because of the value of these scores, you need an understanding of how they are evaluated. A credit risk score is calculated by setting up a "model," which can be described as different numerical "weights" placed on different characteristics in a report. Generally, these characteristics fall into one of the following six categories, listed here in alphabetical order, not order of importance.

1. Application for credit—how recently and how often there's been an application for credit
2. Credit experience—length of time accounts are opened and used
3. Credit mixture—the different types of credit used
4. History of payment—how well the accounts are maintained
5. Total balances—the total amount of money currently owed
6. Utilization of credit—the amount of credit used in relation to the total amount available

Potential Credit Score Flaws

Different credit bureaus will place different emphasis on these characteristics, depending on what that company is developing the model for.

This leads us to one of the main problems with credit risk: scoring. A credit score designed for a specialty credit clientele such as the medical or insurance field would not be the same scoring as, say, the lenders use. So an acceptable score pulled for one purpose could be less valuable than if it was pulled for another purpose.

The Big Advantage

In spite of the main flaw of credit risk scores, they have one big advantage, which is that *they eliminate individual biases from the credit granting decision in an objective and precise manner, with generally accurate results.*

Although it is important to keep in mind that risk scores do not tell with *absolute* accuracy how someone will or will not react in a certain situation (in your case, paying rent), it *will* reflect how thousands of others with similar credit histories performed in the past, therefore giving you a *reasonable* idea of what to expect from your renter.

Your main concern as a landlord is to be aware of where that risk score came from. Or in the words of the credit industry, what model was used to develop the scoring. Let's say you have a friend who can pull scores for you, and you decide to use this service. You want to know if the risk score they are giving you profiles tenant rent

The credit score you really want is called a FICO credit score .This is the score most lenders use. For this reason, I would try to find a credit reporting agency that uses this score. Out of the big three credit reporting agencies (Experian, Trans Union, and Equifax), Equifax has a lock on providing the true FICO score to consumers. The other two agencies also offer a score, but they are different from Equifax. If you order your credit reports through Trans Union or Experian, you can get your FICO credit score at www.myFICO.com.

payments in any way because if your friend is pulling scores based on medical information, insurance information, credit cards, car loans, or even some home mortgage lending institutions, you could be receiving scores that will lead to an ill-informed decision, possibly giving you a tenant you don't need or losing a tenant you do want.

My advice when you pick your credit reporting agency is to discuss your concerns about the risk score they provide you. Ask if their score will do what you need it to do. If you aren't comfortable with their answer, look at other agencies. Understand that the more emphasis you personally place on this scoring, the more precise your scoring source needs to be.

Establishing a Credit Score

As mentioned previously, I run my credit checks through the National Association of Independent Landlords (NAIL). You can reach NAIL at 1-800-352-3395. They are geared only toward helping landlords achieve better results with tenants. When you receive a credit report from NAIL, you will receive a credit score. The higher the score, the lower the risk potential. Their scoring is as follows:

- 680 and up low risk
- 640–679 low to medium risk
- 600–639 medium risk
- 550–599 medium risk to high risk
- Below 550 high risk

This is the scoring NAIL uses. If you get your credit scores from another source, you will need to know how their scoring system works. As an example, your chosen credit bureau's medium-risk score could be 100 points higher or 50 points lower than what you think it is, depending on how their scoring model is set up. Theoretically, you could chose a score of 600 as your cut-off point between good and bad credit but because you may be using a determined cut-off score that doesn't fit the credit scoring of your reporting agency, you may accept or reject tenant prospects based on incorrect information. Do not assume one scoring system is the same for all credit bureaus. Learn their scoring before you set your scoring qualifications.

Of course, once you get a look at your applicant's risk score, you need to determine if it falls into the acceptable range as per the tenant qualification guidelines you previously established. If you don't use credit risk scoring in your qualifications, then simply continue to review the report to further analyze the applicant's credit.

What's in a Credit Report?

Now that we've covered some general knowledge of risk scores and other items credit granters consider, let's review what is typically covered in a credit report itself and how to analyze that information from a landlord's point of view. These items will be covered in the order they are most likely to appear on a credit report with examples used along the way where necessary:

- Personal information. This includes name, current and previous address (which with a little effort, can provide you with a former landlord for another phone call) telephone numbers, Social Security number, birth date, spouse's name, past and present employers, and so forth.

- Information from public records. This includes tax liens from state or county court, bankruptcy records, monetary judgments, garnishments, and sometimes overdue child support payments and evictions.

- Specific account information. As previously stated, each agency may not have all credit accounts listed, but what they do have will include the date opened and/or closed, credit limit or loan amounts, balances, monthly payments, and pay pattern or history.

- Recent inquiries. Record of those who have recently received your credit.

- Active disputes. Creditors may report disputes someone has challenged them with on a credit report until the dispute is resolved.

- Report summary. Overall review of the credit report contents.

Reading Credit Reports

Now that you are armed with the knowledge of what is on a credit report, let's talk about some specifics in each category.

Personal information

Since the personal information is pretty much a repeat of the data on your tenant application, you will most likely have very few concerns in this section unless there was a major difference in what was on the report and what you were told by the tenant prospect.

Name (& spouse):	Joe Renter (Jane)		
Res. Address:	123 S. Miller Ave. Miller IN		
Employment-Occ:	ABC Steel Works/ Furnace Supervisor		
Bus Address:	100 Main, Gary IN	Income	$ 22.65 hr.
Social Security No:	123-456-7890	Date of Birth	7/14/61
Married	Yes	Legal Records	Yes

Verify your rental/credit application against your credit report, including areas such as Social Security numbers, present and previous addresses, and employment. Use this credit report as a checking system for this information. On occasions, your report may give you a warning that the Social Security number or some other issue is inaccurate, needs more attention, or is somehow questionable. Should you ever have this problem, I suggest you call your reporting agency and discuss it with them. They can give you insight on how to follow up on the problem at hand. You also can ask your real estate attorney if the issue needs legal clarification.

Public records

Generally, following personal information are public records.

Serious delinquency and derogatory public record or collection filed
Bankruptcy—chapter 13

The first thing you wish to know is if your tenant applicant has any bankruptcies. If he or she does have a bankruptcy, find out how recent that bankruptcy was and if it falls into your qualification range. You also need to establish if that bankruptcy was a Chapter 7 or a Chapter 13. A Chapter 7 bankruptcy means that all monies due included in the filing of that bankruptcy are totally written off. They owe nothing on their debts. In a Chapter 13 bankruptcy, a percentage of the total dollar amount filed in the bankruptcy is being paid back to the creditors. As of this writing, the average percentage is around 50 percent (although with the change in bankruptcy laws, that almost certainly will be increasing). It stands to reason that when someone is still responsible for that bankruptcy payment, even a partial payment, you need to find out how much that payment is and for how long. Any money going out is an "expense" and should be treated as such on your Cash Flow form. Likewise, any other monetary judgments that are being paid are an area of concern to you because any money that leaves the hands of the tenant prospect is less money they have for their rent payment.

Keep your eye out for any reported evictions listed on a report and understand that many landlords "evict" by paying a tenant to move out of their rental, forgiving whatever debt the tenant owes them, and never going to court, and therefore, never filing a public judgment on the tenant. So, if you have an eviction listed on your report, you can probably lay odds the situation was a rough one. Think twice about accepting these evictions.

Be aware of any judgments or garnishments that look like they could be from a former landlord. The biggest warning sign here is if you have a high dollar amount (a few month's worth of rent) coupled with a name that has words like "management," "realty," "investment," "properties," or even "LLC" in them. Likewise, check out any personal names, property sounding names, or unrecognizable names. If need be, ask the reporting bureau on the tenant applicant what the name is. Also keep in mind that a collection from a former landlord falls under the topic of "landlord credit problems" on your Tenant Qualification form. If you don't accept this problem, you may not need to analyze this report any further. It's also worth noting that public record shows up on a credit report anywhere from 7 to 10 years, depending on what the record is. Generally, the older the record, the less problematic the issue is for you.

Account information

When you begin inspecting the section for account information, the confusion begins to set in. Remember that the account information is the meat of the credit report and it is this section where you will learn the most about your tenants' bill paying habits. With a little practice and patience, you will overcome this confusion and I promise the results will be worth it.

First, any accounts that are in collections will usually be listed before other accounts.

WHO	ACCT. #	STATUS	WHAT	OWED
Doctor Pay	#A1234-0	Collection	ER physician	$237
TV's Now	#A23-99L	Collection	TV	$1258

When I see a single item in collections, I first check the dollar amount and who it is with. Many times, your tenant prospects will have no clue that they have an item or so in collections, especially if the item in question is a small dollar amount or is related to the medical field. Sometimes a change of address or other error can cause bills to not arrive when or where they should, resulting in late pays on a tenant credit report. Often the medical industry sends billing statements to both the insured and the insurance company, resulting in confusion over who has paid it or not. If you believe your tenant applicants are unaware of the collection listed, ask them about it.

When you see multiple items in collection, you can pretty much be sure that your applicant is aware of the situation, at least to some degree. Based on your tenant qualifications, you may decide to end the review of the credit report. Or at the bare minimum, scrutinize what is in collection to establish if the debts are medical or simply bad consumer spending. The difference could help you decide the outcome of the credit report review.

After accounts in collection, you will see a list of the active and closed accounts. (Sometimes these are listed before accounts in collection.)

WHO	ACCT. #	STATUS	WHAT	OWED
Buy A Car	#1234567890	Active	Auto	$10987
Credit Card USA	#1212-ABC	Closed	Credit card	$0

We will look at these more in depth in a moment.

Account ratings. When it comes to reviewing these accounts, other information you will notice is what kind of accounts they are, which generally falls in one of these categories:

- Revolving (can charge as needed and pay minimum once a month as in credit card)
- Installment (fixed payment for a set number of months as in a car loan)
- Open accounts (one-time charge such as a doctor bill or open store credit like the neighborhood hardware store)

On the report, these categories will be represented by R, I, and O, respectively. For the most part, you will not be concerned when someone started the account. What you are concerned about is the payment history of such accounts. Many agencies use a number system, letter system, or combination of both to rate these accounts. Using the number system as an example, the numbers 1 to 9 are used to list the history of that individual account with 1 being the best rating and 9 being the worst. These ratings generally mean the following:

- 1—payment made on time
- 2—payment was 30 days late
- 3—payment was 60 days late
- 4—payment was 90 days late
- 5—payment was 120 days late
- 6—payment was 150 days late
- 7—payment was made under a debtor plan
- 8—repossession occurred
- 9—bad debt incurred

Generally, these rating numbers are listed with an R or I or whatever letter designates the type of account it is. For example,

- R1 means a revolving account (R) that is paid on time (1).
- I8 means an installment account (I) in repossession (8).
- O2 means an open account (O) 30 days late (2).

Most often, you will find these important numbers under a heading named *account status* or *historic status.*

When you review the tenant applicant's report, you want to see primarily 1s for account ratings, although depending on your guidelines, some 2s or occasional 3s might be acceptable.

At the other end of the spectrum, you might see a multitude of 7s, 8s, and 9s on many accounts, indicating accounts headed to or currently in bankruptcy. We will cover this issue in greater detail in a few moments.

Payment history. Another section you should pay attention to is the area with the following listing:

30   60   90

These numbers represent 30-day pay increments, and a number listed under this section will tell you how many times that particular account was paid late for those listed days. For instance, you may have the number 3 under the heading 30, which indicates the payment was 30 days late 3 times. Likewise, a 1 listed under the heading 60 means 1 payment was 60 days late.

30   60   90
3   1   0

Analyzing accounts. Taking the information we have just covered in the accounts section, let's look at a couple of sample accounts you might see. These accounts are taken from no one particular agency, but are patterned after some of the most common reporting systems I've seen. I am using these examples as a training tool, so if they don't resemble exactly what you are used to, don't panic. I will try to pull it all together for you at the end of the chapter.

Generally, accounts are listed in order of newest account being first, so an account opened 12/06 will be read before an account opened 12/02.

To begin with, one of the main problems with trying to read credit reports is that since everything is listed either in an abbreviation (example: opened = OPND) or code (example: revolving repossession = R8), these letters and numbers often seem to run into one another. This makes it difficult for the untrained reader to understand where new information begins and others end, all in all just adding to the difficulty of deciphering these reports.

For this reason, any credit report that is formatted in a "box" system is often by far the easiest report to read. The accounts' individual bits of information are contained in their own boxes and then attached to a corresponding larger box or subject. The first couple of examples are written in this format and we will put a lot of focus on them to better prepare you for the harder-to-read reports.

EXAMPLE 1:

ABC Credit Card 123-4567-890	OPND 01-04	LAST RPTD 07-06	Hi Bal 2,061	30 60 90 0 0 0	PAST DUE 0	BAL 1371
	LAST ACT 04-06	PYMT 128	HI CR 5,000	REVOLVING (R1) CHARGE		

In this first example, you will notice one long rectangular box with numerous smaller boxes inside of it. The whole larger box is all the information pertaining to the name contained at the left portion of the box. In this particular case, we have ABC Credit Card and the card's account number listed below that. (For consumer protection, these numbers are often rearranged or partially eliminated on the actual report.)

ABC Credit Card 123-4567-890

Moving to the right of the name, you will find six boxes total, set up in three columns of two.

OPND 01-04	LAST RPTD 07-06	Hi Bal 2,061
LAST ACT 04-06	PYMT 128	HI CR 5,000

If you have an understanding of the codes contained in the report, this information will tell you the basics of the ABC credit card account. For example, beginning on the left, we see this account was:

- Opened (OPND) on 01/04
- The last activity (LAST ACT) on the card, payment, or purchase was 04/06
- It was last reported (LAST RPTD) to this credit bureau on 07/06
- The monthly payment (PYMT) is $128
- The all-time high balance (HI BAL) ever on this card was $2,061
- And the card's credit limit (HI CR) is $5,000

Keep in mind when you read these reports that what you need to be able to do is pull only the information from this report that will help you make a good choice on the tenant applicant. Out of the six bits of information you've just reviewed, the ones you will be most interested in are last reported and payment.

First off, knowing the last reported activity of each account helps you to understand that there was activity on the account within the last 30 days. It could just be a payment, it could be a charge, or it could be both. I check the last reported column of every account to get an idea which are active and which are closed or inactive (although nowadays many reports will simply list the account status in the account information). This helps me understand what monthly payments are still the obligation of the tenant applicant. I also check the current payment so I can transfer that figure to the Cash Flow sheet, provided it isn't already accounted for when I analyze that particular form.

As far as high credit (HI CR) or high balance (HI BAL), I generally do not worry about these figures because to me, if the payments are being made regularly and on time, then I feel those figures are not that important.

Of course, I'm sure some readers are saying things like, "What if they have high balances and then lose their job?" or "With such high credit limits, they can go make some extreme purchase and then find they can't make the payments."

These are good observations, but keep in mind that you can't predict every situation or run from every possible problem that could happen but has not. The fact is, if they pay their payments every month on time and have a strong employment history, current balances and limits aren't as big an issue as those who have payment history problems.

In fact, that very topic is covered in the next section of the report: the pay history of that particular account. Continuing with the example, we see the following:

30	60	90	PAST DUE	BAL
0	0	0	0	1371

REVOLVING (R1)
CHARGE

Remember what I previously said about increments of 30 days being used to mark late pays? In this section, you see three areas: one for 30 days late, one for 60 days late, and one for 90 days late. In this particular example, you'll notice there are no numbers or marks listed under any of the day headings, indicating this particular account has never been delinquent.

Also notice under that information is another box that says revolving (R1) and the word "charge" under revolving. This tells us the account is a revolving charge account (as most credit cards are) and the account is rated at a (1) the highest rating achievable.

Next, you will see a column listed as past due. This will tell you the amount of money currently delinquent on the account, which is 0 on this particular credit card, as indicated by the lack of any numbers in the space provided.

Finally, we get to the last column, which is balance (BAL), representing the current outstanding balance. In this case, the amount is $1,371.

Let's analyze this tenant applicant's credit card account, which is from the first example. From the gathered information, we can tell the following:

- This person has never been late with even one payment on this card, thus earning him or her a perfect or high score in the rating (represented by the number 1 next to the R in R1).

- This person has never been overdue with a payment (PAST DUE=0).
- The current balance (BAL) is less than $1,400, which is almost $700 less than the highest amount ever owed on the card.
- This person also had a $5,000 credit limit, but only used about $2,100 of it at his or her peak usage.

This is an outstanding report for this particular credit card, and you would be lucky to see this for any tenant applicant. More than likely, you will see an occasional 30-day late pay, possibly coupled with a small past due amount. Generally, one or two of these items are acceptable if they are for a good reason, such as one payment lost in the mail or someone simply forgot to send in a payment on time. Things do happen, so don't be alarmed when you see an occasional occurrence. What should cause a raised eyebrow is the next example. This next bit is going to be tricky, so pay attention.

EXAMPLE 2, PART 1 (for training purposes, this report was pulled on 8-05):

Toys Unlimited ABC-0456	OPND 04-03	LAST RPTD 07-05	Hi Bal 4,112	30 60 90 6 3 1	PAST DUE 3,710	BAL 3,710
	LAST ACT 10-03	PYMT 273	HI CR 4,112	INSTALL I8 JOINT		

Let's look at the Toys Unlimited payment account, starting with LAST RPTD. As you can tell, the last reported date (LAST RPTD 7-05) corresponds with approximately 30 days of the date this report was issued (8-05), indicating it is still a current and active account. You'll also notice the payment (PYMT) is a manageable $273 per month. You can look at the payment history and see numbers under all three headings (30, 60, and 90 days), indicating there might be a problem with this account.

The "8" next to the word "INSTALL" tells you the item is in repossession (8 = repossession). Under the word "INSTALL" is the word "JOINT" (joint account), indicating there was more than one person responsible for this loan. This information tells me that this account is not a revolving credit card but probably a large single purchase shared with someone else. This account is also extremely behind in payment.

Let's examine further. Look at the past due and current balance, and you'll notice those two figures are one and the same—in this case, $3,710. This tells us that the payback time on this loan was relatively short (probably two to three years), and now the whole remainder of the balance is due in full.

Remember back when I said the opened and last active information were not that important? Well, when you run into credit problems like the one above, it will be time to examine the information filed under those boxes because they will give you some good insight about problem accounts, in this case, the Toys Unlimited account. Let's take a closer look: This person opened the account on 4-03 and made only six month's worth of payments. So, by 10-03, the account had no more activity. Consequently, by 7-05, just 20 months later, the account is still about 90 percent unpaid and in default.

Adding insult to injury, since the account was a joint account, you don't know who is supposed to keep up with the payments: the tenant applicant or his or her joint partner. If you ask your tenant applicant that very question, the answer will probably be, "my partner, wife, brother, and so forth," and you will have a hard time knowing the honest truth.

But let's come back to that topic in a moment, because right now, I want you to review the next creditor in example two, Furnishings-R-Us.

EXAMPLE 2, PART 2:

Furn-R-Us	OPND	LAST RPTD	Hi Bal	30 60 90	PAST DUE	BAL
000-111-233	11-98	10-02	7,230	8 3 1		0
	LAST ACT	PYMT	HI CR	INSTALL I9		
	3-00	212	8,000	IND		

For now, skip the basic information and go right to the payment history (30, 60, and 90 days) and account status (INSTALL I9) of this account, in which case you will notice there are again many late pays and an account rating of (9), indicating this account is currently in bankruptcy.

You'll also notice this is an individual account, as indicated by the abbreviation "IND"(individual) under the word "INSTALL." This indicates that the tenant applicant was solely responsible for this account. No one else is on the account.

Remember a few paragraphs back in the delinquent Toys Unlimited account where it was questioned whether the creditor was at fault for the nonpayments or if the problem was the result of the joint partner? By analyzing the second Furnishings-R-Us account, you can tell that this individual was solely responsible for these furniture payments and obviously failed in that obligation. Therefore, you can safely assume this tenant applicant was at least partly responsible for the failed first Toys Unlimited account.

Since it is obvious the tenant applicant had an earlier credit problem, you'd better go back and check out the "open," "last active," and "reported" boxes on this account.

By examining the account information contained within these boxes, you can conclude that after 17 months of payments (11–98 through 3–00 =17 months), this tenant applicant stopped paying on the Furnishings-R-Us account and approximately two and a half years after that last payment was made, this account stopped receiving reported activity. The fact that this account was last reported (10–02), which is almost three years before this credit report was run (7–05), makes it safe to assume this account was written off to bankruptcy.

> If you wish to be sure of this assumption, simply look at the past due and current balance boxes. If there is a 0 in these two areas, chances are this account was a charge off. Some reporting agencies even make it simple and write in the words "included in bankruptcy" or "charge off" in this section of their reports.

Using just the information you reviewed on these two accounts, let's build a credit profile on our tenant applicant.

The overall analysis of these accounts leads us to believe that the applicant had money or responsibility problems that led to bankruptcy of the first account (Furnishings-R-Us) and just a short time later, opened a new account (Toys Unlimited) with a partner (probably because he needed a cosigner), and then he didn't act responsibly with that creditor. This should lead you to the conclusion that this tenant applicant is a bad credit risk because he has a track record of not being accountable for his financial responsibilities.

I made up this example to try to help you not only read a credit report, but to realize that the information contained within credit reports can provide you with a very accurate profile of the tenant applicant's ability to handle money. Often, though, you will have to look in-depth at the stats, dates, and numbers so you can mentally follow the history of those numbers—actually travel the exact path of the bullet so to speak.

As you learn how to read credit reports with fine-tuned deductive reasoning, you will eventually be able to build a pretty solid profile on the way your applicant deals with money. It just takes time and practice.

Armed with the information you now have on reading reports, let me ask you a question: Do you think it is possible to see a good account such as example one coupled with bad reports like example two? Answer: Absolutely.

Generally, when you see this combination, what has happened is that the creditor had past financial problems and regrouped under a Chapter 7 or 13 bankruptcy. Then they began rebuilding their credit and may in fact be doing a superb job of maintaining a good payment history. Consequently, you may see part of a credit report where the last reported dates are a few years old and the accounts have 9s for a rating (often including the words "charge off"). Then the newer half of the report has current (within 30 days) last reported dates and is rated mostly 1s. A situation such as this could indicate a reformed creditor, or at best, someone trying to rebuild their credit. It does happen, and these prospects often work out to be solid tenants.

By now, I hope you have some confidence in your ability to read these credit reports. If so, let's look at one more example so I may further educate you on the art of credit report reviewing. To help keep you on the right path, we will use ABC Credit Card and the Toys Unlimited information and put it into a different format. Look at the example.

EXAMPLE 3:

| FIRM | | RPTD | LIMIT | HI CR | BAL $ | DLA | MR | 30 | 60 | 90 |
ACCT #		OPND	P DUE	TERM				24-Month History		
ABC Credit	R1	7-05	5,000	2,061	1,371	4/5	13	0	0	0
012345-6789		1-04	0	128						
Toys Unlim.	I8	7-05	4,112	4,112	3,710	10/3	25	2	3	2
ABC-0456		4-03	3,710	273						

This example is basically what you will see if you order your credit report through NAIL. You will notice items are still listed two to a column, but they are in different areas. You will also notice a couple of different headings. Let's quickly review them.

- Term. This is the monthly dollar amount to be paid on the loan. It could be a perpetual number as in a revolving credit account or a stagnant number like in an installment plan.
- DLA. The date of last activity.
- MR. The number of months this account was reviewed.
- 24-month history. Here is where the credit report may list a number, one for each month of review for that particular account over the last 24-month history. This history would list late days in 30-day increments, with 0 being on time, 1 being 30 days late, 2 being 60 days late, and so on. Activity might look like this: 000120010000123. (Often this is blank for whatever reason.)

Knowing this information is not that big of an issue for you because it just tells you which month out of a period of time they were late making their payment. You will be more concerned with how often they were late and the account's current status.

Looking back at example three, you can plainly see that all this information is "unboxed" and printed quite closely together. As previously stated, the newcomer to credit report reading will have a difficult time keeping this information separate. That is why learning the abbreviations and codes that correspond with the reports you receive are important in developing the skills to read those reports. The abbreviations covered in this chapter are probably all you'll need, although it is possible different abbreviations are substituted for each other on different reports. It is also quite possible on occasion to see a category I failed to cover.

Remember, if you have trouble decoding anything you feel is important on a credit report, call the bureau that issued it to you. They will probably be able to address your problem over the phone, or at the very least, send you information to educate you on how to read their reports.

Now that we are done analyzing the account information, let's cover the last few items you may find on a credit report.

Recent Inquiries

This area is used for listing anyone who has recently pulled a report on the tenant applicant. Some of these inquiries were initiated by the applicant, and others may be creditors looking at the possibility of extending unsolicited credit to the tenant applicant. All in all, as a landlord, you will probably never really use this section. About the only thing I do with this area is to give it a quick scan to see if this person has any inquiries from other landlords. Again, look for the words "management," "property," "investment," and so forth. Also watch for personal names and LLC titles. Recent inquiries such as these listed on your report could indicate that this particular tenant applicant has been recently turned down by other rental units in the recent past. If you run into this scenario, ask your applicant to explain these inquiries. In my entire landlording career, I've seen very few situations like this.

Active Disputes

Here you will find out if the tenant applicant is fighting any of the account information listed on their report. Sometimes incorrect or even other people's information ends up on someone else's account. When this happens, it is the responsibility of the person who owns the account to correct the mistake. Chances are, when you are first interviewing your tenant applicant and ask them about their credit, they will more than likely tell you if they have a dispute going on. After all, they are currently fighting the dispute, so it is foremost on their mind and they are fully aware it is affecting their credit and rating.

Report Summary

Some credit reports have a summary section and others do not. What a summary does is give a grand total of all things previously listed. Topics covered might include totals for: 30 days late, 60 days late, charge-offs, high balance, high credit, and so forth. Having these summaries is really handy, and I wish all credit bureaus included them. If yours does, consider yourself lucky, as these summaries will act as a checklist to help make sure you read the report correctly.

When you finish reviewing the credit summary, you probably have finished analyzing the report and should have a pretty good idea if your tenant applicant passes your predetermined credit qualifications.

Now that I've completed my explanation and examples of analyzing credit reports, I would like to inform you of some good news concerning the reading of these reports. In my examples, for training purposes, I used what I refer to as "older" formats. The old formats were originally designed to be read primarily by lending institutions and other professionals in the field. Even though you could receive reports in this format (that is the reason I used them as training tools), it is more likely you will review a newer "consumer friendly" version of a report. Recently, the government has stepped in and made it legally easier for a consumer to pull their own credit reports and review them. To abide by these new standards, most credit bureaus have changed their credit report format for the better.

If as a consumer, you order your own report, it will probably come from one of the big three (Equifax, Experian, and Trans Union). Therefore, I would like to give you a brief review of each so you know what to expect.

Equifax

Equifax does a pretty good job of laying out its reports. On the front page, the upper right-hand corner is dedicated to an easy-to-read confirmation number, in addition to all information needed to contact Equifax. The left side is reserved for the personal information the report is about.

The majority of the front page provides explanations for understanding account column titles and account history code descriptions.

Equifax uses a box-type format to list its information; the information is printed a bit close together, making it slightly harder to read then the other two. Equifax does not supply an overall summary report, but it does give a one-line summary of each account after the listed information.

Keep in mind that Equifax is the only one of the big three allowed to supply to consumers the true FICO score as used by lenders. Equifax also supplies NAIL with the information on their credit reports, although NAIL will deliver it to use in their own format along the lines of the third example in the previous account section.

Experian

The Experian credit report is easy to read and may even be the easiest of the big three to decipher. It uses the aforementioned box format, but Experian use more space, larger print, and different fonts to make reading a pleasure for the reader. The first page is laid out with the important information and is easy to locate. Experian does not give you a credit score, although it does list a phone number on the front page where you may order yourself a copy.

The one exceptional thing about Experian is the brochures and pamphlets it sends on request that are loaded with solid educational information about credit and how it applies to the consumer. It has pamphlets covering topics such as "new credit," "divorce and credit," and "home buying credit," in addition to the basic topics of credit risk scoring and credit fraud. I recommend anyone trying to better understand credit in any capacity to call Experian at 1-800-947-7990 and ask for more information.

Trans Union

About once a year, I review my credit reports from the big three, and Trans Union was always the most difficult to read. That has changed. Sometime in the last couple of years or so, Trans Union revamped its reports and they are now much more consumer friendly. Each account receives plenty of space for reported information with the account high-lights easily accessible at the top of that particular account report. Then Trans Union uses a box on the left to report the number of times an account was 30, 60, or 90 days late. To complete the account report, Trans Union will show you the monthly standing of that account for the last 48 months, again in an easy-to-read box format.

The other notable thing about receiving a Trans Union report is that it will give you a Trans Union Personal Credit Score and devote one page to its explanation and usage. The Trans Union score is generally higher than a FICO score by as much as 100 points or so, so be aware if you use this for your qualification. As I explained back in the chapter covering how to fill out credit reports, I'd advise calling each of the big three credit bureaus and ordering your personal report so you can see how each one is presented. While you're at it, ask them to send you anything they have on how to read their reports, in addition to any educational credit information they might have. For your convenience, I've included their contact information again here:

- TransUnion, PO Box 1000, Chester, PA 19022; 800-888-4213; www.transunion.com
- Experian, PO Box 9530, Allen, TX 75013; 888-397-3742; www.experion.com
- Equifax, PO Box 740241, Atlanta, GA 30374; 800-685-1111; www.equifax.com

Why You Need a Credit Report

All this newly acquired knowledge is great, but when all is said and done, you need to remember *why* you're so actively reviewing your tenant applicant's credit. In case it slipped your mind, I'll state the reason again: *The ability for your tenants to pay rent religiously and responsibly is the most important factor in the longevity of your landlording career.*

It is up to you to decide if they can live up to that ability. To reach that decision, you must verify that the information contained in the credit report is acceptable as per your Tenant Qualification guidelines, and if you are basing your pass or fail decision on a credit risk score, you must decide if their score is acceptable as per your preset requirements.

Should your credit decision be exempt from credit scoring, you will need to decide their creditworthiness based on the other decisions within the report. For example, does the bankruptcy fall within your guidelines? Are any accounts currently delinquent? Are the majority of the accounts rated with 1s with only one or two rated a 2 or 3? Will you accept lower ratings on accounts? Do you accept 8s or 9s on any active accounts?

Keep Learning

As you can probably tell with your newly acquired knowledge on credit report analyzing, it can be difficult to decide what is acceptable or unacceptable to you and your comfort level in this category. You might find it worthwhile to reread this chapter and then go back to your tenant qualifications chapter and double-check your stance on acceptable credit, adjusting your qualifications accordingly. Make this a regular practice as you get more familiar with the credit world workings and report reading.

You also may find it necessary to rethink your credit standards regularly as you adjust to the ever changing economic climate in your locale. There are times you may have to accept lower credit scores, possibly coupled with more security deposit. Maybe you'd rather not take bankruptcies, but now you must. To be successful at landlording, you will need to adapt to your surroundings quickly and logically. Just remember to be fair and nondiscriminatory in your changes.

In Closing

As I wrap up this chapter, let me give you a few extra tips in properly reviewing these reports:

- When you collect all the paperwork from the tenant applicant, immediately send off the credit application to get the reporting process underway. The sooner you send for the report, the quicker you'll receive it, giving you more time to analyze the report itself.
- When reviewing these reports, study one section thoroughly before proceeding to the next section.

- Spend extra time decoding and studying the account information. In fact, I advise reviewing this section more than once. Review it. Put it down and walk away. Then review it again. Do this as many times as it takes to understand the information contained within and to build what you believe to be an accurate profile of how the applicant handles money.
- Call your reporting credit bureau and get information on how to read their reports. Do this before you use their services, or at the very least, the first time you order a report from them.
- Read and reread this chapter if necessary. Also, go to the library or the bookstore to get yourself a book that will explain the credit world to you in greater detail.

As I close this chapter I need to tell you, if you reject a tenant applicant based on information from their credit report, you must by law give the applicant, in writing, the criteria for your decision and include the reporting agency's name, address, and phone number. You should also tell the applicant that they can obtain a free credit report within 60 days and dispute any inaccuracies.

Keep in mind that I am far from a credit expert and my explanations are based on my experience and opinion from a landlord perspective. If you feel you need further education on this topic, please research it as needed.

CHAPTER 15

Analyzing Employment Verification

Y ou're at your desk, you've sent off the credit check, you've talked to current and past landlords and three to five personal references per adult, as listed on their rental application. While you were on the phone, you tried to verify the applicant's employment information, but you were not successful. The employer's policy is to see a signed release with the employee signature before they will verify any employment information.

That's not a problem. You are a professional landlord using a professional system and you are prepared for this moment. Remember the Employment Verification form? You and the applicants each filled out a portion of this form when they filled out the rental application, just in case you needed it. Well, now you need it.

You also learned how to fill out this form in step three, chapter 10. But step four, the step you are now in, is dedicated to putting each form to use. Here is how I use the employment verification form to get the best results.

I call the applicant's place of employment and ask for the listed supervisor to verify the information I am seeking. If the supervisor will verify information on the phone, I gather this information as thoroughly and quickly as I can, using the questions previously listed in the chapter about analyzing the rental application. When the supervisor has finished the verification, I then ask if I can send an employment verification form for them to fill out and send back to me so I have some documentation in my files. I let them know that his or her employee has already signed the release and even though the supervisor has verified everything I need to know, by sending this form, the supervisor can also see that the employee is okay with the release of the information.

Often, an employer will warm up to this idea. When that happens, I send out the form and when it comes back, I have the best of both worlds. I had a one-on-one conversation with the supervisor and have another filled-out form for my files.

Should the employer policy be to *not verify* employment over the phone, ask for the correct name, phone, and fax number for the person who can verify the employment. Then follow this procedure: Immediately fax over the form and after waiting for a half-hour to an hour, call the supervisor you sent the form to and ask if he or she received the release form for such and such employee. I recommend doing this because once the supervisor has the form on his or her desk, there is a good chance you may get some constructive conversation out of that supervisor. This again gives you the best of both worlds because hopefully, you will get some of your questions answered and since you know that company requires a form to release information, you will also have a written verification for your file.

If the supervisor still refuses to talk to you, it is no big deal, as the Employment Verification form will tell you what you wish to know.

Once this form has been filled out and faxed back to you, double-check to see if what the supervisor states on the form is close to or the same as what the applicant claims. If there is a difference, use the supervisor's information as your base information unless the applicant has enough current pay stub clarification to prove the supervisor wrong.

Even if the tenant applicant brings me recent pay stubs to prove employment, I still call the employer and verify income as outlined in this chapter. Doing so offers me the possibility of another reference source for my evaluation process.

As a reminder, if there are three jobs contributing to the household income, you may have to do this procedure three times. So be it. Do whatever it takes to verify employment.

After verifying that the applicant makes enough money for your requirements, you need to know they have enough left to pay rent after paying their other bills. Proceed to what should be the last form for you to analyze. The Cash flow form is analyzed in the next chapter and from there, you should be ready to rent your dwelling.

CHAPTER 16

Analyzing the Cash Flow Statement

A s you may have noticed, every once in a while I like to make a reference to a particular movie or TV show that somehow connects me to my search for quality tenants. Well, I'm going to do it again.

Do you remember the movie *Jerry Maguire* and the football player Rod Tidwell (played by Cuba Gooding, Jr.)? Remember how he loved to say, "Show me the money"? It was his catchphrase. Did you notice that for months after this movie came out, those four words were repeated by anyone and everyone who saw it? This phrase quickly fell into everyday society for two reasons:

1. It's easy to remember.

2. Everybody feels this way at some point or another.

Even though this book is about finding a good quality tenant, the underlying truth is we want a good quality tenant because we want to be paid rent each and every month. In other words, just like Rod Tidwell, you as a landlord want your tenant to "show *you* the money!"

Analyzing the applicant's Cash Flow form is where you get to prove to yourself that the money is actually there for your tenant to pay rent with every month. Let's review.

Income

If you remember, the Cash Flow form is split into two sections: Income and expenses. We'll begin by totaling all the numbers in the income section.

STEP THREE

Cash Flow
(All figures monthly)

Name ___Joe /Jane Renter___ Date __8/5/07__

# of adults __2__   # of children __2__   # of pets __1__

INCOME

		Source	Amount
Job 1	Joe	mail Carrier	$ *3100* B.T
Job 2	June	clerk	$ 750 2 wk *1500*
Job 3			$
Gov't Assistance			$
Other Income			$
Misc. Income		1350 3 mo.	$ *450* mo.
		TOTAL	$ *5050* B.T

Before you add up all the income figures, you need to look for a couple of things.

Jobs

First, remember what AT and BT stand for—*after taxes* and *before taxes*. Should you have a before-tax figure next to any of your income figures, you need to make sure you've adjusted for these taxes by having a dollar amount listed on the tax line in the expense column. In other words, be absolutely positive that somewhere on the Cash Flow form you have accounted for income taxes either in the income or expense section. Failure to do so will severely alter the figure your prospect has left for rent—and it will be for the worse.

Also, any figures you have listed under job 1, 2, or 3 should be a monthly figure. If you have a weekly, yearly, or other such figure, be prepared to do the math to come up with a monthly number. This applies to any income figure that is not listed as monthly.

Next, you want all of your income figures put in the proper spaces. Most if not all of this section was probably filled out at the initial showing

242

and therefore should be completed by the time you sit down to review the figures. If during the conversation with employers and personal references you uncover information regarding income that requires you to adjust a figure, then do so, but for the most part, all your figures in the income section should be verified and complete.

All Other Income

Should you have figures listed in the income section that are not verified, call the applicant and ask to see documented proof of the figure in question. (This can be done at lease signing, if need be.) Generally, the figures in question will be alimony, child support, or some kind of government assistance check.

Watch the alimony and child support areas extremely closely. Many people should be collecting in these categories, but unfortunately, they do not. Even if someone does receive this payment on a regular basis, you may well be looking at a gray area when trying to verify it.

Figuring out a self-employed person's cash flow can be tricky because things like a change in seasons can affect their monthly income. For instance, a roofer may make great money seven or eight months out of the year, and a book author may receive a very large check periodically. Besides reviewing two years' worth of tax returns, it is also advisable to review three to six months' worth of bank statements to see if they consistently carry enough money to pay all their bills, not just rent.

For example, the person who claims to receive the alimony/child support check receives the check; he or she then proceeds to cash or deposit the check. That check then goes back to the person who gave the check; not to the person who received the check. What this means is that the proof of the check is in the hands of the ex-spouse—the one who is not renting from you, in this case. Under these circumstances, it could be difficult for someone to show proof that they regularly receive this money.

How does one handle this gray area? Well, if you remember, I explained that sometimes gray areas require a lot of common sense and instinct, so be prepared to rely on these God-given talents. Otherwise, you have a couple of choices to try to dig up proof.

First, maybe the exes are on speaking terms and the ex-spouse writing the check will provide proof of funds to you in regard to the person receiving the check. It is also possible that the funds are automatically deposited into the tenant prospect's account and show up on their bank statements. Last but not least, you can inquire about alimony and child support when you talk to personal references. Personal references are usually people close to your applicant, so chances are, if your applicant is supposed to receive money and isn't, at least one of the references is on the receiving end when your applicant has to blow off steam about not receiving the child support or alimony check.

How you approach this subject is, as you are asking questions to the reference, you mention the fact that you know Jane Renter is divorced and then you say something along the lines of: "Can you verify for me if Jane Renter receives her alimony/child support on time?" Or even better, "It is my understanding that Jane Renter receives X amount of dollars for child support payments. Is that correct?"

If this is true and the reference knows the answer to your question, they will probably verify it one way or another. Of course, sometimes none of the references know anything and this tactic is useless, but don't be afraid to use the references in times such as these. You will often be surprised by what you hear.

After all the income figures are adjusted to a monthly figure, add them up and record this figure in the appropriate space provided at the bottom of the page. This should represent what the applicant has for total cash flowing into his or her hands.

Expenses

Once the total income has been verified, it is time to add up all the monthly expenses. Just like the income figure needed to be adjusted up or down to a monthly figure, so too, should the expense figures be monthly figures.

STEP THREE

Cash Flow

(All figures monthly)

EXPENSES

(Joe)

Taxes	$ 750
All vehicle payments	$ 494
All credit card payments	$ 25
All other loan payments (student loan, boat, personal, etc.)	$ 0
Judgments/garnishments	$ 0
Alimony/child support/other dependent	$ 210
All telephone bills	$ 100
Gas/electric area average	$ 200
Sewer/water area average	$ 50
Garbage area average	$ 30

EXPENSES (continued)

Cable TV area average	$ 60
All food/dining in & out	$ 600
Health care/prescriptions	$ 50
Auto expenses	$ 200
Day care	$ 0
All entertainment/hobbies (movies, vacations)	$ 100
Pet care (vet & food)	$ 50.
All miscellaneous (clothes, toys, holidays, mad $)	$ 300
TOTAL	$ 3219

INCOME $ 5050 - EXPENSES $ 3219 = $ 1831 Available for Rent

245

Taxes

As already mentioned in this chapter and a previous one, you must account for income taxes. The first line in the income section is where you will do this if and *only* if you have not already accounted for this tax.

At this point in the analyzing process, you should have already dealt with income taxes. If you need a review on completing this line, refer back to chapter 11 in step three.

Car and Credit Card Payments

Next, if you run a credit report, the car payment and credit card payments should be listed on that report, as should judgments and garnishments (unless it is a very recent filing). You have to verify that the figures from the credit agencies are the same as the figures recorded by the applicant, and if they are not the same, record and use the figure that is higher. As you analyze the Cash Flow form remember that it is better to be safe than sorry.

All Telephone Bills

One of the questions you may have asked your applicant is what their total phone bills were each month. If you failed to ask that question and need to figure out an answer, just remember that verifying telephone bills is a little harder. When the applicant filled out the paperwork at the dwelling, one of the first things he or she did was list all phone numbers, so look back at the application and see how many personal phone numbers he or she gave you. This will tell you how to go about averaging a figure for a phone bill. Also keep in mind that some people ring up astronomical cell phone bills, and if they are not paying these bills in a timely manner, this could be revealed on their credit report, so be alert.

Gas/Electric/Sewer/Water/Cable

After the telephone figures, you come to four categories that you are responsible for knowing as the landlord. If you haven't already figured out an area average for these categories, do so now. It is in your best interest to know the average costs of these items. Please realize that if you overestimate each category by $20 per item or $80 total, you may eliminate an otherwise good prospect, based on false estimated figures. Likewise, underestimating these figures could allow a prospect to rent your rental unit who really doesn't qualify. Knowing these figures will make your life easier in the future and will be fair to your applicant now.

Up to this point, almost all figures are relatively easy to verify or guesstimate. Unfortunately, verifying the next few categories will be much harder. In fact, you probably used a mixture of common sense, applicant accuracy and honesty, and previous landlording experiences regarding these expenses when you first tried to establish figures in these categories. Since these figures are often guesstimated by you when you filled out this form, be aware of any numbers that you feel you may have blundered on and be prepared to change accordingly.

Remaining Categories

The figures for "All food," "Tenant paid health care/prescriptions," "Daycare," "Entertainment & Hobbies," and "Pet care" were covered in great detail in the previous section, including the many things that could influence those figures. There is no need to run through these again, but there are some points worth mentioning.

First, when you are at this point in the analyzing process, you are almost done evaluating your tenant applicant. If you have not eliminated the applicant at this point, I pretty much guarantee you've found your next tenant. I'm also confident at this point that you do not want this form to stop the process because of inaccurate, untrue figures, so your guesstimates need to be as on target as possible.

What I suggest is to use the figures the applicant gave you on the Cash Flow form *unless*:

- You discover the applicant is underestimating every category for which he or she gave figures.
- You get a sense that the applicant doesn't have a real grasp on the cost of living, such as a divorcing couple where one spouse paid all the bills in the household, therefore leaving the other spouse in the dark about the couple's finances. If the spouse who didn't pay the bills is applying to be your tenant, he or she may not realize how much money goes to pay what bill.
- You know a figure is just too low.

In these cases, adjust any figures you need to. Just be fair to your applicant as well as yourself.

Caution

If *you* estimate a cash flow category based on your expenses and you are a big spender in that category, you must realize that this is a personal trait of yours and do not assume everyone has to spend like you do in that category. People can survive quite nicely in many categories on a small budget. Be fair.

The last category you will not be able to verify so don't even try is the miscellaneous category. As I've said earlier, there are just too many things that can impact this category. Your best bet is to figure out one per-person average and use that unless you get a sound, reasonable figure from the applicant. You might even have two figures, one for adults and one for kids. My suggestion is maybe $100 average per adult and $50 average per child or $75 average per person. These average figures could be drastically lower, depending on your clientele and the economics of the area your rental is in. Be careful not to overstate this category since it could kill otherwise good prospects.

It is also important to remember that whatever averages you choose for this category will need to be adjusted periodically, especially in years of high inflation. Failure to adjust figures every year or so will result in figures that are too low and could possibly throw off your calculations.

After all the expense categories are filled in and verified to the best of your ability, add up the expenses. Record your total in the appropriate spot at the bottom of the page. Now subtract your expenses from your income and hopefully the remaining figure is more than enough to cover rent. If it is enough to cover rent, you have your tenant.

If roommates apply and each will be paying part of the rent, the combined total from each of their Cash Flow forms must add up to be enough to cover rent. Should the figure be short of the amount of rent, don't rule out the applicant yet. You will notice at the bottom of the Cash Flow form that there is a statement that says *"Since some category figures are based on landlord opinions and assumptions, 10 percent of the rent amount can be added to the applicant's total rent money. This can only be applied if applicant passes credit and employment qualifications."*

This means if you are asking $800 rent for your unit, you can add 10 percent of $800 or $80 onto the figure you show as the applicant's money available for rent. If your tenant only has $753 for rent and using the exception, you can tack on $80, then the applicant now has $833 for rent. I suggest you use this rule only if the applicant has good employment history and at the current time has no back debt or credit problem.

If you choose not to use this exception because it makes you uncomfortable, then just put a large N/A through the exception and leave it at that.

Financial Windfalls

On occasions, you will run into this scenario: The applicant doesn't have enough cash flowing into his or her hands on a monthly basis. What he or she does have is a healthy bank account or good pool of money stashed somewhere, and this person is planning on paying rent out of this pool. This does happen. People win lawsuits, hit jackpots of large sums of money, or sell a business. Instead of buying a place to live right away, they wish to rent and see what their next move is going to be. It is okay to rent to this applicant provided you see concrete proof of this money. It could be an approved letter from a bank source with the correct letterhead, names, and phone numbers on it. It could be an actual copy of bank statements. Whatever it is, make sure that proof is current, titled to the applicant, and legit in funds.

The proof must be solid and easy to verify. Don't accept the *promise* of a payoff of a lawsuit or inheritance. Don't count the money unless the applicant has the money at application time.

With this being the end of the chapter, let me add a personal story about knowing how a person's cash flows.

In Closing

As I wrote this chapter, it was mid-December. My wife is part of a church group that fields and assists calls for people needing financial help with rent, food, or utilities throughout the year. How it works is that each member of the group is on a rotation where one answers and handles callers one week and then someone else covers the phones the next week.

Sometimes, a call comes late in the first week where the original person who handled it turns it over to whoever is responsible the next week.

This was the case with my wife. She had to finish a call that was started the week prior. It seems the caller had just moved into a new rental house and her *first* month's rent, December, wasn't paid and she was looking for assistance. While the group member who originally took the call was interviewing this woman in need, she realized it was the tenant they had just put into their own rental house! She told my wife they wouldn't kick her out at Christmastime but would have to start eviction after the New Year.

Basically, this landlord fixed up a house, rented it for December 1, which she was going to get only part of if any, and obviously would lose January's rent as she evicted her tenant. This would probably leave her with some cleaning and painting along with eviction fees, advertising fees, and heating the house so the pipes don't freeze and on top of that, who knows if she could even rent the house in February, since northwest Indiana has a lot of cold and snow during that period.

I tell you this story because this was a real situation for a real landlord at Christmastime. It does happen. If this person had properly interviewed and analyzed the tenant and had used some type of Cash Flow form, she would have known there would be no money for rent.

Don't be like the landlord whose story I just shared with you. Instead, analyze the tenant applicant's cash flow so that when you say, "Show me the money," you will actually be receiving the money. And isn't that really what landlording is all about?

CHAPTER 17

The Checklist—Part Two

I n this brief chapter, I am introducing the second part of the ongoing checklist that I advise using during tenant selection. Successful completion of part two of the checklist means you have your quality tenant and are ready to rent to them.

The Checklist—Step 4

STEP 4

1) ____ Check rental history
2) ____ Check employment history
3) ____ Check personal references
4) ____ Check credit
5) ____ Check cashflow
6) ____ Check bank account verification
7) ____ Run criminal background check

Let's take a quick look at part two of the checklist and of course, remember that a few simple rules apply to this part of the checklist just like they did in part one.

- Do not move onto the next step in the rental process until you complete this portion of the checklist.
- Apply a checkmark or your initials if the corresponding items check out okay, and an N/A if it doesn't apply.
- Use the (-) to delineate that you need more follow up work on that item.

Listed below are the items to be checked over in part two of the checklist.

1. Check rental history
2. Check employment history
3. Check personal references
4. Check credit
5. Check cash flow
6. Check bank account verification
7. Run criminal background check

Analyzing the first six checkpoints has been thoroughly discussed in previous chapters so there is not a lot left for me to cover concerning these areas except use your checklist to verify and double-check that you have completed analyzing these items. These six checkpoints are the primary areas you'll want to know about, because it is this combination of areas that will prove to you your tenant applicant is worthy and capable of renting your dwelling. At the bare minimum, you'll wish to put a check mark in these six categories.

The last checkpoint for step four in the processing step is one that's seldom used at this time. I've included it because I hope once you've read this book, you will put it on your shelf to use for future reference. Since I wanted to make this book the best source of information I could in regard to finding that quality tenant, I've tried to look into the future and give an opinion on what could be problem areas that landlords might have to deal with.

Running Criminal Background Checks

Checkpoint number 7 deals with checking a prospective tenant's criminal history.

As our prisons continue to fill and the taxes we collect to run those prisons dwindle, you will see more offenders back on the street. Many of the offenders will have a history in acts of violence, theft, and sexual assault, among other violations of the law. If you are using my system and forms correctly, you will have a very good chance of filtering out newly released offenders. You will discover these situations because newly released offenders will have "holes" in their important information. "Holes" refer to a period of unaccountable time in the applicant's history, such as lack of a job, housing, or credit activity. Generally, holes in the rental history will probably be covered up by lying on behalf of good intentioned friends and relatives. The work hole and lack of credit, however, will be harder to pad, and therefore, hopefully easier to uncover.

Any kind of large hole in work history should cause you to investigate the applicant's situation deeper. This hole doesn't necessarily mean the applicant did any jail time. They very likely could have been injured, down on their luck, or just plain lazy, but a large hole in the work history could be a red flag for criminal activity.

Should you run into a work history hole, ask to see proof verifying that period of time. For instance, get doctor and insurance information if that hole was injury related or unemployment benefit proof if they were out of work.

The reason I'm introducing the thought of criminal background checks is you might one day realize you are receiving too many calls from people who have too many holes in their life stories. I just want you to know that criminal background checks are available and easy to use, if needed.

Megan's Law

Since I'm speaking about background checks, I should also mention a law, which was passed in 1996. It is called Megan's Law, named after seven-year-old Megan Kanka, who was brutally raped and murdered in 1994. The passing of this law allows the public access to the names of child sexual predators and where they live in a given community. It is a worthwhile law and even though as a landlord you may never use it, I believe you should educate yourself about this law and watch for changes that might affect how you landlord in the future.

Disclaimer

At this time, I wish to say it is not my intention in this book to judge our laws, or penal system, or to pass judgment on anyone who has served their time.

253

It *is* my intention to educate anyone willing to read and study the system and material I provide to help you find the best tenant possible for your rental unit. I will try to achieve this by showing you what tools and information are available and pass on any knowledge I've gained through my hands-on experience.

In Conclusion

If you have every category on the checklist accounted for in step three (paperwork) and step four (process), you should have a highly qualified tenant. Let's move ahead to the next step and start to profit from that real estate investment.

Step Five: Payoff

S tep five is the final step in the tenant selection process. It is the icing on the cake or where we "reap our rewards," so to speak. It is the payoff step. Here you sign your rental unit over to your new tenant and hopefully receive monthly rent on time with very few problems for years to come. The payoff step is what makes landlording lucrative and worthwhile.

CHAPTER 18

Rules and Regulations

Congratulations! Once you've completed step four (processing) of the tenant selection system, you will have found a tenant who should satisfy the tenant qualifications you have established. The first four steps in the tenant selection system all lead to this fifth and final step, and without each of those steps, the fifth might not ever happen. Before we examine this final step, let me remind you of those first four steps:

1. Prepare
2. Prequalify
3. Paperwork
4. Process

Because of the proper application of each of these four steps, the fifth step should be the easiest and absolutely the best step of the process. That step is titled *payoff!* Actually, it is not so much a step as it is a reaping of rewards, per se. The payoff is relatively easy because it only requires reviewing and signing all the appropriate paperwork, collecting of necessary monies, and turning over the keys to the new tenants.

Call the Tenant

The first thing you will need to do to begin the payoff process is call your tenant applicants and let them know they are no longer an applicant but will now be regarded as tenants. In simple terms, *they made it!* After they calm down from their excitement about being selected, you will want to make an appointment with them so step five can be completed in its entirety. Here are a few tips to keep in mind when you set up your appointment:

- Try to pick a convenient time so all parties signing the lease can be present for the paperwork and transferring of keys. You don't want to do this step more than once.

- Allow enough time to do all needed items thoroughly. One to one-and-a-half hours should be sufficient.

- Have the tenants bring any information or proof of items you may not have verified yet. This can include meeting all family pets.

- If you request that utilities are transferred to the tenants' name before lease signing (a good idea), let them know at this time and give out the utilities phone numbers if you have them.

- Before you meet, explain to the tenants how you wish to collect your beginning rent, security deposit, and other monies. Let them know if you want cash, check, or cashier's check. Be prepared to give a receipt for any cash collected.

- Just like I recommended in step three, I suggest keeping a file in your briefcase labeled "step five" or something to that effect. Inside of it, keep copies of the forms you'll need when you review and sign all the paperwork.

The Rules and Regulations

Day of Reckoning

Once the big key-exchanging day arrives, you will explain the procedures, rules, regulations, and all information that will make co-

If it will be some time before the tenant signs the lease, get a substantial nonrefundable holding deposit for the rental. You do not want to wait for them to sign a lease without such a deposit, because should your tenant applicant back out at the last minute, you will be stuck with the costs of holding the empty unit.

existing with your tenants easier and more professional. The first item I recommend reviewing is your Rules and Regulations sheet.

Besides your lease, your rules and regulations are the best way to keep things under control in your rental unit. These rules and regulations instruct a tenant about how to best live in harmony with you as well as with their neighbors for the time they occupy the dwelling. I suggest you review all rules and regulations with your new tenants before you sign the lease or hand over the keys to the rental. You want to make sure they can abide by your rules before they take possession.

Begin this session with two copies of the Rules and Regulations. Give the new tenants a copy of your house rules. You can use a copy of mine if you do not have any already written down. Simply obtain a copy off our website at www.FindThatQualityTenant.com. They can read from their copy as you go over the details from your copy. Cover each topic individually, answering any questions as they pop up. Once all the rules and regulations have been thoroughly reviewed, have your new tenant read the closing statement on the form and if they agree, have them sign the line at the bottom of the last page. That closing statement reads as follows: *I have read and had the house rules and regulations explained to me in their entirety and agree to abide by those set rules. I also have been shown how to use and maintain both the fire extinguisher and smoke alarms and will check them monthly.*

Not only will you want them to sign and date the last page, but make sure their initials are on every rules and regulations page in the space provided. Once every page is signed and dated, you will keep the signed copy for your file. Leave the unsigned copy so the tenants will have easy reference to the rules, should they need them.

Rule Basics

The procedure of reviewing rules and regulations is simple enough, but it would help if you knew what criteria go into worthwhile landlord rules. Generally, rules and regulations can be made up by you, your lawyer, or a collaboration of the two. They are to be tailored to your specific landlording requests and desires, and/or to the property or unit being rented. Allow me to give you a few words of caution as you establish these rules: Don't make them so strict that nobody can live within your specified policies. Ruling with an iron fist will just cause a lot of tenant turnover and undue frustration for you. You want your tenants to respect your rental and the neighbors of that unit, but being too strict will stress you out as badly as not being strict enough. And it goes without saying—don't write rules and regulations that discriminate.

Rules Explanation

To help you compile your rules and regulations, I will give you a list of things to consider and some brief thoughts on each area.

Alterations

This refers to actual changes to the premises. It could cover hanging a ceiling fan to enclosing a porch and all points in between. Generally, when something is altered in a rental, the alteration stays with the unit unless it's removable and the rental can easily be put back to its original condition. A ceiling fan a tenant hung could easily be removed and the original light hung back up upon the tenant's departure. Built-in bookshelves, on the other hand, would probably have to stay since their removal would leave holes in the wall.

The biggest problem with alterations (besides the fact that people sneak them in), is that you do not know the quality of someone's work. I've seen plenty of alterations and most have struck me as below par. Alterations such as these leave you with problems you will eventually have to correct; some could even jeopardize the safety or integrity of your property. Unfortunately, more often than not, you will discover an alteration after the tenant has already performed it. And more often that not, it is an alteration of which you would not have approved. My advice is to realize this will happen and react appropriately. A poorly wired ceiling fan can burn down your investment, whereas removing an added bookshelf can probably be done in minutes.

Fortunately, most leases already have a clause covering this topic and a good majority of tenants simply refuse to spend too much time on an alteration project in a place they do not own.

Appliances

Sometimes you will supply the appliances and sometimes the tenant will. When you supply the appliances, you want them left as clean as when you first rented the dwelling. You also want them to be in the same working order (except for normal wear and tear) they were in when the tenant moved in. When tenants bring in their own appliances, you want to make sure they do not damage the premises as they move the appliances in or out (broken trim or ripped flooring, etc.). Be sure the tenant makes all appliance connections correctly and tightly. Gas connections need Teflon tape on the thread ends and water connections need a rubber washer.

Disposal of Environmental Waste

It is tough to find someone who takes used paint, oil, gas, or other such products (tires) and disposes of them properly. If you get left with these, you most likely will pay to get rid of these types of items.

Fire Extinguishers

I believe landlords should supply a good ABC rated fire extinguisher in every rental they own in addition to an extinguisher in a common area of multi-units, even if not required by law. The ABC rated extinguishers can put out the largest array of fires and a decent-sized unit costs between $30 to $40 at a home improvement store. I also recommend you show the tenants how to use a fire extinguisher when you go over the lease. It would also be worth your while to stop at the local fire station and get any brochures you can hand out on fire safety so you can further educate your tenants.

Furnaces and Filters

The cheaper filters in furnaces should be changed monthly for optimal performance. I recommend you supply tenants with six months worth of these filters in cold weather and have them change them when they send their rent check.

Garages, Sheds, and Basements

These can be nice amenities when renting out a unit, but can turn into a huge problem when the tenant moves out. The main reason is that these areas have the potential to be huge collectors of stuff: often heavy, bulky, hard-to-dispose-of stuff. It is not uncommon to use a dumpster or take multiple pickup truckloads to the dump to clean out these areas. Either of these solutions to a left-behind-stuff problem is time-consuming and costly. Also, it is not uncommon for items left behind to also be environmental garbage, which compounds the problem.

Garbage

You definitely want all trash and garbage to be handled correctly and disposed of quickly. Bags of accumulated garbage tend to breed roaches and other undesirable pests in addition to smelling up the surrounding areas. Make sure garbage gets handled properly.

Guests

At some point in the tenant's stay, he or she will probably have an overnight guest or two. The thing about guests is if they stay too long, they turn into tenants. Then, of course, you have more people than you bargained for living in the dwelling. Another thing to watch for is any damage a tenant's guest does, which is the responsibility of the tenant. Be aware that some guests bring their pets when they visit. If you don't allow pets, watch for this issue with guests.

Landscaping and Yard Maintenance

In a single-family dwelling, landscaping is generally the responsibility of the tenant. Multi-units are usually handled by the management. When a tenant is responsible you want to make sure yard maintenance is done year-round. That means leaves are raked and grass is mowed, even if the tenant is moving out: *especially* if the tenant is moving out, because I've noticed a tenant who is moving in the near future often will not rake leaves, shovel snow, or take care of a yard. This type of situation means you could be doing two months of yard work as you prep for the next tenant.

Locks

Locks should be changed when a new tenant takes over a rental or when a written request is made. This can be a delicate situation, so if confronted with this scenario you should probably talk to your real estate attorney to find out the proper procedure. You will also want to come up with a solution for people who lock themselves out of a residence. Charging them each time you have to come out and unlock a door usually solves the habitual lockout.

Noise

Here you want to regulate the standards for noise. Of course, multi-units might have tighter rules than single-family homes. The problems in this area generally will be loud televisions and stereos, loud mufflers, or other ruckuses. Time limits can be set for when noise will not be tolerated, generally before 9:00 A.M. and after 10:00 P.M.

Notice to Vacate

This is usually covered by the lease, but you may want to state how many days' notice you require before the tenant vacates.

Painting

I buy foreclosed properties all the time and the one recurring theme I notice in these houses is that people generally can't paint. I can safely say that about 75 percent of people, when painting a property themselves, will almost certainly hit the wood trim with paint and splatter paint on nonpainted surfaces. Often, they don't pull off the masking tape on trim work if they used masking tape at all. These habits cause irreversible damage to the premises. If you want to keep your property looking good, I recommend *never* allowing tenants to paint.

Parking

Here you want to regulate the maximum number of cars per tenant, where they can or cannot park, and how unlicensed or improperly parked vehicles will be handled, etc.

Parties Responsibility

The tenant is responsible for the rental's condition with the exception of normal wear and tear. You'll need to establish how this will be decided and when.

Patios, Decks, Walks, and Driveways

Tenants in single-family homes are responsible for their own snow removal and trash pickup. You need to make them aware of the importance of safety in keeping theses areas well lit and free from hazardous clutter.

Pest Control

This directly ties in with the garbage rules, but you want everyone to know that pest control begins in the residence. If tenants leave dirty dishes and scraps of food lying around, they could have pest-related problems. The cost of pest control is expensive, so you might want this cost to be paid for by the tenant, especially if you are renting a single-family residence and therefore can easily prove the tenants are the cause of the problem.

Pets

Pets should be covered in the lease, but you might want to put extra rules in effect to ensure proper cleanup of pet duty, noise regulations, and the normal responsibility of pet ownership. (This issue is covered in more detail in an upcoming chapter.)

Repairs

If this item is not covered in the lease, you'll want to establish guidelines on how to handle repair calls in a timely manner. You'll also want to state that a small problem that turns into a big problem because the tenant failed to report it could be the financial responsibility of the tenant.

Renter's Insurance

Explain that your property is covered for damage but the tenant's personal items are not covered if a catastrophe should strike. They need to know in such cases, a fire or flood would ruin all their personal items with no chance of reimbursement, unless they were insured. In addition, all tenants in multi-units would be wise to carry renter's insurance. You never know when one tenant's negligence could cause damage to another tenant's property. In those instances, the building's insurance probably would not cover the damage, leaving the offending tenant financially responsible. A flood from an overflowing tub, or an unattended candle that turns everything into ashes are just two examples.

Sewer Drain/Toilet Clogs

Generally, the landlord is responsible for sewer backups that are the fault of the building or tree roots, and so forth, and the tenant is responsible if the clog is hair, grease, kids' toys, women's hygiene products, and so forth. Tenants must be taught to use care in what goes down drains and toilets, and it is your job as landlord to educate them.

Smoke Detectors

Smoke detectors are an important safety item that many tenants (and landlords) overlook. Establish rules for how often to check the smoke detectors and how often to change the batteries.

Snow Removal

This should cover all areas of the patio, deck, walks, and driveway. Somewhere, you'll want to designate who takes care of snow and when (as in minimum amount of snow and timeline it has to be cleaned by).

Waterbeds

Even though waterbed technology and craftsmanship have greatly improved over the years, waterbeds *do* leak and can cause quite a bit of damage when it happens. Also, waterbeds take up hundreds of gallons of water and with each gallon weighing 8-plus pounds, they can be a huge strain on floor joists, especially in older structures. Because of these potential problems, you may want to give permission for a waterbed in your rental unit only if they have proof of insurance to cover the damages a waterbed could cause. The topic of waterbeds is an area you may wish to discuss during the phone interview.

Window breakage

Generally, owners are responsible for breakage caused by natural causes, whereas tenants are responsible for any other source of the breakage, including kids in the neighborhood or the tenant's guests.

Vehicles

Many tenants will have one or two licensed vehicles in their name. These vehicles need to be in good running order. They need to be licensed and insured at all times. Also be aware of backyard mechanics who may have nonrunning cars and an accumulation of parts lying around the premises, especially on multi-unit properties. Often, tenants will leave the premises and any nonrunning vehicles are left behind. Usually, these tenants will not give you a title, which means you will almost always need to have these vehicles removed. The only exception you might make to these rules is a collector car they have. Even though a collector vehicle might be unlicensed, it should still be running.

That completes the explanation of some of the different subjects you may want to cover in your rules and regulations. You can pick and choose what you want to use, but I would advise giving tenants some rules as guidelines to live by while they rent from you. Please remember to make the rules appropriate for the clientele you are renting to. Lower-income tenants in a multi-unit would probably have fewer rules than, say, a tenant renting a penthouse apartment.

Overall, quality tenants actually expect and appreciate good guidelines, because good rules let the tenant know you are a professional landlord. These tenants like to know where they stand at all times, what boundaries they have on the important issues, and how things work under your watchful eye. Look these rules and regulations over, and if you like what you see, use them as they are. Should you find something you dislike or that does not apply to your situation, simply cross out that specific rule. Likewise, feel free to alter a rule if you need to. Just cross out the part that doesn't fit and write in what you need. You might want to date and initial your changes just for the sake of a paper trail.

Finally, keep this thought in mind: For whatever reason, tenants are more apt to break a rule than a lease, so you may wish to write those rules you really want to enforce as part of your lease. And it goes without saying that you could list a rule both on the rule sheet *and* in the lease.

As stated earlier, I've included a copy of my rules and regulations on our website at www.FindThatQualityTenant.com.

CHAPTER 19

The Lead-Based Paint Disclosure

T his chapter covers an issue and its corresponding form which may or may not apply to you as a landlord. Whether this topic does pertain to you or not, I would read this chapter so you have some knowledge of lead-based paint.

Lead Paint Pamphlet

I've had many tenants over the years, and any-time I show the mandated government lead paint booklet to them, almost everyone says they have never seen it. Maybe these people rented dwellings built after 1977, so there was no need for this pamphlet. Or maybe the landlords didn't know it was their duty to hand out this information. Whatever the case, I want you to understand this law from a landlord's perspective.

Lead-Based Paint Act

In 1992, the Residential Lead-Based Paint Hazard Reduction Act was passed, also known as Title X. At the time, it was discovered that 1.7 million children had high levels of lead in their blood. To help bring up public awareness and hopefully lower that number, the government passed Title X, which calls for full disclosure regarding lead-based paint on all houses built before 1978.

Why 1978? Because in 1978, the Consumer Product Safety Commission (CPSC) banned the use of lead-based paint for residential use. Houses built after 1977 should not have had lead-based paint used in their construction.

How the Law Affects You

In a nutshell, the way Title X affects you, the landlord, is this:

Before ratification of a sale or *lease*:

a) Sellers and *landlords* must disclose known lead-based paint and lead-based hazard and provide available reports to buyers and renters.

   The government has provided an easy-to-use disclosure form that we will cover, and you should make it part of your lease package if your rental was built before 1978.

b) Sellers and *landlords* must give buyers and renters the pamphlet, developed by the EPA, HUD, and CPSC titled "Protect Your Family From Lead in Your Home."

   This pamphlet is available for sale in bulk (50 copies) from the government or you may reproduce copies of the pamphlet to give out as long as you produce and give out the pamphlet in its entirety.

c) Sales and *leasing* agreements must include certain notification and disclosure language.

d) Sellers, *landlords,* and real estate agents share responsibility for ensuring compliance.

If you are renting to own, you need to beware of one other requirement that applies:

e) Home buyers will get a 10-day period to conduct a lead-based paint inspection or risk assessment at their own expense. The rule gives the two parties flexibility to negotiate key terms of the evaluation.

This disclosure also lists a couple of things not required. They are:

1) This rule does not require any testing or removal of lead-based paint by sellers or landlords.

2) This rule does not invalidate leasing and sales contracts.

Most private housing and public housing are affected by this law. This includes federally owned housing and any housing receiving federal assistance. There are some exceptions to the ruling. They are:

1) Housing built after 1977.

2) Zero bedroom units such as efficiencies, lofts, and dormitories.

3) Leases for less than 100 days.

4) Housing for the elderly (unless children live there).

5) Housing for the handicapped (unless children live there).

6) Rental housing that has been inspected by a certified inspector and found to be free of lead-based paint.

7) Foreclosure sales.

The lead-based paint ruling is a federal ruling and since some states already have lead-based paint regulations in place, these regulations will act as a complement to existing state requirements.

Lead Paint Disclosure

It is your responsibility to give this pamphlet out and explain the basics of it to all tenants who rent a dwelling that was built before 1978. After you give them this pamphlet, you need to fill out and sign the lead-based paint disclosure. When I hand out the lead-based government pamphlet, I do not go over the contents of the

I recommend you go to my website at www.FindThat QualityTenant.com and take a look at the actual pamphlet the government distributes. You can access both the pamphlet and the disclosure though either my "links" or "forms" page. It is available in both English and Spanish.

Disclosure of Information on Lead-Based Paint and/or Lead-Based Paint Hazards

Lead Warning Statement

Housing built before 1978 may contain lead-based paint. Lead from paint, paint chips, and dust can pose health hazards if not managed properly. Lead exposure is especially harmful to young children and pregnant women. Before renting pre-1978 housing, lessors must disclose the presence of known lead-based paint and/or lead-based paint hazards in the dwelling. Lessees must also receive a federally approved pamphlet on lead poisoning prevention.

Lessor's Disclosure

(a) Presence of lead-based paint and/or lead-based paint hazards (check (i) or (ii) below):

  (i) _____ Known lead-based paint and/or lead-based paint hazards are present in the housing (explain).

  _____

  _____

  (ii) _____ Lessor has no knowledge of lead-based paint and/or lead-based paint hazards in the housing.

(b) Records and reports available to the lessor (check (i) or (ii) below):

  (i) _____ Lessor has provided the lessee with all available records and reports pertaining to lead-based paint and/or lead-based paint hazards in the housing (list documents below).

  _____

  _____

  (ii) _____ Lessor has no reports or records pertaining to lead-based paint and/or lead-based paint hazards in the housing.

Lessee's Acknowledgment (initial)

(c) _____ Lessee has received copies of all information listed above.

(d) _____ Lessee has received the pamphlet *Protect Your Family from Lead in Your Home.*

Agent's Acknowledgment (initial)

(e) _____ Agent has informed the lessor of the lessor's obligations under 42 U.S.C. 4852d and is aware of his/her responsibility to ensure compliance.

Certification of Accuracy

The following parties have reviewed the information above and certify, to the best of their knowledge, that the information they have provided is true and accurate.

Lessor	Date	Lessor	Date
Lessee	Date	Lessee	Date
Agent	Date	Agent	Date

document page by page or word for word. There is no need to do this because I am giving them the pamphlet. What there is a need to do is to go over and then sign the accompanying disclosure. Let's look at this form.

Lead Warning Statement

This statement explains why you are giving the tenant the pamphlet and any related information you might have concerning lead-based paint and the rental. Generally, when I pull out this form, I read the new tenants this statement word for word, and if they have no questions, I explain the rest of the form in the following manner. (This gets a little tricky so be prepared to look at the form and reread the explanation a couple of times).

Lessor's Disclosure

"This section here, Lessor's Disclosure, is where I must circle either (i) or (ii) in each section (a) and (b). The first section (a) deals with me having or not having knowledge of lead-based paint, and section (b) deals with any reports I may have concerning this property and lead-based paint."

At that point, I circle the appropriate (i) (knowledge) or (ii) (no knowledge) in each section (a) (presence of L.B.P.) and (b) (records of L.B.P.) at the same that I explain to my tenant why I'm circling my choice. (More on this later.)

Lessee's Acknowledgment

I then proceed to Lessee's Acknowledgment where they initial both (c) Lessee has received copies of all information listed above and (d) Lessee has received the pamphlet "Protect Your Family From Lead in Your Home." Since you have given them the pamphlet, then initialing (d) should not be a problem. On the other hand, (c) may not really apply in many cases. When this happens, have the tenants initial the line anyway because it does apply. If you have nothing to give them, they did receive all information. Get initials at both (c) and (d).

Agent's Acknowledgment

This area is used should somebody else be disclosing this information to your tenant. In addition to the above initials and acknowledging of information, the agent needs to initial his/her position on this form.

Certification of Accuracy

The disclosure ends with everyone signing and dating the form at the bottom of the page.

Everything in the booklet and on the disclosure form is pretty simple for a landlord to acknowledge with the possible exception of (a)(ii). If the house was built before 1978, there is a chance it has some lead-based paint in it. But unless the house has been tested or you yourself have owned the house long enough to know of it being painted with lead base, you have no real proof of the existence of lead-based paint.

It's even possible the dwelling was victim to fire or flood, resulting in a gutting and complete remodel of the premises. So unless you have proof of the existence of lead-based paint, either verbal or in writing, you don't know for sure if there is lead-based paint or its current hazards.

I am not an attorney, so please take my opinion as just that—an opinion. Should you wish to question that opinion or want true legal advice, contact a qualified attorney. Or you can do as I did and call the National Lead Information Center at 1-800-LEAD-FYI or the Center's clearinghouse at 1-800-424-LEAD (hearing impaired call 1-800-526-5456) to find out how they define "knowing." When I called, I was given this answer, "If you have never had the house tested, or have some other equivalent knowledge about the lead-based paint, then you don't know and should check (a)(ii)."

If you are a little nervous about the lead content in your rental, let me give you a couple of thoughts to help ease your mind. Every year puts distance between the 1978 cutoff for lead-based paint. During this year, a large number of rental dwellings get demolished or get totally or partially remodeled. Chances are, the threat of lead in the rental should be decreasing daily. If you wish to decrease the risk further, you could re-paint the unit completely. When I acquire a rental that is pre-1978, I'm aware of the potential for lead-based paint. What I recommend is to clean and paint anything that isn't already freshly painted. By doing this, I keep all the loose dust from becoming airborne. This painting includes windows and trim, walls, doors and trim, and baseboards. If you use quality paint and if you do not paint already loose paint, you should be pretty safe using this approach although this is not a guaranteed remedy.

In addition, during the early 1990s there was a big surge in home improvement. One of the best things that happened during that period was the technology of door and window replacement. Because of the ease and low expense with which doors and windows could be replaced, many people took advantage of the situation and got these items replaced. This window/door replacement greatly reduces the threat of lead-based paint.

Everyone hates to paint windows, so these items do not get the attention they should. When this happens, the window paint cracks and flakes and falls to the window ledge, where kids put their hands. This dust then goes from the kids' hands to their mouths, which puts the lead in their body. Or else the dust becomes airborne and the kids breathe in the dust. Having new windows greatly reduces the lead paint threat.

Next is painted trim. Often the trim gets neglected when people paint the walls. Unfortunately, kids sit in a corner playing with their trucks and other toys and will knock into the base trim possibly causing it to chip. The kids then eat these chips.

As paint gets older, it becomes more brittle and prone to chipping. Of course, different paints and quality paints last longer, so this brittle time will vary. What I recommend is to paint trim anytime you notice the paint is starting to crack, splinter, and chip.

By following these steps, keeping all painted surfaces in good order and cleaning these surfaces between tenants when you don't paint, you reduce your risk of lead-based paint hazards.

In addition to the phone number I gave you earlier, you can also check out the lead-based paint link at www.FindThatQualityTenant.com; it will take you right to the government website. You will find this site listed as the first site on my "links" page. As previously mentioned, you can access both the form and/or pamphlet from this page as well.

CHAPTER 20

The Property Conditions Form

L andlord/tenant disputes happen from time to time, with the most
common ones usually evolving like this: A landlord finds a tenant he
or she likes and who seems to fit the qualifications the landlord desires.
The landlord rents the unit to this tenant and the tenant assures the landlord that he or she is going to keep the dwelling clean and in good repair.
At the time, the tenant likes the property and seems to trust and believe
the landlord so the new tenant is confident the place is in sound shape.
Because of the way they believe in each other, the landlord and tenant
have silently said to themselves that there will be no disputes or misunder-
standings that can't be solved with a handshake. All is well.

Time slowly passes, until one day the tenant moves out of the rental
and to the landlord's dismay, leaves things in worse shape than the landlord had envisioned possible from his perfect tenant. The landlord holds
back the security deposit, leaving the tenants to think they are being taken
advantage of. A dispute ensues.

Who's Right?

In these disputes, sometimes the landlord is correct and sometimes
the tenant is correct. When the landlord is right, the scenario usually is
that the landlord does have a very nice rental unit with no defects, nice
paint, new carpet, and an otherwise very clean rental. The tenants, upon
leaving the environment they have occupied daily for whatever length of time,
don't realize how Kool-Aid–stained carpet, chipped mirrors, scratched
countertops, and broken hardware really make a dwelling look run-down.

275

On the flip side of the coin, some landlords pretend everything is fine, that there are no carpet stains, all hardware and fixtures are in good working order, and yes, 10-year-old paint jobs can last another year or two. The tenants, even though they were very good about doing no damage larger than normal wear and tear, somehow get blamed for the pre-occupant deficiencies.

These scenarios cannot be avoided altogether, but the frequency of the disputes can be greatly reduced and controlled. The best way to do this controlling is to document the condition of the rental unit before your tenant takes possession and after the tenant departs.

Recording the Condition of a Property

Photographs

I know of a couple ways to document the condition of the property First, the use of a camera for photographing details is a very effective solution to recording a property's condition. With digital technology, it is very easy to snap photos with your camera or even your cell phone. Once you get back to your office or home, you can download this onto your computer. You'll want to take before-and-after photos, label them as soon as you download them, and back them up on disk. You can also print copies of the photos and keep them in your files with their application, lease, and other paperwork.

If you like the idea of taking photos but you're not computer savvy, try this: Each time you rent your dwelling, take photos of the place with a disposable camera. These cameras are about six dollars at most retail stores and hold approximately 24 to 27 photos. Take 10 to 15 good shots of the interior, getting as much detail as you can in each shot. Take a couple exterior shots as well. When you get back home, simply label the box and camera with the dwelling address and tenant name. Store until the tenant departs, then finish the roll with the after shots. Should you ever need the photos, all you have to do is develop that tenant's roll of film.

Notes

Many of you may prefer to forgo these methods and use the old standby: pen and paper. You will need the Property Conditions checklist

THE PROPERTY CONDITIONS FORM

STEP FIVE

Property Conditions Form

Page 1 of 3

Names _____

Address _____ Date _____

Following is a conditions checklist for the dwelling you are about to rent. Please take the time and fill out the form in its entirety. You will notice every room lists individual items pertaining to that room. To the right of the item is a small line followed by a larger line. On the small line, simply mark an X if that item is satisfactory. If the item is not satisfactory, write N on the short line and a word or two detailing the problem on the long line. Should two items be listed on an area you have marked N, circle the item with the problem.

Example: lights (fans)   N   blade broken

You will also notice to the left of the listed item is a number. Use this number to give more detail about a problem if more detail is needed. Do this on the notes section provided on page 3.

Example: #4   2 fist holes in E walls

If something does not apply, then simply write N/A for not applicable.

ENTRY

1. Front door
2. Screen door
3. Other

LIVING ROOM

4. Walls/ceiling
5. Floors/carpet
6. Lights/fans
7. Windows/doors
8. Closet
9. Trim/misc.
10. Other

DINING ROOM

11. Walls/ceiling
12. Floors/carpet
13. Lights/fan
14. Windows/doors
15. Closet
16. Trim/misc.
17. Other

Int. _____ Int. _____   Int. _____

copyright 2007 Blue Collar Publishers

277

for this method, and I have provided you with just such a form. This form is to be filled out by the new tenants on the day they sign the lease. Don't wait until after they've settled in to give them the form, and don't give them the form to fill out and mail back to you. You will never get it returned to you. They must fill out the form the day of the lease signing. Do this before you sign the lease.

The Property Conditions Form

The first few lines of the form include general information—the tenant's name, date, and property address. Fill this in before you turn it over to the tenant.

The form then begins with instructions on how to use it. I suggest you become familiar with these instructions and at the lease signing, personally show them how to fill out the form. For your understanding, here are those instructions:

Following is a conditions checklist for the dwelling you are about to rent. Please take the time and fill out the form in its entirety. You will notice every room lists individual items pertaining to that room. To the right of the item is a small line followed by a larger line. On the small line, simply mark an X if that item is satisfactory. If the item is not satisfactory, write N on the short line and a word or two detailing the problem on the long line. Should two items be listed on an area you have marked N, circle the item with the problem. See the illustration for an example.

Example: 6. Lights/fans   N   blade broken

You will also notice to the left of the listed item is a number. Use this number to give more detail about a problem if more detail is needed. Do this on the notes section provided on page 3.

Example: #4   2 fist holes in E. wall

When you give this checklist to tenants, encourage them to open and close doors and windows, turn on lights and fans, and give the property a

STEP FIVE

Property Conditions Form

	#1	#2	#3	
46. Sink/counter				
Vanity				
47. Medicine Cabinet				
48. Mirrors				

MISCELLANEOUS

49. Back door
50. Screen door
51. Garage
52. Shed
53. Laundry room
54. Basement
55. Heating/cooling
56. Hot/cold water
57. Porches/entries
58. Fence
59. Sidewalk/driveway
60. Other

Notes _____
_____
_____

I have found dwelling to be to my satisfaction with the exception of the flawed items listed. I understand it is my responsibility to return property in the same condition minus normal wear and tear.

Signature _____ Date _____

Signature _____ Date _____

Signature _____ Date _____

thorough inspection. Make sure they mark an X or N on every line of the checklist that applies to the dwelling.

When they have completed all three pages, checking all items that are applicable to the rental, they can then proceed to the bottom of the checklist where there is a group of empty lines. These lines are used when an item the tenant found below par needs to be explained in greater detail. All they need to do is write down the corresponding number that can be located to the left of the item, then they simply write more detail about that item's specific problem if more details are needed.

Example: #4   2 fist holes in E. wall

Once they have completed the form, they need to read the closing statement, which reads: *I have found dwelling to be to my satisfaction with the exception of the flawed items listed. I understand it is my responsibility to return property in the same condition minus normal wear and tear.* Then they should sign and date the bottom of the form. You will want to make a copy of the Property Conditions form and give it to your tenant for their files. Of course, you will retain the signed original in the tenant's file in case you need it for reference when they leave the premises.

Keep in mind that either party can do the blaming and finger pointing. From the landlord's perspective you want to win the debate, whether you are accusing or being accused. To do so, you must have this form filled out. I repeat, you must have this form filled out and *signed* by the tenant. The chances of you winning any court dispute without this form are about 1 in 100.

Filling out the Property Conditions form can be time-consuming, but it is vital to proving your case if you go to court. Make its use a regular habit.

You can pull the Property Conditions form off of our website at: www.FindThatQualityTenant.com.

CHAPTER 21

The Pet Addendum

R emember when we touched on the subject of pets in the Tenant Qualifications form? I stated that pets were probably the most volatile
requirement you'll deal with because of the emotional connection pet
owners have to their pets and the fact that pets have the ability to do costly
damage to a rental.

You may choose not to rent to owners of pets or possibly to certain
kinds of pets, but anytime you limit pets, you eliminate many potential
quality tenants. Somehow, you need to fuse the two. You need to be able
to accept pets and acquire quality tenants/pet owners.

The Pet Addendum will go a long way toward helping you achieve
that union. Not only is this agreement your legal tie into pet control, but
the pet rules are established there in black and white for all to see. By
using an addendum for pets you will eliminate a lot of the potential conflicts you could be faced with.

As we've done in other chapters, we will look at the pet addendum
and go over the important points. The pet addendum is designed so each
pet gets its own addendum. I've combined a pet description, owner rules
for pets, and the actual pet lease statement on one sheet. This allows future easy access to all pet information and eliminates tenant confusion
about their responsibility involving their pets.

Reviewing the Pet Addendum

Breed

Most of the pet description portion of the form is self-explanatory, but I will point out a couple of areas to watch for. Pet name, age, and color are simple enough, but double-check the answer for the line "breed." Look for two things. Check to see if the breed is one of the dogs you've put on your dangerous dog list (if you use this list) and then watch for the words "mix" or "mixture." When you see this word, make sure you see at least two dog breeds listed such as Collie/Shepard mix or pit bull/Labrador mixture. Again, you want to make sure both types of dogs are acceptable to you.

Description

Here you ask the owner to describe the pet, or if they brought the animal with them, you describe it yourself. Here you want special identifying marks or traits of the particular pet, such as one blue and one brown eye, extra long hair with white spot on left front leg, tip of tail broken, and so forth. Basically, you want any description that would help you identify this pet if you needed to.

Other Information

After you get a description of the pet, you need to know a few things about the owner's responsible care of their animal. Listed below the form are eight topics you may wish to question the pet owner about. Have him or her circle his or her answers as they apply.

- Outdoor pet
- Updated shots
- Declawed
- Indoor crated
- Licensed/collared
- Sprayed/neutered
- Housebroken
- License or tag number

STEP FIVE

Pet Addendum

Page 1 of 2

Pet Name _____ Age _____ Color _____

Breed _____ Description _____

Outdoor pet	Y/N	Updated shots	Y/N	Declawed	Y/N	
Indoor caged	Y/N	Licensed/collared	Y/N	Spayed/neutered	Y/N	
Housebroken	Y/N	License or tag number				

This agreement is an addendum to the Rental Agreement between (Owner/Manager) _____

and (Tenants) _____

_____ dated (Lease Date) _____ . This agreement is for pet listed above and does not permit any other unlisted pets on the rental premises, including a temporary basis. This includes dogs, cats, birds, fish, reptiles or any other animals without owner consent. Owner grants permission of pet described above with the agreement to abide by these following rules and regulations.

1) Tenant agrees to local ordinances, including licensing, leash law, ID tags, health requirements and mandated vaccinations.

2) Tenant agrees to keep pet under control at all times, including unnecessary noise, aggressive disturbance or annoyance to others. This holds true both during the day and at night. Tenant agrees to remedy any complaint from owner/manager immediately.

3) Tenant agrees to keep pet restrained or fenced when outside the dwelling.

4) Tenant agrees to clean up pet waste and dispose of it properly and quickly, both inside and outside the dwelling.

5) Tenant agrees not to leave food outside dwelling that could attract other animals.

6) Tenant agrees to pay additional security deposit of $_____ and/or monthly rent of $_____ for keeping said pet on the premises. Additional security deposit may only be used after tenant has vacated premises and may be applied to repair of damages, carpet cleaning/replacement, spraying or cleaning of rental or delinquent rent. Unused deposit shall be returned to tenant within _____ days of tenant vacating premises.

7) Tenant agrees to obtain a liability insurance policy with $_____ coverage to cover injury or damages caused by pet. Tenant agrees to list owner as "additional insured".

8) Tenant agrees to find new homes for pet's offspring within 8 weeks of birth.

9) Tenant agrees not to leave pet unattended for unreasonable periods of time.

Int. _____ Int. _____ Int. _____

Pet Qualifications

In fact, depending on your position on pets in your dwelling, you may wish to make all or part of these questions a qualification on the Tenant Qualifications form you filled out in the beginning of your rental process. If you want to, you can include pet qualifications under the "notes" section listed in the pet category.

Such a qualification could look something like this: *Must pass qualifications on pet addendum.* Or maybe you want to loosen the reins a bit, but still have some pet requirement control. In this instance, you could write: *Must answer yes to questions 4, 5, and 7 on pet addendum.*

The more "yeses" on the pet addendum, the harder it will be to find quality tenants who can pass everything. Choose your battles wisely.

I give you these topics to make you aware of some of the issues associated with these pets. How you handle those issues are up to you. You may choose the topics to use as qualifications (if any) according to your area's rental clientele or the actual rental itself. For instance, if you are renting a farmhouse where outside pets would be more common, the declawing and housebroken topics are nowhere near as important as neutering, but declawing and housebroken could be top priority in a ritzy New York apartment.

How you use the pet addendum as a requirement is totally up to you. Use common sense and fair judgment and you should do fine.

License or tag number. You want to include on the form the tag number given to the pet by the city or the pet's veterinarian. If possible, read the number for yourself. The owner may have to remove the tag or collar for you to correctly get the number. You might even get this number off of the city permit papers if the tenant has them. If the pet owner reads the number to you, they may accidentally or intentionally give faulty information. The chances of you ever needing this number are slim at best, but it is nice to have it on file, so should the need arise, you can prove you're a conscientious and thorough landlord.

Legal Agreement

After you learn the pet's history and get a good description of the pet, you are ready for the legal jargon in this addendum, which is stated below.

This agreement is an addendum to the Rental Agreement between Owner/ Manager _____ and Tenants _____, dated (lease date) _____ . This agreement is for pet listed above and does not permit any other un- listed pet on the rental premises, even on a temporary basis. This includes dogs, cats, birds, fish, reptiles or any other animals without owner con- sent. Owner grants permission of pet described above with the agreement to abide by the following rules and regulations.

You will notice there are three lines to fill out in this paragraph. On the first line you put your name as owner/manager. The second line is for the name of the tenant. On the third line, you are looking for the date of the original and currently active lease, *not* the date you are filling out the addendum. Don't put the date you filled out the addendum unless you are just putting these people in your rental. Coordinate the *lease date* to the third blank line in the paragraph. They should be one and the same.

The rest of the paragraph basically states that you as owner/manager are granting permission for *only* the pet described above and only if the following rules are adhered to. Let's look at and discuss each of those rules.

The Pet Rules

1. *Tenants agree to adhere to local ordinances, including licensing, leash laws, ID tags, health requirements, and mandated vaccinations.* Of course, here you are requiring the local ordinances to help you po- lice the health and safety of your tenant's pets. I strongly recommend if you don't know your community pet ordinances, you get yourself a copy. I would keep it in the file for that particular unit so it can be conveniently found when you need it.

2. *Tenants agree to keep pet under control at all times, including unnec- essary noise, aggressive disturbance, or annoyance to others. This includes day and nighttime. Tenants agree to remedy any complaint from owner or manager immediately.* Here, you're allowing the abil- ity for you to police the tenant's pet if they cause any kind of neighborhood problems. These problems include barking day and night, running through neighbors' yards, knocking over trash cans,

or things of that nature. Failure of the pet owner to respond to your complaints could cost them the pet or use of the rental unit

3. *Tenants agree to keep pet restrained or fenced when outside the dwelling.* This rule is self-explanatory although some locales have fence requirements that might pertain to certain breeds of dogs.

4. *Tenant agrees to clean up pet waste and dispose of it properly and quickly, both inside and outside the dwelling.* You will notice two important words in the rule and those words are "properly" and "quickly." "Properly" does not include piling it behind the alley where the sun can cook it or kids can play in it. This is not safe or sanitary. In fact, since children get tetanus from animal feces, you could possibly be setting yourself up for a lawsuit if you know but allow improper pet waste removal to happen anyway. "Quickly" means what it says. One does not wait until the litter box is overflowing or the backyard has more landmines than a war zone. Animal waste needs to be cleaned up in a common-sense, timely manner. It should be removed according to the ordinances established in your community.

5. *Tenant agrees not to leave food outside dwelling that could attract other animals.* In addition to keeping a food dish on the back porch for Rover, some pet owners throw their pets' leftovers, which are heading for the trash bin. Generally, this is acceptable, but the problem arises when these food items are uneaten and left overnight. Stray dogs, cats, and other unwanted visitors tend to find these food sources. Actually, it is the other unwanted visitors that cause the big headaches, especially if the other visitor is a raccoon. Once a raccoon begins to hang out at your rental, you will understand this rule. Following this regulation also helps to keep away rats, mice, and other pesky rodents.

6. *Tenant agrees to pay additional security deposit of $_____ and/ or monthly rent of $ _____ for keeping said pet on the premises. Additional security deposit may only be used after tenant has vacated premises and may be applied to repair of damages, carpet cleaning/ replacement, spraying or cleaning of rental or delinquent rent. Unused deposit shall be returned to tenant within _____ days of tenant vacating premises.* The form goes on to explain that the additional

security deposit required may only be used after tenant has vacated premises and may be applied to repair or damages, carpet cleaning/replacement, spraying or cleaning of rental, or delinquent rent. Unused deposit shall be refunded to tenant within a certain number of days (be sure to specify) of tenant vacating premises. This is where you fill in the amount you are collecting for extra security deposit, monthly rent, or both. You will notice that tenants cannot get the extra security deposit back until they have *vacated* the premises. This helps give you extra money when you need it most: when they have moved out and all damages are apparent. Most states have laws on how long you can hold a security deposit. Ask your lawyer what the maximum limit is and put that time limit in the appropriate spot.

7. *Tenant agrees to obtain a liability insurance policy with $ _____ coverage to cover injury or damages caused by pet. Tenant agrees to list owner as "additional insured."* Animals as pets are wonderful. They provide us with comfort, protection, and companionship. They help give a purpose for our existence. The reason they are able to do that is because they have their own personalities. Unfortunately, just like humans, animals have personality flaws and if one of those flaws causes the pet to bite someone, you could find yourself in a lawsuit. The form specifies that tenants with pets must obtain liability insurance to cover such problems. You should have your name listed on this policy. One way to handle liability insurance is to charge the tenant for the policy and you set it up with your agent. This way, you know it gets done.

8. *Tenant agrees to find new homes for pet's offspring within eight weeks of birth.* Pets sometimes have babies, so include a clause that requires the tenants to find a new home(s) for offspring within eight weeks of birth. This will help ensure they are not a new permanent occupant in the rental.

9. *Tenant agrees not to leave pet unattended for unreasonable periods of time.* Also specify that the tenant agrees not to leave pet unattended for an unreasonable length of time. This rule will vary with each pet. "Unreasonable length of time" could mean three hours for an

old dog with a weak bladder, or two weeks for a well-fed snake. When you get to this rule with your tenant, you need to explain the rule with something along these lines: "Unreasonable length of time can greatly vary from species of pet to the pet's training and personality. What we mean by this term is that the length of time a pet should be left alone is the amount of time a pet can handle without needing their waste facility cleaned up, their food replenished, or where they get bored and begin to do damage." This cannot guarantee that tenants will abide by this rule, but it will let the tenant know where you stand on pets who are left alone.

10. *Pet identification tags are to be worn at all times.* This regulation is more for the tenant than you. This rule will ensure that should a pet escape, they have a better chance of being returned to the rightful owner.

11. *Tenant agrees to furnish owner/manager with picture of said pet.* Ask that the tenant furnish you with a picture of their pets. Having a picture of the pet will go a long way in a lawsuit. This will also help to ensure that you do in fact have a collie in your rental if they say they have a collie. I recommend you take a picture of the pet yourself and when you take the picture, try to get the owner's face in the frame as well. This will go a long way should you ever need the tenant's picture for future reference.

12. *Tenant agrees that this addendum is for that specific pet described above and there are no pet substitutions, including "pet sitting" or harboring of any other pets. Any unlisted animals are to be removed at tenant's expense.* Make sure the tenant agrees that this addendum is for that specific pet described above and there are no pet substitutions, including pet sitting or harboring of any other pets including guests' pets. Any unlisted animals are to be removed at tenant's expense. This regulation reaffirms that the described pet is the only pet allowed under this addendum.

13. *Tenant agrees to pay for any loss, expenses, or damage caused by said pet. Nonpayment of such damage will be listed as additional rent.* Specify that the tenant agrees to pay for any loss, expenses, or damage caused by said pet. Nonpayment of such damage will be listed as

additional rent. This rule lets the tenant know they are financially responsible for any expense their pet costs you and how damages will be listed.

14. *Tenant agrees to the owner/manager's right to revoke permission to keep said pet should tenant break this addendum. Breaking of addendum shall be grounds for termination of rental agreement.* Finally, the last rule on the form spells out to tenants what could happen if they break this agreement. Simply put, they could lose their pet or their right to rent from you.

Closing Statement

After all the rules, the contract is closed with the following statement: *I have read the above rules and regulations and am willing to comply with all of the above. I also state that any information I gave about said pet is truthful and complete to the best of my knowledge.* If all parties agree to everything on the addendum, date it with the date you are filling it out, and then you and the tenants will sign it.

Now that you've been over the addendum form itself, there are things to keep in mind as you use it.

Applying the Form

Naturally, you can use what you need on the form and delete what you don't need. To delete on the form, simply cross out or put N/A over the ruling you don't like or need. Place your initials by the number of the ruling you wish to delete. If you find you need to add some terms that are not covered here, please add as needed. You can also use this form as a layout for your own form and come up with the perfect addendum for you.

It goes without saying that you can skip using this form altogether, but if you need an addendum to anything, it will probably be pets. Unlike waterbeds, parking, key accountability, or any of the add-ons you could tack onto a lease, pets will cause you problems the fastest and most often. Using a pet addendum will go a long way toward giving you protection from the variety of problems you could face.

Last but not least, you may wish to go over this form and rules with the tenant at the time you interview them on the phone. By doing so, you give them an opportunity to see if they can abide by these rules. At the very least, you may wish to expose them to it at the time they fill out their application. You don't want to get to the lease signing and have them back out because of a pet rule they couldn't live with.

Obtain a copy of this form off our website at
www.FindThatQualityTenant.com.

CHAPTER 22

The Lease

I f you are going to be a landlord, I strongly advise having a well-prepared lease. A good lease will solidify the verbal agreement and important criteria between the landlord and the tenant. It will also be your strongest link in that paper trail I've been trying to get you to develop, should a dispute arise between you and your tenant. A properly entered lease will go farther in solving landlord/tenant disputes than any other document you have. In 99 percent of the cases, it is your first weapon and strongest ally in a courtroom battle.

Finding a Lease

So once you understand what a lease is, the next question becomes, "Where does one find a good rental lease?"

That's an excellent question—one, in fact, I was having trouble solving for the scope of this book. I have a lease that serves me well in my state and locale in which I live. But unfortunately, that leaves 49 other states and tens of thousands of locales for which I'm not prepared to offer leases. Factor in the fact that this book will probably be shipped to Canada and other countries around the globe, and you can see why putting a generic lease form in this book would probably be pointless.

Fortunately, I was determined not to let the problem stop me from helping you find or develop a good lease. Therefore, let's begin with me telling you how you go about finding a lease. There are basically three ways. I'll list each of them along with the advantages and disadvantages associated with each choice.

1. *Draft your own.* The advantage to this is that it is cheap. The disadvantage is that you could make some costly legal mistakes by not having enough information or the wrong information in your lease. If you choose to draft a lease yourself, there are books you can purchase that will walk you through the process, although I cannot say how well they work, because I have personally never tried to draft my own lease.

2. *Pick one up at an office supply store.* The advantage to this is that it is easy to do. When you need a lease right now, these store-bought leases can do the trick since they are so easy to find. The disadvantage is that it could be too general to offer adequate protection. They are cheap and simple but will offer the least amount of protection out of the three lease options.

3. *Have a real estate lawyer draft you a lease.* The advantage to this is that it is tailor fit for your situation, offering you the best overall protection. But it is more costly—although not nearly as costly as a poorly drafted lease followed by a tenant dispute.

I recommend using a real estate lawyer to draft a lease. When you are a landlord, you have at least some financial net worth—probably more than your tenants will have. This automatically makes you prone to frivolous lawsuits and unwarranted demands by those tenants. A properly drafted lease will offer maximum custom protection against many of the possible lawsuits and demands landlords are exposed to. Therefore, I advise you to have a lawyer draft your lease and to do it from the time you put that first tenant in your first rental.

I know money can be extremely tight when you are first entering your landlording career, but I highly recommend using a lawyer from the beginning for this reason: If you draft your own lease or use a store-bought one and you have reasonable success with it for a couple of tenants, you could be lulled into a false sense of security. When you reach that point, you will never pay a professional to draft a lease for you until you end up with a legal dispute, which will, of course, be too late. Take my recommendation and spend the money initially on a lawyer structured lease

Contents of a Lease

No matter which way you decide to come up with your rental lease, you'll need some tools to help you get the best lease possible. As you know by now, I like checklists, so it only makes good sense to use one on your most important paperwork. Therefore, a checklist is what I'm offering to you as a guide to your leasing needs.

This checklist is probably very close to the same one a lawyer would use for reference if he or she were drafting a lease for a client. This checklist will be extremely consistent, wherever you live.

We will go through the checklist and I will give a brief explanation of each item as I list it. Keep in mind that not every item will be necessary but should be considered.

Finding a lease that fits your every need will be tough to do. In addition to my recommended lease options, check into one of the real estate investment groups that dot the country. These groups have many benefits for the new investor, including ties to area appropriate leases. Please visit www.FindThatQuality Tenant.com for a listing of such groups.

1) **Parties**—the people involved in the lease (Each person or entity is a party to a lease. You could have two parties or many parties to a lease.)
   - Names—all parties or entities on the lease need to be named
   - Address—of the parties if different than the leased address
   - Other identification—as needed

2) **Subject of the lease**
   - Address or legal description of the property; address of the property being rented
   - Lessee's purpose—whether residential, commercial, farm use, and so forth
   - Restrictions on use of property—limits on use and occupancy

3) **Duration of agreement or option for lease**—length of contract including starting and ending dates

4) **Provisions to be included in subsequent lease**
   - Parties—usually refers to names of minors/pets
   - Subject term—fixed day when rent is due and when considered late
   - Rental payments—amount of payment and security deposit
   - Access to property—right to enter property for emergency, repairs, or timely condition review
   - Designation of party responsible for repairs—who's responsible for what repairs and action taken if repairs not completed in a timely manner
   - Identification of appurtenances—what goes with or is related to the rented premises (appliances, equipment, etc.)
   - Liability for utilities—who pays sewer, water, garbage, and so forth
   - Liability for taxes and assessments—in some leases, the tenants are responsible for these items
   - Renewal option provisions—conditions and time frame for lease renewal of premises
   - Purchase option provisions—conditions and time frame for purchase of premises
   - Transferability of lease agreement—whether you can sublease or not

5) **Date of execution**—when the lease was signed by parties

6) **Signatures**—signatures of parties

This completes the checklist you may use to structure your rental lease. It is likely that you will include provisions in your lease other than those listed. For instance, many people write their rules and regulations into the lease itself. These regulations cover such things as noise, lockouts, pets, and parking. Other landlords simply hand out the rules as an afterthought, but might write out amendments to their standard lease as they feel it's needed.

Amendments are changes added to the standard lease as you learn about your property, business, and general habits of renters. You write an amendment to cover a potential problem not addressed in the lease. The addressed problem may pertain only to the specific rented location or the addressed problem could be something you as a landlord have experienced and wish to have better control of in the future. You add amendments because it is easier than rewriting an entire lease. Since these amendments come from learning the landlord business, don't be afraid to write an amendment or change as you see fit.

Optimizing the Lease

Now that we've covered what a lease is, where you can obtain a lease, and a checklist to help you develop a sound lease, let's talk about other "need-to-know" lease information.

First, no matter how solid you believe your lease to be, your real estate attorney should review it periodically to make sure everything in that lease is still valid. Tenant laws change all the time and you need to keep abreast of those laws. Also, as talked about in the paragraph about amendments, as you learn the landlording business, some of the changes you wish to enact could be better represented in a professional lease, therefore you'll want your lawyer to structure the change correctly. I personally double-check the legal end of my business every January, and this includes leases. This keeps me aware of the easy-to-forget but important things in my business. I advise you to do something along the same lines.

Second, be careful that the lease you or your lawyer draft makes sense to both you and the tenant. Sometimes, lawyers put so much legal wording in their lease that neither party truly understands what the lease says. You want and need a lease that you can honestly and thoroughly comprehend so you can tell your tenant what every part of the lease means.

And third, make your lease as legal as you can within the jurisdiction where you live, but at the same time, keep your lease reasonable enough so you and your tenants can abide by it for the length of their tenancy.

Lease Length

With all the previous information, you should be a little more comfortable with the constructing of a lease, although the one thing we haven't covered yet is lease length. There are two basic lease choices: month-to-month and specific-time leases. They each have distinct advantages and disadvantages.

A month-to-month lease is good for one month but at the end of the month, the lease automatically starts over unaltered unless one party makes some kind of change. In my personal opinion, it is this automatic renewal that makes a lease of this type nice for landlords. If they need to raise rent or make some other changes, they only have to give 30 days' notice of said change. This is a real plus when you see a sudden increase in taxes, and insurance, or decide you have a much needed policy change for your tenant. With a month-to-month you can enact your change immediately. Month-to-month leases can also theoretically go on forever.

With a specific time lease (one year is the norm for residential rentals), that lease cannot be changed unless both parties agree in writing or until it expires. So if you receive a hefty tax increase in the third month of a 12-month lease, you will probably have to wait until that lease is up before you can legally pass the tax increase on to the tenant.

Some landlords like a long lease because they effectively know when a tenant is going to vacate the premises. These landlords believe if a tenant were to break the lease then they could sue for the remainder of the lease. This is fairly solid and accurate thinking, but when you consider the time and frustration involved in a lawsuit, it makes suing a tenant more trouble than it's worth.

Tenants, on the other hand, generally want at least a year lease because they know there can be no enforced legal changes for the duration of the lease. Therefore, specific time leases offer good security for the tenant.

Nowadays, most long-term leases have a policy of converting over to a month-to-month lease once the initial agreement time is up. This conversion actually works out quite well for both landlords and tenants. It gives tenants their desired security until they are comfortable in their new habitat. And then when the lease converts to a month-to-month, the landlord gets more flexibility.

Deciding if you want a month-to-month or a length lease is an issue you might wish to discuss with your attorney. Whatever you choose, choose wisely because you have to be comfortable with your decision for the duration of that lease.

Signing the Lease

Of course, once you have your tenant choice made, the renting of the unit is not official until they have signed your lease. Following are some important points to remember when this lease signing takes place:

- All parties who will sign the lease need to be present when you review the lease. This includes cosigners. My lawyer recommended everyone over 18 who will reside in the dwelling sign the lease.
- I recommend having at least two copies of the lease at lease signing—one for you to read and one for the tenants to follow. You may want one for all responsible parties.
- Know your lease so that you can review each and every topic covered in that lease. This may require a call to your lawyer or some reference digging to learn what some specific, hard-to-understand areas really mean.
- Cover each topic one item at a time. Speak slowly and don't get so long-winded you lose the concentration of the tenants.
- Do not move to the next topic of the lease until everybody understands the previous topic.
- Do not leave blank spaces on the lease to be filled in later. This is unprofessional of you and unfair to the tenant.
- Once the whole lease has been reviewed, double-check that all parties have no unanswered questions.

Once all parties understand the lease, have everyone sign and date one copy for you and one for the tenant. The tenants should also initial each and every page of the lease.

Renting to roommates or unwed couples generally has more risk than a husband and wife. The main reason is because the legal ties that bind are not there, meaning it is a lot easier for one person to leave the other holding the bag. Therefore, I suggest you include a clause in your lease stating that each person who signs the lease is responsible for the lease in its entirety. I would make this a regular clause for every lease for everyone, married or not. That way you're less apt to discriminate. Remember, I'm not a lawyer and the above is only an opinion. If you have questions concerning this topic, contact your real estate attorney.

However you decide to handle your leases, remember this: a lease is absolutely no good if it can't do its job where it is supposed to: in court. Get yourself a sound, enforceable lease, one that will hold up in court.

CHAPTER 23

The Cosigner Agreement

B ecause of the way the systems in this book have worked for me, I seldom need to have a cosigner for my tenants. I'm hoping that if you use this system or at least the parts that will enhance what you currently are using, this will be true for you, also.

But should the occasion arise where you need a cosigner, it would be nice to have the paperwork to help make the cosigner agreement stick. This way, if something happens with a tenant who is somehow not living up to his or her financial responsibilities, and you have to work to get your monies due, at least with a cosigner, you have an extra option for "turning up the heat" to retrieve your money.

When to Use a Cosigner

Before you look over the cosigner agreement, you need to realize when you should accept the use of a cosigner. A cosigner is not the end-all answer to putting just anyone in your rental. A cosigner is used when you have someone who passes all of your qualifications, but the individual's scenario needs a little extra reassurance for you to feel secure about renting to them. For example, let's say you have a college graduate who is a first-time renter. He or she has a strong, good-paying job near your rental unit. Unfortunately, you figure out through a Cash Flow form that this person is about $75 shy of rent every month. This comes out to about $20 per week. Logically, most college graduates are used to living on very little money, surviving on cheap beer and ramen noodles, so you think you could make this work. On the other hand, this is probably the first

STEP FIVE

Co-Signer Agreement

Addendum to rental agreement dated _____ for (address) _____

as agreed between owner/manager _____ and tenant(s)

_____

As co-signer for above tenants and residence, I understand and accept the following:

1) I have filled out a rental application for the purpose of allowing the owner/manager to check my credit.

2) I will not and have no intention of occupying this residence now or anytime in the future. Should I wish to occupy said residence, I need written consent from owner/manager.

3) I may be liable for rent due, cleaning costs and/or damage and repair charges should tenant fail his/her obligation under the terms of this agreement. I agree to pay such costs within 10 days of notification.

4) I understand this agreement will remain in force throughout the term of lease, including an extension of said lease or changes within said lease.

Notes _____
_____
_____

Owner/manager _____ Date _____

Tenant _____ Date _____

Tenant _____ Date _____

Tenant _____ Date _____

Co-Signer _____ Date _____

Co-Signer _____ Date _____

300

time he or she is receiving consistent, serious cash, so the desire for new furniture and such for a new place might overwhelm the new graduate. This type of scenario is perfect for a cosigner agreement.

When Not to Use a Cosigner

Do not use a cosigner agreement to justify renting to someone who you know is not qualified to rent from you. For instance, the prospect is one week on a job that doesn't pay enough, but for this person, it probably won't matter since he or she has changed jobs three times in four months and probably won't keep this one either. This person has a boat and a motorcycle payment, both of which are behind, but assures you the rent is always paid. And if this person does miss a month, the cosigner will help out. This is not a cosigner-friendly atmosphere.

Also be aware of a tenant prospect who seems to fit the criteria but would need a cosigner who, for some reason, you cannot seem to contact. I had a situation where a young man and his fiancée wanted to rent from me. He admitted to money problems in the past, but had recently obtained a good job and really was getting it together—or so the story goes. He had a great personality and was very likable and convincing. He went on to state that his father would have no problem cosigning for him. Well, I didn't yet have an adequate reason to eliminate him, and I hoped he was what he said was. So I let him fill out the paperwork. The next day, I put a call into his dad and left a message with reason for my call. I also sent in for his credit report.

To make a long story short, three days later, I got his credit report and still hadn't received a return call from his father even though I called daily. Upon opening the credit report, I discovered this young man had a $3,000 judgment against him from an apartment complex filed just two months earlier. No wonder his dad wouldn't talk to me. To make a long story short, the kid charmed me, lied to me, and tried to entice me with the use of a cosigner.

Reviewing the Cosigner Agreement

Let's look at the cosigner agreement. Where it says, "addendum to rental agreement dated _____," you will put the date of the original, current active lease for the tenant. Almost without exception, you will be filling out the cosigner agreement at the same time you fill out the lease.

In fact, a word of warning: Do not sign a lease and then sign a cosigner addendum on a later or different day. If the cosigner decides to back out, you could have an iffy tenant without the necessary financial safety net. Should you have to sign a lease agreement a couple of days before the cosigner agreement, write in this wording on your lease: "Keys will not be given to tenant and lease is not valid until completion of cosigner agreement."

In a nutshell, if you feel you need a cosigner for a tenant, do not give that tenant the rental unit until you have the appropriate paperwork filled out and signed by the cosigner.

Cosigner rules

Next on the addendum are conditions the cosigner needs to read, understand, and accept which are listed here as they read on the form.

As cosigner for above tenants and residence, I understand and accept the following:

1) I have filled out a rental application for the purpose of allowing the owner/manager to check my credit.

The cosigner may not want to fill out a Rental Application, but legally he or she needs to fill one out so you can check his or her credit. I advise you to have the cosigner fill out an application even if you decide not to run a credit check. The reason for this is that with a filled-out application, you now have more leads if you need contacts to help you locate or gather information on a problem tenant. If you find the situation worth a cosigner, the situation is worth that cosigner filling out an application and credit report.

2) I will not and have no intention of occupying this residence now or anytime in the future. Should I wish to occupy said residence, I need written consent from the owner/manager.

Since you are using the cosigner as financial reassurance and not doing a complete analysis from a tenant perspective, you do not wish to grant permission for the cosigner to occupy the rental unit. This clause also states that if they wish to occupy the dwelling, then they need to okay it with you. Of course, if that were to happen, you would run a complete paper and background check just like you did on the original tenant.

3) I may be liable for rent due, cleaning costs, and/or damage and repair charges should tenant fail his/her obligation under the terms of this agreement. I agree to pay such costs within 10 days of notification.

If your tenant skips out, owing you rent, then chances are you will have to clean the unit and probably repair damages as well. Since you are using a cosigner to help cover this tenant's failure to comply with the lease, you might as well make the cosigner financially responsible for all of the noncompliance. This is fair and legal as long as the cosigner is aware of the potential financial obligation beforehand. This clause brings attention to those obligations and explains how quickly you expect them to respond should they find themselves financially responsible.

It only makes sense that if you have a cosigner for a particular tenant, you might as well keep the cosigner as long as you can. The previous clause does this for you. Should you wish to add, delete, or change anything on the cosigner agreement, do so on the empty lines that follow your four clauses. Remember to initial and date your change. Have everyone sign and date the form.

A strong cosigner in addition to a solid tenant is a good combination to have for your rental unit. Just keep in mind that a cosigner is not the cure-all for a weak or substandard tenant. It is also not a guarantee that a cosigner will pay any money they might owe you from your tenant's failure to live up to their obligation. In short, work to find the strongest tenant prospect you can and use the cosigner as a little extra insurance if needed.

A copy of this cosigner agreement can be obtained at
www.FindThatQualityTenant.com.

CHAPTER 24

The Checklist—Part Three

I f you recall, we began using the checklist as we completed step three (paperwork) and step four (process) in the search for a quality tenant. As we conclude step five (payoff), we will use the last and final part of the checklist to ensure we have completed all the necessary paperwork before we hand over the keys to our new tenant.

STEP 5

1) ____ Rules and regulations initialed and signed
2) ____ Fire extinguisher use and maintenance reviewed
3) ____ Smoke alarm use and maintenance reviewed
4) ____ Tenant given lead based paint pamphlet
5) ____ Lead based paint form signed and dated
6) ____ Property condition form signed and dated
7) ____ Additional/missed information verified
8) ____ Information contact, form received
9) ____ Utilities transferred

    a)   gas
    b)   electric
    c)   water
    d)   sewer
    e)   garbage
    f)   other

10) ____ Explained property workings
    a) ____ individual water shut offs
    b) ____ main water shut offs
    c) ____ all gas shut offs
    d) ____ furnace filter change
    e) ____ appliances
    f) ____ all others

11) ____ All lease items reviewed
12) ____ Lease initialed, signed & dated
13) ____ Pet addendum signed & dated
14) ____ Co-signer agreement signe & dated
15) ____ Copies of photo ID/SS# collected
16) ____ All monies received
17) ____ Celebrate!

Signature _____ Date _____

Just like we did in steps three and four, we will cover the items in the checklist and I will briefly talk about any items I believe need further clarification.

Take a look at part three of the checklist:

1. Rules and regulations initialed and signed

2. Fire extinguisher use and maintenance reviewed

3. Smoke alarm use and maintenance reviewed

305

4. Tenant given lead-based paint pamphlet
5. Lead-based paint form signed and dated
6. Property condition form signed and dated
7. Photos/video taken
8. Additional/missed information verified
9. Tenant received Important Contacts form
10. Utilities transferred
    a. Gas
    b. Electric
    c. Water
    d. Sewer
    e. Garbage
    f. Other
11. Explained property workings:
    a. Individual water shutoffs
    b. Main water shut offs
    c. All gas shutoffs
    d. Furnace filter change
    e. Appliances
    f. All others
12. Pet Addendum signed and dated
13. Cosigner Agreement signed and dated
14. Copies of photo ID/Social Security number collected
15. All lease items reviewed
16. Lease signed and dated by all parties
17. All monies received
18. Key exchange
19. Celebrate!

When first looking over the checklist, it appears that there is an awful lot to do, and quite frankly, there is. But everything on this list is important to cover and doing so will make your landlording job easier during the life of the tenancy. Fortunately, many items on this list can be completed very quickly, and from start to finish, the entire process generally takes me about an hour. Believe me, it is an hour well spent. Let's begin discussing part three of the checklist by looking at the first three items on that list. They are:

1. *Rules and regulations initialed and signed.*
2. *Fire extinguisher use and maintenance reviewed.*
3. *Smoke alarm use and maintenance reviewed.*

I already spoke of the correct way to review the rules and regulations with your new tenant in that particular chapter, so I won't say anything more except make sure each page is initialed and the whole form is signed and dated.

But it is important to discuss again both the fire extinguisher and smoke alarm and their proper use and maintenance. Whatever you do, make sure you cover these items with your tenant. If you've seen the movies *Backdraft* with Kurt Russell or *Ladder 49* with John Travolta—or experienced a fire yourself—you realize how devastating a fire can be. I actually had a house burn, and believe me when I say it is no picnic. Do yourself a favor and cover these items with your tenant.

4. *Tenant given lead-based paint pamphlet.*
5. *Lead-based paint form signed and dated.*

These two checkpoints were thoroughly covered in their corresponding chapter should you have any questions. Please use them if they apply.

6. *Property condition form signed and dated.*
7. *Photos/video taken.*

Many landlords never do either of these important items. It's unfortunate because even the use of just one would probably win a financial judgment against a tenant if you had to sue for damages. Do yourself a favor and get in the habit of taking care of these two checkpoints.

8. *Additional/missed information verified.*

Often you will need to collect a copy of an ID or other piece of important paperwork for your file on the new tenant. This will be your last opportunity before you hand over the keys to do so.

9. *Tenant received Important Contact form.*

I haven't discussed the Important Contacts sheet thus far. This particular form is one I've yet to mention or introduce to you because it is so short and easy to fill out, I couldn't warrant writing a complete chapter around it. Basically, the contact sheet is just a simple form you fill out and give to your tenant at lease-signing time. All this form does is make their move in a little easier as the form lists all the phone numbers for basic utility turn-ons, such as gas, electric, water, and so forth. Of course it also makes you look more professional and caring, which can go a long way in a tenant/landlord relationship.

There is also a place for your mailing address and your emergency contact number. It is best to keep the numbers in a handy location and fill out this form before you meet with the tenants. You will find a copy of this form on our website at www.FindThatQualityTenant.com.

10. *Utilities transferred.*

Some landlords require that all utilities are transferred to the new tenant before the lease is signed. Depending on your clientele, this can be a good idea. If the tenants are going to be paying for the utilities anyway, why let them move in and then make the transfer? Most utilities can be transferred in minutes by a simple phone call, therefore, you would be wise to have the tenants make the transfer before they take possession. If this is not your policy and the tenants have not transferred the utilities by lease signing, let them know you will order the utilities turned off in two days from the day the lease begins. You are being courteous by giving them two days so as not to interrupt their service, but do not go beyond that.

11. *Explained property workings.*

Explaining the property workings will help the tenant get settled into his or her new residence, but it also can make your life easier as a landlord. What this checkpoint does is remind you to review with the tenant all the little nuances of that particular dwelling. You want them to be able to respond quickly and correctly in case something happens, like a pipe breaking or other sudden emergency.

This topic covers things such as how to shut off each individual water valve or even the whole dwelling if necessary. Gas shutoffs, correct toilet plunging, and keeping hair out of a shower drain are other worthwhile issues to discuss. You might even want to explain how to check and change a furnace filter or clean the coils on a refrigerator or air conditioner.

This checkpoint also covers quirky items like a light switch that activates an outlet or switch in a remote place or a sticking window you can't seem to fix. Basically, this checkpoint is designed to remind you to explain all the little things you expect the tenant to maintain or to provide enough information about the unit to head off those pesky "How do I?" and "Where are?" phone calls. I've listed some of the important issues for your convenience.

12. *Pet addendum signed and dated.*

If you are renting to someone with pets, you would be wise to use this addendum. Make sure the new tenant understands your position on pets using this form as your guide.

13. *Cosigner agreement signed and dated.*

You will seldom use this form, but when you do, you want it filled out correctly and completely. Now is the time to make sure it is done.

14. *Copies of photo ID/Social Security number collected.*

Like many items in this checklist, there will be things you may not wish to do. Collecting a photo ID and Social Security numbers may be one of them, but should you choose to exercise this option, simply tell your new tenant to bring a copy of these items to the lease signing if you have not already collected them. I recommend getting a copy of each adult and then you will have a copy for your records should your quality tenant go astray in the future.

15. *All lease items reviewed.*

16. *Lease initialed, signed and dated.*

By the time you get to the signing of the lease, you are probably reaching a point of fatigue. When this happens, don't be tempted to let your guard down and become lax. The lease is too important a document to not give 100 percent attention to.

17. *All monies received.*

When you reach this checkpoint, you want to collect whatever monies you require for move in. This includes security deposit, first month's rent, last month's rent if you ask for it, and any other money you require. Remember to collect individual funds if you are choosing to keep these funds in separate accounts. I recommend you collect these funds in either a money order or cashier's check. Don't take personal checks for the first month and don't get into the habit of collecting cash because of the safety issues involved with walking around with a pocket full of cash. However, if you do collect cash, count it as soon as the tenant hands it to you to verify there is no shortage of funds.

18. *Keys exchanged*

After all the forms are properly signed and dated and the monies are in your hand, you can then and only then turn over the keys to your new tenant. Some landlords give two to three sets of keys to their tenant and collect a key deposit for each key they hand out, hopefully guaranteeing their return. I personally think all this is just one more item to worry about and just not worth the effort. Since I always change locks with each new tenant, what I do when I change these locks is make three complete sets of keys distributed the following way:

- Set one—my set for maintenance purposes
- Set two—my backup set
- Set three—used for showings (so I know they work)

I hand my tenants set three when I rent the dwelling. By handling keys in this manner, I don't have to worry about what keys I get back, although I notice I generally am given more keys back when tenants leave than what I gave them in the first place.

As I conclude the final chapter on the checklist, let me go over some suggestions for optimum usage:

- Print a few copies of the checklist and keep them in the same file or folder as your rental application, employment verification, and so forth. Proper use of the checklist begins at the showing, which is step three. You can put a check mark on each item as you finish it, although I recommend

> If you are renting a dwelling in an apartment, once you have collected your first month's rent and turned over the keys, do the tenant a favor. Put their name in the window of their mailbox door (if applicable). Only include last names to help conceal the gender of the occupant. Once all the keys are handed over, it is official: You have new tenants. Shake their hand and welcome them to the neighborhood.

putting your first and last initial on each spot, especially if more than one person is working to complete the checklist (husband and wife team, for example). This will help you recall who did what if you run into a problem or must communicate important information between the two of you. Of course, use N/A if items don't apply.

- Since you filled in a date at the top of the sheet when you first began using the form, I suggest you also sign and date the bottom of the page when you complete the form. You never know when you'll need to prove something to somebody. Now that all forms are signed, make sure the tenants have a copy of everything they signed and you take all the signed originals, along with the checklist, all original step three and step five paperwork and place it in a file in your home with the property address and the word "Tenant" on the flap. You will occasionally be referring to these papers for information, so keep them handy.

- You can now take your copies of the Tenant Qualifications, Ads and Tracking, all completed Caller Interview forms, and any failed applications you have accumulated as you tried to rent this unit and staple them together. Put them in a file labeled "Failed Applications" and keep them at least three years in case you ever need them.

In Closing

This concludes the five-step process that has evolved through my landlording career over the last decade or so. I'm sure there are many more ways to "skin a cat," but I have had relatively good luck finding quality tenants using the system you've just learned. This is not to say that I haven't had my share of problems, lost monies, or aggravation, but I can safely say that I seem to have experienced them a lot less frequently than many of the people I've talked to over the years.

Whether you choose to use part, all, or none of my system, I hope you have gained some useful knowledge from the pages you've just read. I also invite you to read the appendix in the back of the book to further that knowledge just a wee bit. I sincerely hope you have the best possible success in your landlording career.

Congratulations! Your work here is done. Now it is the time to do the very final item on that checklist.

19. *Celebrate!*

You deserve it!

The entire Checklist form is shown below.

STEP 3, 4 & 5

Checklist

Name _____ Date _____

Address _____

STEP 3

1) ____ Verify driver's license number and picture
2) ____ Verify social security number
3) ____ Landlord information complete
4) ____ Employment information complete
5) ____ Reference names and phone numbers complete
6) ____ Rental application signed and dated
7) ____ Credit application filled out completely
8) ____ Credit application signed and dated
9) ____ Credit monies received
10) ____ Employment verification signed and dated
11) ____ Cashflow form filled out
12) ____ Co-signer credit check completed, signed and dated
13) ____ Co-signer credit check monies received
14) ____ Co-signer cashflow filled out

Signature _____ Date _____

STEP 4

1) ____ Check rental history
2) ____ Check employment history
3) ____ Check personal references
4) ____ Check credit
5) ____ Check cashflow
6) ____ Check bank account verification
7) ____ Run criminal background check

Signature _____ Date _____

STEP 5

1) ____ Rules and regulations initialed and signed
2) ____ Fire extinguisher use and maintenance reviewed
3) ____ Smoke alarm use and maintenance reviewed
4) ____ Tenant given lead based paint pamphlet
5) ____ Lead based paint form signed and dated
6) ____ Property condition form signed and dated
7) ____ Additional/missed information verified
8) ____ Information contact, form received
9) ____ Utilities transferred

    a)   gas
    b)   electric
    c)   water
    d)   sewer
    e)   garbage
    f)   other

10) ____ Explained property workings
    a) ____ individual water shut offs
    b) ____ main water shut offs
    c) ____ all gas shut offs
    d) ____ furnace filter change
    e) ____ appliances
    f) ____ all others
11) ____ All lease items reviewed
12) ____ Lease initialed, signed & dated
13) ____ Pet addendum signed & dated
14) ____ Co-signer agreement signe & dated
15) ____ Copies of photo ID/SS# collected
16) ____ All monies received
17) ____ Celebrate!

Signature _____ Date _____

Government Assistance

T here are many government assistance programs designed to cover all
or part of the rent payment for the participants. It is not my intention to cover each program since there are many such programs out there,
and I'm far from being an expert. But I *have* had tenants on these subsidy
programs, so I can fill you in a bit on how government assistance affects
finding a quality tenant.

I believe any income bracket of people can produce both bottom-of-
the-barrel tenants or cream-of-the-crop tenants, so it doesn't matter if a
tenant is "low income government subsidized" or not. I believe you can
find a good tenant in any income category. I say this with confidence because one of the absolute best tenants I ever had was on Section 8. She
would schedule her own government inspections. She herself would fix
and clean anything she felt might cause her to fail an inspection. She would
call if rent was going to be one day late. Yes, you heard right: one day and
she would call. She never, ever gave me a problem or worry, ever. And you
know what? She was my very first Section 8 tenant I ever had, and I found
her with this system.

My intent is not to educate everyone on all the government programs
available, because there are countless books available and/or government
people to help you muddle through them. Instead, I will show you how
using a subsidiary program will affect the system that you are studying in
this book.

As you probably know, everything in life has positive and negative
aspects, and as often is the case, to reap the positives, we must learn to live

with and control the negatives. This rule applies to government rent assistance programs just like it applies to everything else.

The main positive of such programs is the guarantee you are going to get all or part of the rent on time each and every month. Actually, as far as I'm concerned, it is really the only true positive worth mentioning. But boy, is it an enticing one. I mean, you have one of the strongest governments in the world sending you money consistently month after month and all you have to do is follow their system of rules and regulations. If for no other reason at all, this positive reason may be enough to make you at least think about a government program.

If you choose to use such a program, the question you need to ask yourself is how it will affect your tenant search, especially since you are using a concrete formula for selecting quality tenants. First off, accepting government programs could change the income portion of your Tenant Qualifications sheet drastically. How? Well, why do you want to know the income on *anyone* interested in renting from you? Because you want to know they can consistently pay their rent. But wait a minute: Do you really care about income if all or most of their rent is covered by the government? I don't know about you, but I sure would. Here's why: Just because rent is covered doesn't necessarily mean all other expenses are covered. Some of the expenses they may have will pertain to your rental unit. For instance, heat, water, sewer, and garbage bills all can cause you very painful headaches if they are not handled properly by the tenant.

If you don't know what income the tenant has and let's say they can't pay their heat, how does that affect you? I'll tell you. In the winter, *you* will be the one repairing broken water pipes if the tenant's heat gets turned off or a pipe freezes. If they don't pay the sewer bill, will it affect you? Of course, because a sewer bill can put a lien on your property if it goes undetected. And how about not paying garbage? What would that do to your rental? Here's a hint: Call the Orkin man!

I know some landlords roll those bills into the rent and charge a higher price to rent your unit. Some government programs allow this and others do it automatically. Doing things this way would ensure that you are in control of the bills, but I'm sure you'd find tenants who never shut the water off because they are not paying the bill. Or you'll find all the windows open on a 0 degree day because the tenant is hot and never thought about turning the thermostat to below 85 degrees.

Often you have people whose income is government subsidized, but since they don't earn enough money for the bills they are responsible for, they move other, unqualified residents into the unit to help pay those bills. These residents may have kids or pets that are outside of your established guidelines for the rental. So just because all or some of your rent is government subsidized doesn't mean the tenant prospect income is a nonissue. They still will have bills and you must determine how much income is needed to pay those remaining bills and other necessities of life.

Refresh your memory and take a look at the income portion of the Tenant Qualifications form:

Major Qualifications

1) **INCOME** Minimum per month Gross pay $ _____   Take Home pay $ _____
   or government assistance   Y/N   Must pass **"Cash Flow"** form   Y/N

Notes _____

As you can see, in the section "or government assistance Y/N" the word "or" is very important. If you chose Y in deciding to use government assistance, the word "or" excludes the gross and take-home pay. Why exclude this income? Because you are allowing someone to guarantee that the tenant's rent will be paid in a timely manner, and if the tenant made your minimum pay required, chances are he or she would not need to take advantage of a government assistance program in the first place. You will very seldom get your minimum income required *and* government assistance, so don't even try. What I would recommend is that you fill out a Cash Flow form on those using government assistance, so you at least have some clue as to their money habits. The catch here is that generally people using government assistance have very little "traceable" income. What this means is that they might not have a checkbook, established credit, or a steady source of pay stubs.

In fact, often they work an assortment of side jobs, many of which pay in cash, so you can't verify what they truly earn. In addition, many people who have their rent subsidized use other sources of government assistance to pay bills, as in food stamps or a government allotment toward heat.

One thing I suggest doing with any government-assisted applicant is this: Since most applicants are allowed to earn some money, find out the income of the applicant including government assistance. You need solid proof of any of this claimed income. Then, run a cash flow analysis based on their proven income and probable expenses. Things like food stamps or government medical care would alter the category they are associated with. In other words, if the applicants had complete government health coverage, then you would put $0 in that space for health insurance.

If they get food stamps, find out how much their food stamps total per month and deduct that from their food total to tell you what they pay out-of-pocket for food. Let me also say that all food items are not covered by food stamps, so you will have to estimate a figure in this area. Remember, you might have a $0 figure in the sewer/water, gas/electric, or garbage categories if you are paying these bills.

Use the Cash Flow form, but adjust it accordingly. Use common sense and verify all that you can. Once you've worked the Cash Flow form with their stated income and expenses, you'll have an idea if they are capable of paying their current bills. This is a big concern because, as previously mentioned, if they are not able to pay bills, they may move other people into your dwelling to help cover the cost of living. Pretty soon, you could have a bunch of unrecognizable tenants in your rental.

When you look at the big picture financially, what all this means is that by choosing to use a government rent assistance program, even though all or part of your rent is guaranteed, finding out how much money that tenant truly makes and how they really pay all their bills could be tough to do.

I don't wish to discourage you from using these programs because, let's face it, your rent is guaranteed and deep down, that is really what you want. What I am telling you is that in order to find the best possible tenant when dealing with government assistance programs, you may have to eliminate bad tenants through some of your other qualifications. Let's review a couple of them.

Prior landlord references and evictions are a good place to start. First, if you refuse to take evicted applicants without government assistance, then you should probably keep that policy for those on government assistance. Think of it this way: Most people lose their rental unit to eviction for nonpayment of rent. Almost any landlord will begin eviction after they start to lose rent money. Most landlords on the other hand, will put up with pets in a nonpet lease, or extra people in the unit or too much noise in the building, etc. as long as they get their rent. If your government-funded tenant—the one receiving free or almost free rent—is getting evicted, for what are they being evicted? It probably isn't money-related since their rent is covered, so they are breaking a lease or landlord agreement in other areas, and if they are being evicted for breaking a lease, you can probably assume they are *really* breaking the lease. You don't need the hassle. So again, my advice is do not take evicted applicants.

Personal references can supply some insight to your applicant, but as mentioned previously, personal references are usually the applicant's closest friends and family, so naturally you will expect to hear many positive things about the tenant, which may or may not be true.

Current landlords and previous landlord references hold the same prestige as in any applicant search. Definitely hold a previous landlord in higher esteem than a current landlord. Talk to as many previous landlords as possible and in each case, find out why the applicant moved and how well they paid their bills.

Another thing to really watch out for is frequent movers. You will find that some government-assisted tenants seem to move quite often and generally without good reasons. Of course, every time they move, these tenants must find a new landlord who will work with their program, as well as make frequent trips to their caseworker to go through all the paperwork for the move. The question that enters my mind is if it's such an extra hassle to move, why do it so often?

It seems to me that if your rent was covered each and every month, you'd move less often than normal, unless you had a very unstable life. The point I'm trying to make is that you would probably be much farther ahead as a profitable landlord if your government subsidy tenants had a stable rental history.

The last requirement I want to touch on is the running of a credit check on government-assisted tenants. Most if not all will have no or very poor credit, so you might feel that running such a check would be useless. For the most part, I tend to agree, although by running a credit check, you get to find what judgments they have and possibly what type of people they owe money to (landlords, medical, or material items), which will give you a clue about their character. Also, when you run a credit check, you often get a criminal check as well.

Before I close out this section, let me give you a couple clues about government-assisted programs: These programs work on their own time schedule. You can't change it, so don't try. Your rental unit must meet specific safety and habitable standards. These conditions will be re-inspected at least once a year. Be prepared to keep your rental up to par. The government has preset standards for each program so the dollar amount you expect, hope, or think you will get could be a lot higher than the amount you'll actually receive.

All in all, government assistance programs are a very powerful and popular way to guarantee all or at least part of your rent payment. And as I know from experience, you can find highly qualified and wonderful tenants in these programs. The best way to ensure you find a quality tenant using these programs is to make sure you stay in control of the situation by sticking to solid, sensible requirements, adjusting only those requirements that your particular government program and its related clientele pertain to. Be fair, use good common sense, and learn the specific program you plan on using, and your chances of finding a good quality tenant will vastly improve.

INDEX

Give the Gift of

How to Find That Quality Tenant

The Five Simple Steps of Tenant Selection

to Your Friends and Colleagues

CHECK YOUR LEADING BOOKSTORE OR ORDER HERE

❑ **YES**, I want _____ copies of *How to Find That Quality Tenant* at $22.95 each, plus $4.95 shipping per book (Indiana residents please add $1.38 sales tax per book). Canadian orders must be accompanied by a postal money order in U.S. funds. Allow 15 days for delivery.

My check or money order for $_____ is enclosed.

Please charge my: ❑ Visa ❑ MasterCard
❑ Discover ❑ American Express

Name _____

Organization _____

Address _____

City/State/Zip _____

Phone_____ Email _____

Card # _____

Exp. Date_____ Signature _____

Please make your check payable and return to:
Blue Collar Publishers
c/o Port City Fulfillment
35 Ash Drive • Kimball, MI 48074

Call your credit card order to: (888) 452-0765

Fax: (810) 388-9502   Email: fulfillment@portcity.com

www.FindThatQualityTenant.com